CW00348421

STIRLING MOSS'S MOTOR-RACING MASTERPIECES

ACKNOWLEDGEMENTS

The authors wish to thank the copyright holders for granting permission to reproduce from: *The Dawn of Motoring* by Erik Johnson (Mercedes-Benz UK Ltd, 1986); 'Mansell Breaks Through' from *British Grand Prix* by Maurice Hamilton (The Crowood Press, 1989); 'Brooklands 1926' from *The British Grand Prix 1926–1976* by Doug Nye (Batsford, 1977); 'The French Grand Prix 1934' from *Great Motor Races* ed. B. Carter (Weidenfeld and Nicolson, 1960); 'The Old Devil Nürburgring' from *Fangio: My Racing Life* by Juan-Manuel Fangio and Roberto Carozzo (PSL, 1990); *L'Equipe* 'Le Mans 1955' from that newspaper's coverage of the race; 'Casablanca 1958' from *Champion Year* by Mike Hawthorn (William Kimber, 1959); Peter Garnier for '16 On The Grid' from his book of the same name (Cassell, 1964); 'Clark Wins 500 At 150.686' and 'Hill Wins Disputed "500"' from the coverage of the *Indianapolis Star*; 'Mirage At The Masta' from *The Day I Died* by Mark Kahn (Gentry Books, 1974); 'Six Days in August' from *Six Days in August* by Michael Cooper-Evans (Pelham Books, 1968); Frederick A. F. Petersens for 'The Tragedy of Ronnie Peterson' from *The Viking Drivers* by Fredrik A. F. Petersens (William Kimber, 1979); 'Mind And Body' from *Anatomy of a Grand Prix Driver* by Richard Garrett (Arthur Barker, 1970), and 'My Philosophy and Tragedy At Spa' from *Jim Clark At The Wheel* by Jim Clark (Arthur Barker, 1964); *Principles Of Performance Driving* by Jackie Stewart (Hazleton Publishing, 1992); 'The Pride Factor' from *Keke: An Autobiography* by Keke Rosberg and Keith Botsford (Stanley Paul, 1985); 'The Believer' from Allievi's interview in *La Gazzetta Dello Sport*, 1990; 'In A Different Dimension' from *Grand Prix People* by Gerald Donaldson (MRP, 1990) and 'Time Runs Out' from *Villeneuve* by Gerald Donaldson (MRP, 1989); 'The Car Game' from *Hailwood* by Ted Macauley and Mike Hailwood (Cassell, 1968); 'Principles Of Competition Driving' from *Competition Driving* by Alain Prost and Pierre-François Rousselot (Hazleton Publishing, 1990); 'The First Champion' from *The World Champions* by Anthony Pritchard (Leslie Frewin, 1972); 'A Gentle Guiding Hand' from *Jim Clark: Portrait of a Great Driver* (chapter by Walter Hayes, book editor Graham Gauld); 'Racing Is Also This' from *Racers Apart* by David Tremayne (MRP, 1991); 'Master James' from *Grand Prix British Winners* by Maurice Hamilton (Guinness, 1991); 'There's A Way' from *The British Racing Hero* by Derick Allsop (Stanley Paul, 1990); 'When the World was Young' from *Williams: The Business of Grand Prix Racing* by Alan Henry (PSL, 1991); 'A Different Kind of Life' from *A Different Kind of Life* by Virginia Williams and Pamela Cockerill (Doubleday, 1991); 'The Other Side of the Hill' from *The Other Side of the Hill* by Bette Hill with Neil Ewart (Hutchinson/Stanley Paul, 1978); 'Bad Blood At Maranello' and 'Oh Deer Me' by Nigel Roebuck, 'Mexican Stand-Off' by Jeff Hutchinson, 'Hogging The Limelight' by Joe Saward, all from *Autosport*; 'Thereby Hangs A Tale' from *The Guinness Book of Rallying* by John Davenport (Guinness, 1991); 'An Initiation Test' from *Peugeot 205: The Story of a Challenge* by Jean Todt with Jean-Louis Moncet (Flammarion, 1985); 'Hawthorn and Moss' from *Champions!* by John Blunsden and Christopher Hilton (MRP, 1993); 'Pockets in the Pockets' by Innes Ireland from *Road and Track* July 1985; 'Mille Miglia Report, 1955' by Denis Jenkinson (*Motor Sport*).

While every effort has been made to trace the copyright holders, in some cases it has proved impossible. The authors are happy to hear from any copyright holder whose work has been reproduced here.

INTRODUCTION

I must say one thing immediately. This is my idea of what a motor-racing book should be: you can pick it up and delve or move through from the beginning. Whichever way you choose, you'll find, I hope, intriguing and significant material. You can read about the immortal Jimmy Clark and the awesome Nürburgring, you can feel the tragedy of Le Mans in 1955, listen to Ayrton Senna thinking aloud in an almost mystical way, glimpse the mythical Tazio Nuvolari, have a lap of Goodwood with me and a near-petrified passenger . . .

I've done it in a selfish way. These are the sorts of thing I'd like to read, and I feel there must be many other people who'd like to as well. With my co-author Christopher Hilton, we discussed, narrowed down, argued the merits of this and that. The result, I trust, is a careful selection covering as much ground as you reasonably can without producing an encyclopaedia – which would have been the exact opposite of the exercise, anyway.

Some of the material hasn't appeared in English before and some, like the *Indianapolis Star*'s reporting of the Indy 500 race, hasn't appeared on this side of the Atlantic. I've tried to strike a balance between history and the present day, which is why you have Nuvolari and Senna and much in between. I've reached beyond Formula One to Le Mans, the Mille Miglia, rallying and the world land-speed record because each in its differing way is part of the same family, governed by the same impulses. I've included, for your interest (and perhaps amusement), a chapter on what others thought of *me*.

My Career

I'm surprised to be famous still. You must remember that my competitive life virtually ended when I crashed at the Goodwood circuit in Sussex in 1962, which is a while ago however you look at it. I'm helped by quite a few things, one being that few people stay to make history – they're not there long enough. They win the World Championship and then they go. They're usually at the top for only one or two years, I was in motor racing at Grand Prix level between 1951 and 1961.

I was lucky to have the name Stirling, thanks to my father Alfred. Otherwise I'd have been called Hamish! One of my greatest assets is my name. Everyone remembers it. My mother Aileen wanted to call me Hamish because she was a Scot. My father said, 'No way, think again', and my mother said, 'All right, Stirling with an i', because she had connections in Stirling, Scotland. He said, 'OK, I'll go for that.' Maybe it set a precedent in that you don't know if it's a masculine name or a feminine name, but I've certainly been lucky to get it. For me, the name was important.

Racing ran in the family. My father competed at Brooklands and Indianapolis and my mother in trials and rallies. When I was small she'd allow me to steer the family car along the drive of our home at Bray by the Thames. I enjoyed the exhilaration of speed. I was brought up with cars, nice cars. For example, my father had an Alfa-Romeo. I also had a pony, so my competitive life began early – at gymkhanas. Before I'd reached the age of ten father bought me a very old Austin Seven and I'd drive it in the fields nearby. I suppose the whole family – including my sister Pat – were competitive, and certainly Dad encouraged me to play as many sports as I could. I liked winning.

Dad also wanted me to follow him into dentistry but academically I wasn't, let's say, brilliant and I left school before taking what was then the passport to a profession, matriculation. I opted for hotel management but motor racing attracted me more and more strongly, particularly when I got my driving licence and could go out on the open roads. Up to then I'd ridden a motor bike and thereby hangs a tale. When I was too young to take *that* on the roads I was nevertheless attached to my father's Home Guard unit as a despatch rider with the proviso that I *could* use it on the roads in the event of invasion!

Paradoxically, the fact that the war had happened and there was no racing proved to be my next stroke of luck. Just as it restarted – and I think the first race after the war was at Zandvoort, Holland, in 1946 – I was coming up to the age when I could think of racing myself. I hadn't any established heroes in the way that a youngster of today might follow Nigel Mansell. The only heroes you could have were drivers like Nuvolari from the 1930s but they'd aged and hadn't been written about for a long time. Therefore I was able to go into racing in a completely fresh, uninfluenced way. Even more than that, I was young and if a journalist had to write something, it was easier to get a story out of an unknown seventeen-year-old than a comparatively old man – say of thirty-five or thirty-six – who'd been written about a long time before.

There weren't many races in Britain and I competed virtually every weekend somewhere on the continent. For the first couple of seasons I drove air-cooled Coopers and they taught me the basics, then I went into Grand Prix racing with HWM. In my whole racing career – and this I think is important – I never saw my result appear on the sports pages, and I've eighty volumes of press cuttings to prove it. The newspapers never did it. They always put motor racing on news pages. Now, of course, it is on the sports pages, but in those days the general reader – whether interested in motor sport or not – would see that old so-and-so had won a race.

At the time I was doing up to fifty-seven races a year and, as I've said, most weekends I competed. Because I was a racer by instinct, I'd always be trying. Even if I had to drop out, I'd be leading or contesting the lead – or perhaps I'd win. All those things add up, and then you put on top of them a name that's easy to remember! But deep down am I still surprised to be famous? Yes, I am. I receive letters marked *Stirling Moss, England* and they get here. Funnily enough, I'm more likely to get them with just that than if you write the wrong postal district on the envelope!

British people are all for the underdog and most of my career I was that – but an underdog with a chance of winning. I'd never take the easy way out because I enjoyed the fight, whether it was driving for a privateer like Rob Walker or whoever.

My very first event was a speed trial in 1947, where I drove a BMW, although as a novice I had no idea how to exploit the potential of the car to the full. I reached Formula One in 1951 but in fact my only 'easy' year was 1955 with the Mercedes, a very superior car. My team-mate, Juan-Manuel Fangio, won the Championship with 40 points. I came second with 23 and Eugenio Castellotti, with a Lancia, came third on 12.

Underdog? When Mercedes withdrew I went back to Maserati – I'd been there in 1954 – but we were always battling against the Ferraris. Later I drove a Cooper or a Lotus for Rob Walker, but the cars I had were always at least a year old. That didn't stop me having a go and I think the British public likes to see that. They respond to it. I habitually drove British cars when they were available, too, because I happen to be very pro-British. These days patriotism doesn't seem to be high on the list of people's priorities any more but it was then.

Some thoughts on speed

It's interesting that when I was young I enjoyed the exhilaration of speed and until you begin to race that exhilaration remains. When you race, the speed element matters less, so to speak. As a kid I loved to lower the windscreen to feel the wind on my face. The thought of that appals me now – and would have done when I'd reached the age of twenty-five! The whole idea, the concept of the wind in your face, isn't really what speed is. The definition of speed is this: you go round a 30 m.p.h. corner at 31 and that's too damned fast, you go round at 29 and that's too slow; same thing if the corner is 130 m.p.h. Speed is purely relative to the situation in which you find yourself and is a necessary by-product of controlling the car. To get a car on the limit, you must make the car go faster than you'd normally do on any corner – and it doesn't matter if it's a 30 m.p.h. corner or 130 m.p.h. corner. There is a limit for even the finest drivers – Fangio, Clark, Senna, whoever.

That limit is different from one man to another and, depending on the ability of the driver, can be pushed higher. The exhilaration comes at the point when you are on the limit and still controlling the car. It is an enormous feeling. How fast you're going is really not relevant until you get to speeds which frighten you. Speed frightens more when you're going fast purely because your reaction time begins to drop back. However fast you can react, it will still be too slow. At slower speeds you can anticipate having to make a correction because, say, the car is giving you messages through the steering. If you don't make the correction early enough you are in trouble. If you can interpret the signal from the car – however big or small – that makes you safer.

This business of racing drivers' fast reaction times is true. They do have them, but it isn't to make you go faster, it's to make you go more safely. The quicker your reaction, the quicker you can make up for the problem you're already into.

Some thoughts on versatility

I drove in many, many different kinds of car in many, many different kinds of race and event, but I never found the slightest problem in moving from, say, a Formula One Lotus to a sports car. For me to drive a Mark 7 Jag, get out and step into a Formula One car was no more difficult than for someone to put down a newspaper and pick up the *Radio Times*. Every car has a heart, every car will tell you something about itself.

When you start it up and drive it, it gives you messages. When I go round corners in any car it's telling me, for example, *I'm losing adhesion and you've lost the front end*. When you put the brakes on, you may feel one of them grabbing. All the time the car is relaying these messages. It is the ability of the driver to interpret them which makes one driver better than another.

You can put this another way. If I get into the Mark 7 Jag and push it to the limit it gives me some answers, in the same way that a Formula One car does. The Formula One car will say *yes, I can go like this if you want*, whereas the other will say *sorry, I can't, I'm a bit heavier*. When you interpret that, there really isn't much difference.

Sometimes a car will have the gear lever on the left, sometimes on the right. I don't worry unless I forget which side! What I won't ever drive – and I did once, only once – was a car with a central accelerator pedal. I need to know automatically where the pedals are and I could never get on with the central accelerator. That once I had a shunt.

The more you know about a car, the more you steer it with the throttle. A steering wheel is to *present* the car. You say to the vehicle *you are going to go right*, and then you take over with the throttle. There are right-hand corners where I'd use more left-hand lock than right to go round [this is called opposite lock, and to savour it in action see Godfrey Smith's piece in Chapter Ten. C.H.].

You only need two or three laps and you know what the character of the car is. Once you know that, you start to hone it to go faster. Mind you, it can be difficult: a car might understeer in one place, oversteer in another and you have to make amends for that.

It all came quite naturally to me. I only thought about it afterwards, when I wanted to explain what I was trying to do. I'd go round a corner, things would happen and if someone asked me, 'How did you do that?' I'd have to think about it. I'd ask myself, 'Yes, how did I do that?' and I'd start watching what I was doing. Most people have some natural ability. If they go into a corner and the back end comes out to the left, they'll turn the steering wheel left as well. That's completely natural. As you go up the ladder of motor sport other factors come in – like a brake locking on, a bit of wheel spin, an oil surge – but you instinctively compensate for them in much the same way as a normal motorist does when the back end comes out.

S.M.

Stirling Moss is without question the greatest driver never to win the World Championship. His career coincided with that of Fangio, to whom he finished second in 1955, 1956 and 1957. He lost to Mike Hawthorn by a single point in 1958 – which you can read about in 'Casablanca', Chapter Two. Such statistics pay scant homage to the immensity of Moss's career. He drove an astonishing array of cars, won the fearsome Mille Miglia in Italy and would surely have won Le Mans but Mercedes withdrew during the race – as described in 'Le Mans 1955', also Chapter Two.

The name his mother chose became synonymous with speed and struck deep chords in Britain. Traffic police would stop speeding motorists and ask, 'Who the hell do you think you are, Stirling Moss?' Perhaps they still do. He provoked fierce arguments (I remember some in my household) because he raced so hard and if the car broke down, someone would ask, had he been racing too hard? That struck deep chords, also, not just of controversy but of a kind of open admiration. Isn't this what real racers should be doing? Through all this Moss remained what he was, a restless, polite, perceptive man.

The furores which have surrounded drivers such as Mansell, Alain Prost and Senna never broke over him because he wasn't like that and the era wasn't like that. He speaks of how the Grand Prix drivers went on strike in the early 1980s and his voice trails away, lost in disbelief that it could have happened – an absolute violation of the ethics which govern his life.

In another sense, Moss is a very modern man. At sixty-five he still follows motor sport closely from the *inside*, reads the latest currents and nuances, will discuss the merits and de-merits of young Ferrari driver Jean Alesi as knowingly as he'll discuss

Jackie Stewart. He adores gadgets, itself a forward-looking matter: normally people in their sixties are baffled by anything more than an on-off switch. Moss's London home is frankly futuristic, with moving walls, intercoms and a piano which plays itself. It plays restfully . . .

His attention to detail makes working with him fascinating and rewarding. If he can't remember something he forages in his scrapbooks for information; if it's not there he starts firing off phone calls to people who might know (I've seen him using two phones simultaneously) and keeps on until he has it. That done, his mind moves incisively on to the next problem. In the background his fax machine spews out messages, keeping him closely in touch.

A strong impression forms. Once upon a time Stirling Moss became known throughout the world for racing against time on tracks. He hasn't really altered. He's still racing. It's just that he doesn't do it on the tracks any more. He expanded on the quotation which he has placed at the beginning of this book, *movement is tranquillity*. It means, he said, movement in your daily life – *and every minute of it gives me great satisfaction*.

C.H.

STIRLING MOSS'S RECORD

Country: England
Born: 17 September 1929
First competitive event: speed trial, Harrow, 1947
Married: Wife Susie

Major milestones

He competed in nearly 500 events of all types and won 200 of them.

Crashed at Goodwood, Sussex, in 1962 and was in a coma for four weeks.
It ended his professional racing career.

First Grand Prix: Switzerland 1951 (HWM)
First victory: British Grand Prix, 1955
Finishing place in the World Championship
1954   12
1955   2
1956   2
1957   2
1958   2
1959   3
1960   3
1961   3
Grand Prix career: 66 races, 16 poles, 16 wins, 20 fastest laps
Drove for HWM, ERA, Connaught, Cooper, Maserati, Mercedes-Benz,
Vanwall, BRM, Lotus

Won the Mille Miglia 1955 (with Denis Jenkinson)
Withdrawn from Le Mans 1955 while leading

CHAPTER ONE

IN THE BEGINNING

How the Car came to Britain

Erik Johnson

We take the motor car so much for granted nowadays that it is hardly possible to conceive of a time when it was not with us. Yet 1986 marks only the first hundred years of its being. A hundred years ago, there were no petrol stations or garages, no automobile associations, no Grand Prix racing stars, or any business empires built on the sale of tyres, spark plugs or radio-cassette players for cars – because there were no cars.

This is why the year 1886 is so important in contemporary human history. It was in that year that mankind took its first faltering steps towards the age of the motor car. In January, Benz was granted a patent for his motor vehicle, and a few months later Daimler installed one of his experimental petrol engines into a 'horseless carriage'.

If we look back to the middle of the last century, we see a Britain at the peak of industrial development and strength. Yet it was on the Continent that the motor car first became established in 1886, and it was to be almost a full decade before it really started to get going in the United Kingdom.

While there had been earlier successful attempts at providing mankind with locomotion, these depended on huge, clumsy and often dangerous steam engines. Indeed, so dangerous were they that

Erik was one of the great men at Mercedes-Benz. He acted as Press Attaché, as did his counterpart in Germany, Artur Keser – both terrific guys. It's significant to me that Mercedes-Benz were in at the start of the motor car because you can understand how they acquired so much experience. I always felt when I drove for them that I could ask for anything and they would either have it fitted the next day or they'd look in their big book. Say I asked for square wheels! They'd consult the book and say, 'Ah, we tried that in 1924, the car vibrated, and you can't have them.' They not only had an enormous history but learnt from it.

S.M.

Keser had a nice line in generosity. At the Swiss Grand Prix, 1954, the British magazine *Autosport* reported: 'Just before the start, Mercedes-Benz supplied some comic relief. Artur Keser, their PRO, presented several drivers with slices of cheese cut from a huge 100-kilogram affair. Stirling Moss carried his off muttering that he would be able to keep all the mice in England in luxury for weeks!'

C.H.

successive British governments passed restrictive laws which hampered the beginning of motorization in this country. Fortunately, once the door was opened, the British engineer was able to benefit from the experience of his Continental counterparts.

Through a fascinating process of cross-fertilization, Britain was eventually able to reap the rewards of work started by famous Englishmen such as James Watt and Richard Trevithick. Watt first used the term 'horsepower', and Trevithick showed the way towards locomotion with his steam carriage. It was the pioneering work of men such as these which later opened up the way for Otto, Daimler, Benz and Maybach to develop the internal combustion engine.

Just before the appearance of the first railways in Britain, there had been a brief flowering of steam-powered road-going vehicles. In 1834, Mr Hancock started a steam coach called the 'Era', running from Paddington to Regent's Park and the City at 6d (2p) per head, and carrying fourteen passengers. In 1835, Mr Church built an omnibus for forty passengers for a company called the London and Birmingham Steam Carriage Co. But the success of the railway movement drove all such traffic off the roads, sped on their way by punitive Acts of Parliament.

Although a Parliamentary Commission of Enquiry sat in 1836 and reported strongly in favour of steam carriages on the roads, the famous 'Man with the Red Flag Act' of Parliament was passed in 1865. Four years earlier, a Locomotive Act had limited the weight of steam wagons to twelve tons to limit damage to roads and bridges, and had imposed a speed limit of ten miles per hour. The Man with the Red Flag Act was to hold up vehicular development in Britain for many years. The Act stated that each vehicle had to be preceded sixty yards ahead by a man carrying a red flag. This enforced a walking pace, and was intended to warn horse riders and horse-drawn traffic of the approach of a fearsome 'self-propelled machine'.

The restrictive effect of such legislation on the power of British engineering ingenuity may be seen in the fact that, although engineers were working on combustion and electrical engines at the same time as Daimler, Maybach and Benz, these amounted to nothing. So it is to south-western Germany that we must look for the first steps which were to lead eventually to the motorization of Britain. At either end of the Neckar Valley – some sixty miles apart – two men worked assiduously through the late 1870s and early 1880s to bring the car into being. They were Gottlieb Daimler and Karl Benz, who have been jointly credited with having almost simultaneously developed the world's first practical car in 1886.

The essential difference between the two great early pioneers was that Daimler was a visionary who dreamed of his engines serving mankind, while Benz only ever wanted to be a car-maker. Each was successful in his own way, Daimler living to see his engines at work in the three elements of land, water and air, while Benz was almost certainly first into the field of manufacturing cars in 1894.

Although today past differences have long been forgotten, it is important to realize that both men were rivals in the race to produce the car, and subsequently in the drive to win customers all over Europe. However, in 1926 the firms were merged and the company of Daimler-Benz AG continues to flourish today.

The Mercedes car of 1901, created by Wilhelm Maybach, Daimler's collaborator, captured the public imagination, not least because of its euphonious name. The car was so successful that the name stuck, and was later adopted by the Daimler factory as a trade mark. This car more than any other can be said to have dragged the infant motor car kicking and screaming into the twentieth century. Overnight it made the frail and spidery creations of the late nineteenth century, which looked more like carriages without horses than cars, obsolete. With its powerful four-cylinder engine driving the rear wheels through a four-speed gate-change gearbox and with its cooling provided by a honeycomb radiator, it became the pattern for conventional car design for many years to come.

It is interesting to speculate which of the two great pioneers contributed most to the motorization of Britain, a question which can never be properly resolved. Daimler became a strong Anglophile following his early student visit to Britain. Thanks to his friendship with young Englishman Frederick Simms, the principle of the internal combustion engine was first demonstrated in Britain in 1891.

Karl Benz almost certainly built the first ever petrol-driven car to run on British soil. Either the 1888 Benz in the Science Museum in London or the model imported by Henry Hewetson in 1894 must have been Britain's first car. Men like Simms, Walter Arnold and Hewetson were to bring the fruits of Daimler and Benz's work to an unwilling Britain, only through considerable self-sacrifice. They believed passionately in their cause, and often broke what they saw as unjust laws in order to achieve their objectives. Although the wretched Man with the Red Flag had been removed by 1878, right up until 1896 there was still a requirement for a pedestrian to proceed a motor vehicle on the public highway, limiting progress to four miles an hour. Motorists were still expected to give way whenever they encountered a horse and rider, which was very often. It was not something they appreciated greatly, given the difficulties of stopping and re-starting.

Simms, Arnold and Hewetson worked tirelessly to change the law, and mounted a brilliant campaign to get the motor car accepted in Britain. In order to achieve their objective they attracted the interest of the Royal Family, organized motor shows, and even started up a magazine purely for automobile interests. Their first major achievement was the passing of the Emancipation Act of 1896. This event marked the true start of Britain's motoring history. However it only removed the preceding pedestrian requirement, and merely lifted the speed limit from a walking pace to twelve miles per hour, where it stayed until 1903. There was therefore still plenty of work for the pioneers to do.

These three men could be said to have been the founders of the British motor industry and trade. Simms helped to set up the Daimler Motor Company of Coventry, from which sprang the giant that today is the British motor industry. Hewetson and his partner Walter Arnold could be said to have been the forerunners of today's indispensable friend of the motorist – the motor trade. All this grew, however, from the activities of Daimler, Benz and Maybach. It was their genius and stubborn perseverance in the face of many difficulties which were to take man out of the horse age and enable him eventually to put his wheel tracks on the moon.

From *The Dawn of Motoring* by Erik Johnson (Mercedes-Benz UK Ltd, 1986)

CHAPTER TWO

RACES AND PLACES

Nigel Mansell Breaks Through at Brands Hatch

Maurice Hamilton

Dramatis personae: Nigel Mansell is in his sixth season of Grand Prix racing, Nelson Piquet in his eighth; Piquet twice World Champion, Mansell still establishing himself as a leading driver. They were team-mates at Williams, and they came to the British Grand Prix on 13 July 1986 with Piquet officially the Number One in the team.

The season got off to a terrible start for the team from Didcot when Frank Williams was severely paralysed as the result of a road accident. Fortunately for Frank, he had surrounded himself with excellent people and the team barely broke its stride on the race track.

Piquet won in Brazil; Mansell in Belgium, Canada and France. On the surface, it looked good. Underneath, the growing tension between the two drivers was threatening seriously to undermine the team's championship momentum. Brands Hatch would be the scene of a dramatic confrontation as Piquet claimed pole position with Mansell joining him on the front row.

Within fifteen seconds of the start, it was all

It's difficult to get to know Nigel particularly well because he is a private man. I find that commendable. Nigel is a good honest guy, which leads some people to conclude he's boring. That's one of his problems. However, having met him since he went to America to race IndyCars in 1993, I must say he's improved by a factor of ten in just one year. I thought that when he went his drab accent might put them off but he had a golden opportunity to do global motor racing so much good and he took it.

S.M.

An Ulsterman, Maurice Hamilton fell for motor racing when, at the age of seven, his father took him to a race at Dundrod, the circuit north of Belfast. Hamilton is one of the most respected of journalists and writers – formerly of the *Guardian* he now covers Formula One and rallying for the *Observer* and has written several notable books, including meticulous histories of the British Grand Prix and the RAC Rally. A quiet man with a warming sense of humour, he knows the subject intimately.

C.H.

over. A drive-shaft coupling failed as Mansell snatched second gear. Motoring disconsolately up the hill towards Druids, Mansell radioed the bad news to his pit. They replied with good news. The race had been stopped.

Behind Mansell, there was chaos. As the mid-field had rushed into Paddock Hill Bend, they had been confronted by Thierry Bousten's Arrows-BMW, broadside in the middle of the road. Seven cars collided. Worse still, Jacques Laffite had been forced off the track and the Frenchman, having just started his 176th Grand Prix to hold the record jointly with Graham Hill, suffered serious leg and pelvic injuries when his Ligier rammed the crash barrier.

Unlike the confusion which had surrounded a similar stoppage in 1976, the situation was quite clear. The rules had been clarified and the race would start from scratch. There was no doubt that Mansell could use the team's spare car, but the fact that it had been set up for Piquet did not bode well for the Englishman. But he was prepared to give it a go. The estimated 120,000 spectators, not to mention the man himself, breathed a sigh of relief.

Since he was relatively unfamiliar with this car, having driven it only briefly on the first day of practice, Mansell made a circumspect start and finished the opening lap in third place behind Piquet and the Benetton-BMW of Gerhard Berger. He remained there for two laps and then, with an impressive burst of speed, overtook the Benetton and set after his team-mate.

On lap 20, Mansell recorded the fastest lap of the race thus far and closed right up on Piquet. Three laps later, the Brazilian missed a gear as he accelerated out of Surtees Bend. It was the error Mansell had been waiting for. The spectator enclosures erupted when he appeared at Clearways in the lead. The next phase of this in-house battle would be the scheduled pit stops for fresh tyres.

Piquet came in first. The stop took a scant 9.04 seconds. Two laps later, at the end lap 32, Mansell made his stop. It took half a second longer.

As Mansell booted the Williams-Honda out of the pits, Piquet was rushing towards him along Brabham Straight. Mansell's tyres had been pre-heated – but Piquet's were at working temperature and he knew he had to make the most of that fact before Mansell got into the groove once again.

Piquet attempted to move alongside as they approached Surtees but Mansell refused to be budged. They ran nose to tail for the rest of that lap and, at the end of it, Mansell employed a legitimate blocking tactic as they sped towards Paddock. It kept Piquet at bay but Mansell, holding the tighter line, had left himself open to attack on the run up the hill to Druids. Piquet wisely look the conventional line through Paddock, made the faster exit and lined himself up to take the lead.

The move would have paid off – except that Alessandro Nannini, dutifully staying on the right-hand side of the track in order to let the leaders through, was in the way! Piquet had no alternative but to back off and tuck in behind Mansell who, by now, had his tyres working perfectly. That was the last challenge Piquet would be allowed to make.

For the remaining forty-three laps, the pace was unrelenting. First Piquet would establish a new lap record, then Mansell would improve on it. The gap was never more than a couple of seconds. On lap sixty-eight, Piquet made one last effort. Mansell responded instantly with another lap record. With four laps to go, Piquet realized Mansell had the measure of him.

For the second time in nine months, the entire assembly within the Brands Hatch bowl stood and cheered Nigel Mansell home. Mansell wrote in his book *Driven to Win*:

I could sense the euphoria in the car. I was carried home by waves of cheering fans. The previous year at Brands had been very special, and yet this one surpassed it. It was such a hard race. I'd never had to drive at that speed so consistently. I hadn't had a fluid bottle (there had been no time to fit the drink supply to the spare car) and I was worn out at the end. I didn't feel too steady at the top of the podium, but I knew where I was all right – I was on top of the world.

He led Alain Prost by four points. Piquet was fourth, fourteen points behind Mansell.

Then Piquet won three races to move into second place, five points behind Mansell, but Nigel redressed the balance by winning in Portugal. He threw away an opportunity to clinch the title in Mexico when he failed to put the car in gear at the start. The pressure was mounting. With one race, the Australian, to go, Mansell still led, but Prost and Piquet were within striking distance.

With fifty miles to go, it seemed certain Mansell would take the title. Piquet was leading but second place would be good enough for the Englishman. Then Mansell's rear tyre exploded as he sped along the back straight at 180 m.p.h. Fighting the car all the way, he brought the Williams to a halt, his race and championship wrecked. Piquet was called into the pits for a precautionary tyre change – and Alain Prost motored serenely by to win the race and become the first driver since Jack Brabham to win the title in successive years.

As Mansell made his weary way from the paddock at the end of a gruelling season, the elation of Brands Hatch seemed to be from a different age. But eight months later at Silverstone it would be obvious that he had put the bitter disappointment of Adelaide behind him.

From *British Grand Prix* by Maurice Hamilton (Crowood, 1989)

It was an extraordinary feeling. I drove maybe the last twenty laps at ten-tenths, right on the limit, and I don't really like to do that on such a quick circuit but I knew that was what it was going to take to beat Nelson, and the support from the crowd really inspires you.
Mansell after he'd beaten Piquet by 1.918 seconds, Silverstone, 1987

Why risk a big accident and put myself out for the rest of the year?
Alain Prost after he retired at a wet Silverstone, 1988

I'd love you, Alain, to come to Ferrari – you can be my Number Two! Actually, in all seriousness, I reckon there's only one person I can learn from in the pit lane. And that person is Alain Prost.
Mansell, now Ferrari, after finishing second to Prost, Silverstone, 1989

It's the British Grand Prix and it does make me very sad but I'm announcing my retirement today.
Mansell, Silverstone, 1990

In the end I was just relieved to make the finish. I was missing gears, not getting any gears, getting stuck in gears – you name it.
Mansell after returning and winning, Silverstone, 1991

I am not going to knock them. In a way I would like to compliment them. I think that today has been the most wonderful day for the sport in the history of Formula One at Silverstone.

Mansell after the crowd invaded the track before the end of the British Grand Prix, 1992

Brooklands 1926

Doug Nye

Doug is a tremendous historian, an absolute fountain of knowledge. We were doing a book together [*My Cars, My Career*, PSL] and he asked me about a certain car. I said I'd never driven it, but he said, 'Yes, you did, here is a picture.' He knew more than I did! Any human activity needs such historians, which is why Doug is such a necessary man.

S.M.

This is the story of Britain's first Grand Prix, run at the fabled banked circuit near Weybridge, Surrey. It was the centre of our motor racing between 1907 and 1939 and appeared on the social calendar in the same way that Ascot and Henley did. BBC commentator Murray Walker encapsulates its appeal as: 'The right crowd with no crowding.' The race was 110 laps of 2.61 miles – a total distance of 287.76 miles.

C.H.

The RAC's first British Grand Prix rejoiced in what was, for the time, an outstanding entry of no less than thirteen cars.

The STD combine reserved three entries for the debut of their brand-new Italian-designed, French-built straight-eight Talbots, and opted for a coat of green paint in this 'home' event. A fourth Talbot, an old 4-cylinder model, was entered by Captain Malcolm Campbell. Louis Delage promised three of his exciting new straight-eight cars; J. G. Parry Thomas was hastily completing his two 'Flat-Iron Specials' in his Brooklands workshop; Alvis entered their sophisticated new straight-eight front-drive; and two private entries, came from captain George Eyston – for his Anzani side-valve-engined Aston Martin with Powerplus supercharger – and from Major Frank Halford, whose Halford Special featured his own 6-cylinder engine mounted in an ancient Aston Martin chassis. Campbell managed to buy a new Bugatti Type 39A during the summer, and substituted it for his Talbot entry, which was then listed for Alastair Miller but which did not run.

In the week preceding race-day the brand-new Talbots arrived from Suresnes, together with the Delages freshly rebuilt at Courbevoie following their torrid debut in the European Grand Prix at San Sebastian, three weeks previously.

Up in Coventry the Alvis was behind schedule and the entry was withdrawn, while Parry Thomas was also forced to scratch his cars for Clive Gallop and 'Scrap' Thistlethwayte due to gearbox machining errors.

This left only nine cars to line up for A.V. Ebblewhite's famous red starting flag, yet that was three more than had run in Spain and six more than had started in the French Grand Prix 'classic' which had opened the World Championship season.

The rakish, wicked-looking Talbots had been tested briefly at Montlhéry before crossing the Channel to England, but drivers Albert Divo, Henry Segrave and ex-riding mechanic Jean Moriceau were horrified to find desperate braking problems during their first practice laps. As they swept off the Byfleet Banking and down to the first sandbank chicane, the Talbots' front axles blurred into a savage chattering judder the instant the brakes were applied. Segrave said: '... one saw the front wheels bouncing up and down about a foot from the ground and the car swaying about in an alarming manner'. While the Talbots could storm away along the straights and round the bankings, the Delages held them easily just under braking into the chicanes.

Nothing could be done to rectify the problem without returning to Suresnes, so the new Talbots went into their first race at a distinct disadvantage.

This was lost upon the large crowd which gathered that dull but warm Saturday morning. They had two home heroes to cheer – Campbell and Segrave – both of whom had made their names by breaking the World's Land Speed Record within the previous eighteen months, while the latter had the notable distinction of having won the French Grand Prix itself for Sunbeam in 1923. The Delages were to be handled by Robert Benoist the veteran Louis Wagner and Robert Senechal, with the wealthy enthusiast André Dubonnet present as reserve.

The field formed up in line abreast at the end of the Finishing Straight, beneath the loom of the Home Banking. Senechal was on the inside, flanked by Benoist, Divo, Eyston, Halford, Moriceau, Campbell, Segrave and Wagner, and as 'Ebby' dropped his flag it was Divo's Talbot which rapped away crisply into an immediate lead with Campbell, Moriceau and Eyston next away round the foot of the Banking. Both Senechal and Wagner were slow off the line, and trailed badly as Divo led his Talbot team-mates, Moriceau and Segrave, through the mile-long sweep of the Byfleet Banking.

As they dived down towards the gaping mouth of Finishing Straight, Moriceau felt his car lurch and watched thunderstruck as its front wheels leaned drunkenly towards each other. The Talbot weaved wildly, slowed, then juddered to a halt on the left of the track. Its badly machined front axle had broken just like the V12 Formule Libre car's in Spain, two weeks previously. One down, eight to go . . . and one hundred and nine laps remaining.

For the first six of those laps Divo towed Segrave at an average of 82 m.p.h. with Benoist's pale blue Delage sitting contentedly in their joint slipstream. Senechal was firing the crowd with lurid cornering in the chicanes, and had passed Eyston, but Wagner was in deep trouble with his Delage misfiring. He stopped and changed plugs, stopped and changed again, but still the car popped and banged, and what was worse his foot-pedals and the cockpit panelling were being scorched by the exhaust. After four stops in six laps the veteran Frenchman stopped for good, hopped out in enraged agony and hobbled to the pit counter in disgust.

Segrave's second-place Talbot began spitting flame from its exhaust on the over-run, '. . . and his brakes were a calamity . . .', and only seven laps had been run when Divo's leading car began misfiring and he swept into the pits. This allowed the grim-faced Segrave into the lead, while Benoist sat back in second place, '. . . a slightly satirical smile on his face'.

Segrave's lead lasted six laps until a stop to change rear wheels and tyres dropped him behind Benoist. Senechal had punched his Delage up into third place, and three leaders in the opening thirteen laps was almost unbearably exciting for the spectacle-starved crowd. Halford's snarling Special was sounding very healthy in fourth place, and Divo was back in the race and rushing round to make up lost time.

At twenty-five laps Benoist led Segrave, Senechal, Halford, Campbell, Eyston and Divo – the seven survivors. The sun shone out from an overcast sky as Segrave's brakes deteriorated, and desperate down-changing took the edge off his engine's vivid exhaust note. While he, Divo and Benoist flashed low around the bankings, the theatrical Senechal swooped high around the lip. Divo's car was trailing blue oil smoke from its forward oil cooler, which had split over the Brooklands bumps.

On lap 35 Benoist dived into his pit, changing rear wheels and rejoining before Segrave's ailing Talbot could catch him. Segrave stopped and the Talbot's rear-hinged one-piece engine cowl was flipped back to investigate 'carburettor trouble'. He rejoined, but four more stops followed in the next seven laps. His brakes were entirely shot, and on one occasion the Talbot slithered straight past the first chicane, and Segrave had to snatch reverse to take another bite at the cherry.

Eyston went out with a blown gasket, but Segrave's problems had given the gallant Halford Special third place behind the leading Delages of Benoist and Senechal, and Campbell was chiselling away at his lap times in the wire-wheeled Bugatti.

Divo was still hurtling round in his delayed Talbot, and after fifty laps Benoist began to suffer. His car's exhaust system had split, and as the fractured edges began to glow and crumble so twinkling little flames played on the dash-panel and pedals. Senechal had made his stop and was throwing his car around with Gallic abandon, and when Halford made a slow stop for fuel and tyres on his fifty-fifth lap he gave third place to Campbell until that little martinet of a man made his own call at the pits. This promoted Halford once more, but he was passed almost immediately by Divo whose superb fight-back was gaining him four seconds a lap on Senechal.

Segrave's time had come. In a stop to change plugs spirit had spilled on the track beneath the car and caught fire, and once that was smothered the Talbot refused to start. Driver and mechanic 'achieved unheard-of revolutions with the starting handle and pushed until exhausted', when the straight-eight suddenly fired, and Segrave stuttered away for one final lap before retiring with the supercharger casing split.

During this drama Benoist stopped for fuel and tyres, and for an attempted exhaust repair. The Delage refused to restart, plugs were changed and it fired only after a lengthy push. Despite this delay Benoist still led at seventy-five laps, from Senechal, Divo, Halford and Campbell. The second-place Delage had now blown its exhaust box, and holes had burned in Senechal's shoes! Benoist's car was slowing as its driver was in acute discomfort, and Divo's Talbot sounded flat but was lapping much faster than the Delage.

Divo stopped on his eightieth lap, and Senechal came in simultaneously, handing his car to the redundant Wagner and plunging his burned feet gratefully into a tray of cold water. As the bearded Frenchmen recovered, Wagner led Divo's recalcitrant Talbot away through the second chicane and out on to the broad oil-soaked concrete of the Home Banking.

Halford's steady and impressive drive stumbled as his gear-changing seemed reluctant, and on the eighty-third lap the Major couldn't find a gear at all into the first chicane, then found one, the engine revved, but there was no drive. The front prop-shaft UJ had parted, and as the Special rolled to a stop Wagner dodged by through the centre bridge arch. Campbell was fourth.

On lap 88 the fast-moving blue speck which should have been Benoist's Delage swooping off the Byfleet Banking resolved into detail as Wagner's car, and then Benoist was spotted touring in trailing smoke. He stopped amid a flurry of excitement then rejoined, chased, caught and passed his team-mate for two laps, then stopped again. Wagner regained the lead briefly, then he too stopped, plunged his feet into the water trough, then restarted!

While his feet were still steaming, Divo's Talbot at last refused to restart after a long pit-stop, and was retired with the supercharger casing ruptured and probable internal engine damage from oil loss. Dubonnet – wearing a lounge suit – relieved Benoist in the Delage which had led for so long, and drove gaily away without benefit of practice.

Both surviving Delages were in a sorry state, and the Benoist/Dubonnet car was now back on the same lap as Campbell, in third place with the Bugatti. Campbell was cheered every time he rasped down the short straight between the chicanes, weaved through the sandbanks below the Home Banking and then bucketed away after the Delage towards the Hennebique Bridge over the Wey. Dubonnet was having to learn the circuit as he drove, and this gave Campbell the chance he wanted. Into lap 102 the Bugatti and Delage were closing along the Railway Straight, and out of sight behind the aerodrome buildings. Up on the Members' Hill spectators strained to see the outcome of this last-minute battle, and as the two cars drew together on the Byfleet Banking and the taller machine drew ahead a great cheer told the Campbell pit that their man was second.

Wagner made a quick final stop at this time, and he toured the last uncomfortable, anxious laps in the smouldering Senechal Delage to pass under 'Ebby's' flag and win the first British Grand Prix, the car having averaged 71.61 m.p.h. for a merciless four hours' racing. The Bugatti came home second to a joyous reception for its famous English driver, having made only two stops in the entire distance, and Dubonnet enjoyed his third place hugely in the Benoist car.

The Delages had been lucky winners in many respects, for the

Talbots had the legs of them early on, and Campbell's Bugatti was certainly the healthiest finisher. Segrave had the consolation of fastest lap, at 85.99 m.p.h., and he won Sir Arthur Stanley's special trophy for that performance. When he had cleaned off his coating of oil and grime, Segrave went to a champagne lunch laid on by STD manager Alan Fenn to revive the team's spirits. He arrived late, and was amazed to see a terrific row in progress, with everyone bawling out Bertarione, the designer. Divo and Moriceau were loud in their opinion of the Italian's parentage and a suitable demise for his new car, and eventually Segrave drove them all back to London where he deposited them – still cursing in voluble French – on the pavement in St James's Street. Much the same scene could have greeted Lory of Delage, but for the fortitude of his drivers and the problems of his opposition, and as night fell over the Weybridge track the first British Grand Prix was hailed as 'a magnificent battle . . . a memorable motor race'.

RESULTS
1   R. Senechal/L. Wagner (Delage No 14) 110 laps in 4 hrs 0 mins 56 secs, 71.61 m.p.h.
2   M. Campbell (Bugatti No 7) 4 hrs 10 mins 44 secs, 68.82 m.p.h.
3   R. Benoist/A. Dubonnet (Delage No 2) 4 hrs 18 mins 8 secs, 68.12 m.p.h.

FASTEST LAP   H.O.D. Segrave (Talbot) 85.99 m.p.h.

RETIREMENTS   J. Moriceau (Talbot) front axle failure; G. Eyston (Aston Martin Anzani) blown gasket; F. Halford (Halford Special) broken forward prop-shaft universal joint; L. Wagner (Delage) persistent misfiring and exhaust heat damage; A. Divo (Talbot) split supercharger casing and incurable oil leaks; H.O.D. Segrave (Talbot) split super-charger casing.

From *The British Grand Prix 1926–1976* by Doug Nye (Batsford, 1977)

The French Grand Prix 1934

Barre Lyndon

We must never forget the importance of France – and the French Grand Prix – in the history of motor racing. The French were in at the beginning and of course held, and still hold, the Monte Carlo Rally and the Le Mans 24-hour race. In my career I drove in a lot of other places – like Bordeaux and Caen and Aix-les-Bains – and we raced on roads: many were great roads to race on.

S.M.

That July day an immense crowd gathered at the Montlhéry circuit near Paris – partly banked – to witness the giants of the age in combat. Although neither of the authors knew Barre Lyndon we felt the race report is so evocative of its era that it demanded inclusion.

C.H.

The flag was due to fall at two o'clock. A quarter of an hour before this time the machines were marshalled to the line-up, every driver being greeted with applause as his name was announced through loudspeakers. The enormous grandstand at one side of the track was completely filled, the nearby enclosures were packed, and all around the circuit spectators were crowded behind fencing set among the bushes at the fringe of the road.

The machines were placed in rows. Achille Varzi, with his scarlet Alfa-Romeo, and Hans Stuck with his white Auto-Union, were in the front rank, and these two indicated the real quality of the event. The Italian machine was typical of the existing racing car – low-built, with a blunt radiator to catch a cooling stream of air, a high seated position which gave the driver complete control, and everything about the machine efficiently designed to meet the demands which experience had shown would be made upon it. Against the red bonnet was the yellow shield and the black horse which formed the insignia of the Scuderia Ferrari, a badge which had been carried to victory at least once in every Grand Prix in the calendar.

Standing beside it was the Auto-Union, silvery-white and strange in appearance. Instead of sitting well back in the car, the driver was placed forward, almost within hand-reach of the front wheels. From behind his cockpit a fairing ran down the streamlined tail which shrouded the engine; where the tail ended, a swastika was painted on one side, with the colours of the German national flag on the others, as if it were intended that drivers following the car should have the origin of the machine brought home to them. The radiator was at the front, rounded and cowled, adding to the perfection of the machine's streamlining, and behind this were openings to allow the escape of air after it had passed through the radiator. The strangely shaped body made the machine futuristic and peculiar in appearance, stressing the fact that it was an altogether new racing car, challenging the older type of machine.

Behind waited Momberger on another Auto-Union, with Rudolf Caracciola beside him on a Mercedes, and these cars revealed a second aspect of the race as a fight between representatives of the new-style machine. The Mercedes was a little more orthodox in appearance than the Auto-Union, because its engine was at the front; the cowling for the radiator merged with the streamlining over the front springing, the rear of the cockpit also being faired off into a very short and stumpy tail.

A row of three cars followed, formed by the Bugattis, which Benoist and Nuvolari were driving, and by Chiron's Alfa-Romeo. The French machines were very low-built, characteristic of the cars which had carried the racing blue of France for so long. Count Trossi's Alfa-Romeo and a Bugatti, with Dreyfus at the wheel, formed the fourth row, then came Etancelin and Zehender with their Maseratis and von Brauchitsch on his Mercedes. Etancelin, as a Frenchman, had painted his car blue, but Zehender's was a deep red, and these machines were very typical of the older school of motor racing – low-built like the Alfa-Romeos, but longer in appearance because their radiators were carried well forward. The line-up was completed by Fagioli's white Mercedes, which stood by itself at the back.

These were the fastest road-racing machines that the world had ever known, and they remained silent as the minutes passed. The Mercedes drivers adjusted ear-plugs, intended to damp out the shrill and penetrating whine given off by their superchargers; the rest shifted impatiently against the hot concrete until, one after another, each man slipped down into his cockpit.

Not until barely sixty seconds remained were the engines started up, mechanics using crank-handles, because the rules of the race permitted no other method of rousing the engines. Exhaust notes roared out, rising swiftly to a blast of tremendous sound which echoed across the great track and reached the crowd lining the *circuit routier*, beyond the narrow exit towards which the machines faced. Mechanics ran from the cars as a starter poised his flag and, during the moments before the flag dropped, Chiron's Alfa-Romeo began to roll forward as if its driver was impatient and eager to get away. Suddenly the flag fell and, at that, Chiron's scarlet machine hurled itself away from the line in one magnificent burst of acceleration.

The car shot past Caracciola's Mercedes before the German driver had moved a yard, then raced by Stuck, snatching the lead almost before the folds of the flag had brushed the concrete. By that time every car was moving, each driver trying to gain ground as the machines converged on the narrow opening ahead. Chiron dived into it, Caracciola bringing his white Mercedes to his tail while Varzi followed, with Dreyfus and Stuck. The rest came behind, and the low walls which bordered the exit from the track caught the sound that the machines made, merging it to a vibrant, echoing scream which faded only as the cars dashed on to the road ahead. Spectators, leaning over the palisades, drew back as the massed machines rushed level, then shielded their faces from the grit and dust which they kicked behind.

As they cleared the track, Fagioli – who had been last in the line-up – drew his Mercedes to the road-edge, passing the two Maseratis, challenging von Brauchitsch and gaining on the group which pursued Chiron. The leader was ten yards ahead when he placed his machine for the first long bend, then sent the red Alfa-Romeo through it into the straight that led down to the curves at Couard. Caracciola held him through the turns, while Stuck passed Dreyfus and came up to challenge Varzi for third place. These four went through the hairpin at Bruyères with no distance between them, and only a few yards behind came the rest, struggling together and remaining close in the short straight down to Les Biscornes.

Chiron was still in front when he entered the long straight away to Forêt corner. Caracciola was with him, his Mercedes howling furiously; Varzi and Stuck were still fighting behind. Von Brauchitsch, Trossi, Dreyfus and Nuvolari were in a bunch a few yards further back, then came the others, with only Momberger's Auto-Union slowing a little and falling away.

The cars went down the switchback road in streaks of colour that flashed in the hot sunshine: scarlet, silver-white, scarlet again, dead-white, then red and then two flashes of French blue formed by the Bugattis. These colours represented the nations – Italy, Germany and France. They raced level with the spectators behind the fencing, instantly to be gone in a haze of dust which rapidly blotted them out.

All that was left was the falling of grit and small stones which had been kicked high in the air by spinning tyres – that, and the wild roar of exhausts, lessened with increasing distance.

Along that straight, Fagioli gained ground, and at Forêt corner he passed Dreyfus. Beyond the Virage du Gendarme, he overtook Trossi, then passed von Brauchitsch, to challenge Varzi and Stuck by the time that they were near the final corners before the cars ran back to the autodrome.

The crowd in the grandstand heard them approach, and craned to watch the point where the road entered the track on the north side. From between red posts set on yellow-painted walls there came a flash of scarlet. It was Chiron's car, and he was still leading; from a standing start he had covered the course at 85.3 m.p.h. Hardly was he clear of the walls when the drilling scream of a Mercedes sounded and Caracciola shot into sight, flying after the Alfa-Romeo on to the high banking. Two seconds passed, then Fagioli appeared with his Mercedes, to be followed instantly by Stuck's Auto-Union, which came from the opening like a torpedo fired from a deck gun.

Chiron had his Italian machine high on the sloping concrete banking by that time, and the car was curving round towards the flat stretch in front of the grandstand. Close behind were the three German cars, then Varzi's Alfa-Romeo, with von Brauchitsch and Count Trossi. The placing of these machines showed how stern was the challenge to the supremacy of the Scuderia Ferrari. Chiron certainly held the lead, but there were three German cars very close to him; all were well ahead of the blue Bugatti driven by Dreyfus, who led the remainder of the field – Nuvolari, Zehender, Etancelin, Benoist and Momberger – whose Auto-Union was visibly slowing.

Chiron dived for the narrow exit to the road, and the rest dropped off the banking behind him. All were faster down the outward straight – much faster. Stuck opened out, making an attempt to overtake Fagioli who, in the same moment, began to challenge Caracciola. He caught the German champion at Les Biscornes, and went in front of him during the rush to Forêt turn, travelling with Stuck hard on his tail, also passing Caracciola. In the dash back towards the autodrome, Fagioli and Stuck began to fight for second place, running wheel to wheel for a mile, then the Auto-Union slipped ahead.

When Chiron brought his Alfa-Romeo on to the concrete again,

Stuck was no more than half a second behind him; he had picked up two places and had lapped at 89.47 m.p.h. They roared round, with Fagioli third and Caracciola now fourth. As the field appeared, Nuvolari slowed and drew to the side of the track, stopping at his pit. He changed plugs while the rest roared away from him, and when he started in pursuit he had been delayed nearly two minutes.

It was on this third lap that Stuck launched an attack designed to establish the supremacy of his Auto-Union. Chiron held him off until they reached the short straight down to Les Biscornes, and here Stuck passed, taking the lead and drawing away. At Forêt corner, the Auto-Union was two seconds ahead, and at the end of the return straight he had doubled this lead. By the time his white machine raced aslant along the banking of the autodrome he was five seconds in front; he had covered the lap at 90 m.p.h., the highest speed ever set up during a race over the Monthléry circuit.

When Chiron appeared at the tail of the German machine the crowd in the grandstand roared, urging the Frenchman to greater speed. They wanted a Bugatti to win, but these cars were falling far behind. Chiron was driving an Italian machine, but he remained the most popular of French racing men, so they gave him encouragement, waving him after Stuck. Fagioli and Caracciola were together, one hundred yards behind the Alfa-Romeo, with Varzi and Trossi two seconds further back. They disappeared along the *circuit routier*, while the rest came round the banking, and now it seemed that Etancelin was finding trouble; his exhaust was giving off excessive smoke, but he continued.

The situation which had existed at the end of the first lap had changed. Now a German car was leading, followed by an Italian, two more German, then two Italian cars. The white machines held three of the first four places in the race – but Chiron did not attempt to overtake and regain leadership. Hardly twenty miles had yet been covered, and the Frenchman was satisfied to open up a little, not allowing the German to get far ahead and not overstressing his own machine. He let Stuck make the pace, content to wait until he could see how the Auto-Union withstood the strain.

The end of the fourth lap found the position of the machines unaltered. Stuck maintained his speed, and raised the average for the whole race to 88.3 m.p.h., while Chiron – holding him – increased the gap between himself and Fagioli, who led by ten yards from Caracciola.

On the next laps Stuck's average speed rose to 88.6 m.p.h., to 88.8 m.p.h., and then to 88.9 m.p.h. He was working desperately to shake off the Alfa-Romeo, but Chiron remained with him, and even closed the distance between them a little. At the end of the eighth lap the Frenchman was less than a hundred and fifty yards behind, while Fagioli was out-distanced by nearly a quarter of a mile, with Caracciola another hundred yards further back. Varzi, von Brauchitsch and Count Trossi were struggling together, and the field had fallen well away. It was led by Dreyfus, and more cars were in trouble. Zehender stopped for water and oil. Etancelin checked. Nuvolari again pulled in to change his plugs: he was also in difficulties with his gearbox, and the Bugatti reserve driver – Jean-Pierre Wimille – took over.

The order of the leading cars was Auto-Union, Alfa-Romeo, Mercedes, and at the start of the ninth lap Fagioli was signalled to go faster and carry a challenge to the machines ahead. On this lap, too, Chiron decided that he had the measure of the Auto-Union. He opened out and gained steadily upon Stuck while, behind him, Fagioli lapped at 90.6 m.p.h. closing in but remaining third.

The tactics of the drivers had entered another phase. At the outset, Chiron had made the pace, luring the Germans to real speed. When Stuck passed him, Chiron had remained at his tail, forcing the German to a yet higher rate of travel. Now the Mercedes drivers were coming into the fight, afraid that the Auto-Union and the Ferrari machine might get too far ahead. The gaps between the machines narrowed, and when the ninth lap ended, Chiron was within fifty yards of the Auto-Union, the crowd applauding him as he passed the grandstand, obviously intent upon regaining the lead. Fagioli went by, then Caracciola passed and he, too, had closed up; Varzi followed and von Brauchitsch appeared behind him, slowing and running to his pit, where mechanics worked for nearly two and a half minutes on his supercharger; the car restarted, but it had lost much of the stirring roar with which it had begun the race.

On the straight to Forêt corner Chiron caught Stuck. Along the return road he passed the Auto-Union, and the crowd roared when he circled the eastern end of the autodrome, leading. As the two went around the banking, Stuck gradually dropped back while Fagioli appeared behind, rapidly closing the gap between them. As the field followed, Momberger drew into his pit, and he did not restart; the German machine was announced as forming the first retirement of the race.

Answering the pit signal that he had received, Fagioli caught Stuck and passed him, moving at such speed that he set up a new record for the race, covering the circuit at 91.8 m.p.h. When the lap ended he was close upon Chiron while, behind him, both Caracciola and Varzi had also gone in front of Stuck. When the Auto-Union appeared, it ran to where Momberger's car was being pushed away from the pit; Stuck's rear tyres were giving out as a result of his fast driving, and he lost time over the wheel change. When he started purposefully into the race again, he had fallen well behind. The Auto-Union had made its challenge, and had been beaten, and now it was the turn of a Mercedes to race for Germany.

Fagioli was gaining fast, and Chiron knew it. He put his foot hard down, and the average speed of the race rose yet higher. At the end of the twelfth lap it stood at 89.4 m.p.h. – and still Fagioli closed in. Chiron burst into sight on the autodrome once more, his scarlet machine whipping in a red flash along the concrete, then zooming up the banking, climbing high and pursued so closely by the white Mercedes that there was a gap of no more than fifty yards between them.

In their duel, the two had outdistanced Caracciola, who appeared with Achille Varzi hardly two seconds further in the rear. They were followed by Count Trossi, then by Dreyfus and Stuck – who was driving hard to make up ground, and who came round all but wheel to wheel with Benoist's blue Bugatti.

Behind these were Zehender, and then Wimille on Nuvolari's car, and it was while the field was passing that von Brauchitsch appeared, slowing, stopping at the Mercedes pit. His car had been running badly since its last stop; mechanics examined the supercharger again, then the car retired. The crowd watched the Mercedes pushed towards the 'dead car' park, to which Momberger's Auto-Union had gone only two laps before, then attention turned to a double duel which developed during the thirteenth lap.

Chiron was fighting it out with Fagioli's Mercedes; behind them, Caracciola on the second Mercedes was struggling with Varzi on his Alfa-Romeo. On the thirteenth lap Chiron lifted the race average to 89.6 m.p.h., while he and Fagioli both covered the course at a speed of 91.8 m.p.h. – equalling the lap record. Each driver was striving to set a pace which would bring trouble to the other machine, and Fagioli's pursuit was unremitting – but he lost the fight.

When the two started the fourteenth lap Fagioli gained along the outward straight, then suddenly fell away. Chiron drew further and further ahead until at Les Biscornes he was far in front. He completed the lap at a speed of 91.9 m.p.h., all but equalling the record set up during practice over a cleared course, and he passed the grandstand alone.

Seconds dragged out, and still his challenger did not appear. When the shrill drone of an approaching Mercedes sounded, it was Caracciola who came into view – and Varzi was in front of him. The Ferrari men had won the double duel. Fagioli was at Les Biscornes, standing by his car, which was out of the race; it was reported that a pipe line to his hydraulic brakes had broken.

With Fagioli's car disabled, the German attack was broken. Chiron led, and Varzi was second, and both Alfa-Romeos were drawing well ahead of Caracciola, who was slowing. When he next appeared he pulled up at his pit, to remain there for ninety seconds while he took on water and fuel and the wheels were changed. He restarted – but he did not come round again. He vanished, just as Fagioli had done. The car stopped at Les Biscornes near its teammate, and it remained there, abandoned.

Von Brauchitsch had retired on the twelfth lap. Fagioli had fallen out on the fourteenth, and on the sixteenth Caracciola had halted finally, so that the whole of the Mercedes team had dropped from the race in the course of six laps. Momberger had retired with his Auto-Union, and of the Germans only Hans Stuck was left, running a full lap and more behind Chiron.

The Scuderia Ferrari had beaten the German machines, and only eight cars were still in the race. Of these, the two leaders – Chiron and Varzi – and Benoist on a Bugatti were travelling steadily and well. The rest had been brought to difficulties through efforts to hold the pace which had been set.

The gearbox on Trossi's Alfa-Romeo had developed a defect which made it possible only to use two speeds; young Moll had taken over the car and was driving well, despite the defect. Zehender's Maserati lost time through pit stops; the clips holding one rear spring had broken, and mechanics tried to effect a repair. Dreyfus brought his Bugatti in, misfiring badly; when plugs had been changed the mechanics had difficulty in restarting the engine, and the car covered only one lap more before it retired, later to be followed from the track by Wimille's Bugatti.

Soon afterwards Chiron, now leading handily, dashed up to his pit to change all wheels and replenish in ninety-two seconds. His halt allowed Varzi to take the lead for a lap, then the second Ferrari car checked for similar attention, and Chiron went ahead again. Stuck began to gain ground now, driving hard in the hope that he might yet overtake the cars ahead. He began to gain an average of fifteen seconds on each lap, then pulled in to replenish. While he was halted, Moll passed him so that – with the race well beyond half distance – the Scuderia Ferrari held the first three places, and now the drivers began to fight between themselves. Varzi closed on Chiron, and Moll began to overtake Varzi, so that a situation was created similar to that which had existed towards the close of the Tripoli Grand Prix. On the twenty-fourth lap Chiron had a lead of four minutes twenty-one seconds, and Guy Moll was thirteen seconds behind Varzi. Two laps later, Chiron's lead had been reduced to three minutes fifty-two seconds, while Moll had closed down to eleven seconds with Stuck twenty-seven seconds further back. Behind the first four only Benoist and Zehender were still running, so that but six machines were still on the course. The rest had cracked up under the tremendous pace, the effects of which remained. Benoist brought his Bugatti in for a change of plugs, and mechanics had such difficulty in starting his engine that he spent nearly four minutes at his pit. While he was there, Zehender paused to replenish the radiator of his Maserati, then Stuck pulled in, for mechanics to refuel the car and endeavour to repair a water leak.

As the Auto-Union stood by its pit, there was an atmosphere about the machine and the working men which suggested that the car's race was almost run. It made one more lap, then stopped again and, this time, it remained there – withdrawn. The last of the German cars was out of the Grand Prix.

Only seven laps were required to complete the race, when Zehender's Maserati stopped again. Men laboured over the machine, but the back axle had come adrift from the spring at one side, and they could not repair it. This car also retired.

Four laps from the finish, Chiron was leading and Moll held

second place, gained while Varzi checked once more for replenishment. With Varzi third, Benoist's Bugatti was the only other machine left on the track, running a very long way behind and misfiring badly.

Two laps from the end, Moll stopped at his pit, and Varzi went into second place just before Chiron entered his final lap. He covered the *circuit routier* for the last time, to win the race at 85.8 m.p.h. Varzi finished three minutes seventeen seconds behind him, and Moll was a little less than a minute further back. Benoist was flagged in when he had four laps still to cover, which meant that only three machines actually finished the full distance of the event.

FRENCH GRAND PRIX 1934 RESULTS

1   L. Chiron (Alfa-Romeo) 85.8 m.p.h.
2   A. Varzi (Alfa-Romeo)
3   G. Moll (Alfa-Romeo)

From *Great Motor Races* edited by Bruce Carter (Weidenfeld & Nicolson, 1960)

172 Corners – the most frightening track in the world

Cyril Posthumus

Cyril was a very, very nice, know-
ledgeable enthusiast, a quietly spoken
man and it's apt to have him describing
the Nürburgring, a circuit which
through history has been considered
the greatest challenge of all. Going
round it you'd see a lot of holes in the
hedge and you'd think, 'That is where
so-and-so got killed, this is where so-
and-so went off.'

S.M.

The Nürburgring remained a Grand
Prix circuit until 1976, when Niki
Lauda crashed horrifically in a Ferrari [*see* Fuji 1976 page 82] and the
risks became unacceptable. A new,
shorter – 4.542 kilometre – and
infinitely safer circuit was subsequently constructed there and
used for two Grands Prix, in 1984
and 1985. Interestingly, Fangio [in
the extract which follows this one]
estimates the number of corners on
the 'old' Nürburgring as 176! The
disparity demonstrates the enor-
mousness of the place and turns, I
suppose, on quite what you consider
a corner.

C.H.

There is no circuit comparable with the Nürburgring today. Only the Targa Florio circuit
in the mountains of Sicily is longer and more
rugged (and certainly more primitive) but it is not
suitable for Grand Prix racing. Czechoslovakia
used to have her Masaryk-ring, an 18-mile net-
work of bumpy public roads outside Brno, but
that course is no longer used; while Italy has the
15½-mile Pescara road course, nowadays all too
rarely raced on.

Nürburg is unique, and the Germans are justly
proud of it. It all began as a means of alleviating
the crippling unemployment in the Coblenz-
Cologne areas, credit for the idea going to Dr
Creutz, who was District Councillor of the rural
Eifel district west of the Rhine. Several far-sighted
civic dignitaries in the area, led by the *Oberbürger-
meister* of Cologne, one Konrad Adenauer – later,
Chancellor of the West German Federal Republic
– supported Creutz and made strong represent-
ations to the German Government to back the
project financially. They argued that the unem-
ployed had to be paid anyway, that a racing and test circuit would
provide the German car industry with a permanent testing base
which it greatly needed, and that it would open the poor but very
attractive Eifel district to tourists.

To their credit, the Government agreed to assist the City of
Cologne and other local corporations by contributing a sizeable
proportion of the 15 million marks needed to put down some
eighteen miles of circuit through virgin country in the forested Eifel

mountains, and on 27 September 1925 Dr Fuchs, Supreme President of the Rhineland, laid the foundation stone of 'the first German mountain speed and essay track'. Within its tortuous boundaries stood one of the Rhineland's oldest castles, the ruined twelfth-century *Schloss Nürburg*, so they called the circuit the Nürburgring.

In its full 17.58-mile length, including both the 14.17-mile *Nordschleife* and the 4.8-mile *Sudschleife* it contains no less than 172 corners of infinite variety, 88 being left-hand and 84 right-hand. The two *schleifen* share the same dual parallel strips on a high plateau, containing the grandstands, timing boxes, paddock, pits and other facilities, all loftily overlooked by the *Schloss Nürburg* on its own mountain.

Describing the Nürburgring always provides a vigorous exercise of superlatives, and sometimes expletives from those learning its intricacies the hard way. Sir Henry Birkin said: 'It is an absolute switchback, the abruptness of the corners, their frequency, and the undulation of the road being quite without parallel.' Said Raymond Mays: 'I went to bed wondering if I should ever learn that bewilderingly intricate circuit ... There are fantastically fast downhill stretches, several blind pieces where you climb sharply and the road disappears into the skyline. . . .' Said Mike Hawthorn: 'The fantastic twists and turns are as difficult to negotiate as they are to pronounce. . . . I'm told there are 172 corners. I didn't stop to count them . . .' Said Tony Brooks: 'My favourite circuit. . . . You don't find yourself coming up to the same corner every three miles. . . . But it is also very tough . . . the most fatiguing circuit of all . . .' Said well-known motoring journalist W. F. Bradley: 'The dominating impression is that a drunken giant was allowed to reel around the Eifel mountains, and then road contractors followed in his tracks.' To describe it in full detail corner-by-corner would almost fill this book!

The *Nordschleife*, today the only circuit used, contains only 4 km of straight in its 22.18 km, and that straight is interrupted by hump-backed bridges. Apart from the broad *Startplatz* between the pits and the huge grandstand, it is of normal road width; cars blast down to the wide sweep of the *Sudkehre* (South Curve) and back behind the pits to the slightly banked *Tribunenkehre* or *Nordkehre* (North Curve) where they sweep left and vanish from the grandstand view.

Plunging downhill through the *Hatzenbach* and *Quiddelbacher*

Höhe in the forested Hocheichen valley, up past the *Flugplatz* and the *Schwedenkreuz* (Swedish Cross), the road writhes its way down to the *Fuchsröhre* (Foxhole), then up again to *Adenauerforst* (Adenau Forest). A series of fast curves then brings cars in a downhill rush to Adenau Gate, then they climb past the cliff-like walls of *Bergwerk*, plunge through a valley, then steeply uphill to the *Karussel* (Merry-go-round). This is the most famous corner on the Ring, turning almost a full circle, with a concrete-banked ditch on the inside. (Caracciola's mechanic Wilhelm Sebastian is credited with discovering the time-saving method of using the ditch as a banking in 1928–29.)

After the *Karussel* a long, winding climb follows to the *Höhe Acht*, then dives down twisting and turning to *Brünnchen*, through the fast *Pflanzgarten* bend and on to the *Schwalbenschwanz* (Swallowtail) double turn. Up, then, to the *Dottinger Höhe* and a left-hand sweep on to the home straight with its humpbacked bridges, a last 120 m.p.h. curve under the *Antoniusbuche* (Antonius Beech) and so back to the start and another tortuous 14.17-mile lap.

Such a course demands complete concentration and fitness from a driver. In truth, he (or she) can never practise enough. Its mountainous location makes rain and fog frequent hazards, aggravated because they may visit one point of the circuit and not another, so that a driver has always to be wary. There are steep drops, trees and banks to trap the errant car, while the massed overhanging pines drip on to the course and delay drying. These same pines, imparting what American journalist Henry Manney once called 'a general air of impending doom', also contribute to the Ring's matchless scenic splendour.

The Germans take their *Grosser Preis* very seriously. Thousands upon thousands trek to the Ring the day and night before the race, camping in the sloping meadows and woods bordering the circuit. Clad in the *lederhosen*, bush shirts and Bavarian hunting hats with little feathers or badger's brushes that make up the uniform of the average Teutonic open air lover, they pass the hours singing round their campfires, while the local taverns and cafés ring with drinking songs, and the noise of arriving traffic goes on all night, until at last the dawn, generally rather chilly, creeps over the Eifel and *der Tag* has arrived. That brings many thousands more to queue for the car parks, while yet other thousands have already taken up their positions around the course. The grandstand opposite the pits alone holds 10,000 people; another 20,000 fill the enclosures around the *Startplatz*, and 15,000–20,000 gather in the *Karussel* area.

This tremendous mass enthusiasm pervades the entire place with that indefinable 'racing atmosphere' which the short British circuits so manifestly lack. In the vast *Start und Ziel* area countless multi-coloured flags flutter; there are stalls selling *milch*, *wurst*, *schokolade*, *frankfurters*, *bier*, racing postcards; countless advertising devices adjure one to use Continental, Dunlop or Fulda tyres, Bosch plugs, Gedore spanners, or to *trink* the ubiquitous Coca-Cola. Balloons taking the shape of a Varta battery or one of Dr Hiller's *pfefferminz* or *Edel-drops* hover and bob above the busy scene; there are hordes of police and armletted officials wielding the usual German efficiency – too much of it sometimes – bands play, loudspeakers bray, and everywhere are people en masse. It is a heady atmosphere, and when at last the cars come swooping up one by one through the tunnel from the paddock and make for the pits or the grid, excitement really mounts, and one begins to understand why Nürburg attendances are so high.

From *The German Grand Prix* by Cyril Posthumus (Temple Press Books, 1965)

The Old Devil Nürburgring

Juan-Manuel Fangio

This is one of the classic drives of all time by perhaps the greatest driver of all time. I was witness to it. I know the word incredible is much devalued these days but what Fangio did on 4 August 1957 was, and remains, absolutely that. The thing about Fangio is that he's the greatest driver of all. He had enormous stamina. He was a very humble man, courteous. In a car he had genius. Frankly I can't put it any other way. I co-drove with him at Mercedes, I drove the same cars, and his absolute forte was Formula One. I could beat him in sports cars and I did beat him in the British Grand Prix at Aintree in 1955 when we were both with Mercedes. I don't know to this day whether he let me win and to this day he won't say. All he will say is that, 'It was Stirling's day.' Frankly that's not an answer!

S.M.

'If I hadn't moved over, I'm sure the old devil would have driven right over me.' The words are those of the Englishman Mike Hawthorn. He had just lost the German Grand Prix to Juan-Manuel Fangio by a mere 3.6 seconds. The Argentine had passed him on the penultimate lap, on the mixed curves before Breidscheid, at the entry to the first curve to the left. He explained by means of gestures exactly how the champion had carried out the manoeuvre by means of which he was crowned champion again for the fifth time. While his right hand (his Ferrari) keeps to the right, his left hand (Fangio's Maserati) shows how he kept on the inside of him while he was braking, and how he got onto the inside of the track, forcing him to pull over with a sudden and startled movement. To the 'S' shape traced by his right hand, he added the phrase quoted above, which in time became famous.

Twenty-seven years after that historic race, Fangio laughs at the memory of Hawthorn's words: 'Yes, I might have done, I might well have done. That day I had everything turned on and firing on all cylinders. I was ready to do anything. Whichever way you look at it, it was an extraordinary race. When it was all over, I was convinced that I would never be able to drive like that again, never. I had reached my limit of concentration and will to win . . . Those were the two things that allowed me to take the risks I took that day; I knew I could win, but I knew equally well that I could lose. But I knew exactly what I was doing, and what risks I was taking. The Nürburgring was always my favourite track, from the first day I drove on it, in an Alfetta in 1951. I fell totally in love with it, and I believe that on that day [in 1957] I finally managed to master it. It was as if I had screwed all its secrets out of it, and got to know it once and for all . . .

Perhaps some other day it might have turned against me and beaten me, but that day I was stretching myself to the limit, as was my car. I was testing myself, testing the machine. I was trying out new things during those last laps of the race, pushing myself further at many blind spots where I had never before had the courage to go to the limit. I was never a daredevil, never a spectacular driver. I would go just so fast and no faster. I never tried to shoot far ahead, or to be stylish for its own sake. I always tried to be well positioned, weighing up the opposition. Quite simply, I had always been a man with faith in my own abilities and in the machines that were prepared for me to drive. Till that race, I had demanded nothing more of myself or the cars. But that day I made such demands on myself, that I couldn't sleep for two days afterwards. I was in such a state that whenever I shut my eyes it was as if I were in the race again, making those leaps in the dark on those curves where I had never before had the courage to push things so far . . . For two days I experienced delayed-action apprehension at what I had done, a feeling that had never come over me after any other race, a feeling that still returns to me to this day when I think about that time. I had never driven as I drove then, but I also knew that I'd never be able to go so fast again, ever!'

The story of Fangio and the legendary German circuit begins in 1951: 'We arrived at Nürburgring with our defeat at Silverstone fresh in our minds. Since 1946, the Alfa-Romeo team had not lost a race, but that day had to come . . . I had told Froilán González that we would have a showdown in England. I had no such feelings at Nürburgring, where I felt attracted to the circuit from the very first moment. Perhaps this had something to do with my admiration for Tazio Nuvolari, and the memory of his triumph here in 1935 in an Alfa-Romeo, against the faster Mercedes-Benz and Auto-Union cars, or perhaps the feats of Rudolf Caracciola. What happened to me at the Nürburgring was like what happens when a friend speaks to you about a woman you don't know, and she turns out to be much more attractive than you had imagined when you actually meet her. The relationship wasn't easy, of course. Getting to know the Nürburgring was like getting to know a woman. You can't memorize 176 curves over more than fourteen miles, just as you can't memorize 176 feminine wiles after a short acquaintance.

'It's impossible to get to know it all in a short time. All you have are reference points: "Up to there, I can go at such and such a speed.

From then on, there is a difficult succession of curves." For example, after the "carousel", the first and second curves could be taken with confidence, accelerating; then came a downhill stretch where you saw a wooden hut; this was an alarm signal for difficult "S" bends . . . It is difficult to keep fourteen miles in your head, so for that reason I tried to blot from my mind all the slow parts. What you had to keep in your mind were the fast bits, because dealing with slow curves is like driving in the mountains – you go by what you see, and take them as they come. That's why I always say that mountain driving is not so difficult; what is difficult is dealing with high speed curves. There you can't afford the luxury of confusing one with another . . .

'That is exactly what happened to me in 1951 with the Alfetta in practice. I came up to a left-hand turn faster than I should have done, was taken by surprise, tried to change down, and the clutch didn't respond. I went off the track sideways. In the end the tail hit a mound of earth that was between me and a line of trees, and that stopped the car. I'm glad that mound was there. Over the rest of the circuit, I had to struggle with the first and second gears that wouldn't engage no matter how hard I slammed them, so I pulled into the pits in a foul mood. This happened when I had already managed one of the fastest times, and I did better later.'

However, Fangio fought Ascari and González for the lead, until the time came to stop to refuel. He joined the race again, did the fastest lap, and regained the lead. When Ascari stopped to refuel, he had an advantage of almost two minutes over him, but his turn for a pit-stop came round again:

'The clutch was dragging so badly that the engine stalled on me when I was about to rejoin the race. That's when I lost any chance I had of winning. While my tyres were being changed, Ascari increased his lead from a minute to a minute and a half. In the end I was second, a bit over half a minute behind, and aching in every bone of my body. When I got out of the car, I wondered if I was still all in one piece . . . In those days, we didn't strap ourselves in. Seat belts didn't exist, and at the Nürburgring, what with flying up and down when going over humps, and knocking from left to right when cornering, we ended up pulverized.

'At the factory, when they dismantled the clutch again, they found that the groove in the flywheel where the spring was supposed to seat was not deep enough. So, when you accelerated and de-clutched, the spring came out of the groove, stayed out, and you had no more clutch. That meant that you could only use first and second at the start.'

In his first race at Nürburgring, Juan-Manuel Fangio had to be content with a second place and a fastest lap. That was the year in which he became world champion for the first time, at Barcelona.

Being unable to take part in 1952 because of his accident at Monza, Fangio returned to Nürburgring the following year, when Ferraris had things all their own way. Germany was no exception. Ascari achieved a record practice time and the fastest lap. Farina won the race, beating Fangio by a minute and five seconds.

That second place of 1953 was the last time Fangio followed anyone to the line in the German Grand Prix. From 1954 on, he set about finally conquering the Nürburgring and winning the Diamond Star.

The start of this epic was marked by one of the hardest blows he suffered in his career. Onofre Marimón, the son of his old friend Domingo, who had asked him to take the lad under his wing in Europe, was killed during practice on Saturday 31 July 1954:

'Moss had done very good times in his privately entered Maserati, and I think this had agitated Pinocho [Marimón's nickname], who was the number one team driver now that I had transferred to Mercedes-Benz. On Friday night I had told him to keep calm, and that I would show him the way for one or two laps on the following day. I don't know how it happened. When I went to the pits to get into my machine, he was already on his way.'

Neither Fangio, nor González, nor Mieres, nor Clemar Bucci, who were also competing, saw him alive again. The Grand Prix of Europe and Germany, which should have been a time of rejoicing for this group of Argentine drivers, had turned into a tragic drama.

During practice, Fangio bettered the times he had done in 1951 in the Alfa-Romeo. In spite of the greater power of the Alfa's supercharged engine, the 2½-litre Mercedes-Benz cars could count on the world's most advanced engineering. He managed to beat Hawthorn's Ferrari by more than three seconds, and Moss's Maserati was in third place on the front row of the grid. However, it was Froilán González, starting in the second row, who made the running over the first miles:

'Froilán set off as if taking part in a stampede, and I only managed to pass him on the fast section at the end of the first lap, where the track dips under a bridge and bends to the left. This was the first time we raced the Mercedes-Benz with its wheels uncovered in the normal way. We had started off in France and England with totally streamlined cars, but after the poor showing at Silverstone, I insisted that we should have cars so set up that you could see what the wheels were doing. Kling, Lang and I had cars with uncovered wheels. Herrmann had to make do with a streamliner.

'Once I had caught Froilán, I began to regulate the pace, which was far from forced. For a number of laps I had him on my tail, but then he was overtaken by my team-mates Lang and Kling. The pit-board later told me that Kling was in second place. Soon enough, he showed up in my mirrors, and I was none too pleased when he overtook me. I wasn't worried, though, because my car was in perfect shape. I began to follow him and wait for an opportune moment to take the lead again. But Kling was racing in front of the home crowd, and that was making him go decidedly fast. I therefore had no choice but to press him harder, in order to take advantage of any mistakes he might make . . . In the pits, Neubauer was frantic, because this was not how the race was supposed to be run. But I was not responsible for this state of affairs, so every time I passed the pits, I pointed my finger at Kling, as if to say he had no right to be there. Luckily for the health of our competition manager, something went wrong with the suspension of Kling's car, and he almost slid off the track in the middle of a curve; he stopped at the pits for attention, and my lead was more than comfortable. I finished more than a minute and a half before Hawthorn in his Ferrari.'

There were no celebrations, however, for all the Argentines, who were mourning the death of Onofre Marimón. Ironically, Stirling Moss had retired in the second lap, and the best-placed Maserati was Sergio Mantovani's, which was fifth, almost nine minutes behind Fangio. If only Pinocho had not been so swayed by the hastiness of youth on that last Saturday in July!

As there was no German Grand Prix in 1955, Fangio returned to the Nürburgring in 1956, this time as a Ferrari driver. In the middle of a difficult season, Juan came back to his beloved circuit heartened by his win at Silverstone.

'During the race, as happened so often, my only real rivals were my team-mates. That time, on the track, it was war. Castellotti retired at the pits with magneto trouble and took over Musso's car, and then ended up in a ditch. Collins was challenging me for the fastest lap ... I had to reduce my practice time by ten seconds in order to beat him and to break that record, as I had promised I would! In the end, Collins pushed his car too far, and retired at the pits. He took over Portago's, but he didn't get very far in that one, either. Halfway through the race, my Ferrari was the only one doing any laps of any kind, so I was easy on the engine right to the end.'

He was followed by a procession of Maseratis. These cars had proved themselves to be very reliable, suggesting that they could be developed still further. Moss, as usual, led them, but at no time in the race was he able to get anywhere near Fangio.

Having been the winner with Mercedes-Benz and Lancia-Ferrari, Juan-Manuel Fangio had yet to show what he was capable of aboard a Maserati 250F, with which he had dominated (albeit with difficulty) the Ferraris and Vanwalls:

'At the Nürburgring in 1957, we were expecting a great show of force from the British Vanwalls, but from the first day of practice they suffered from suspension and road-holding problems. That meant that we only had to beware of the Ferraris, which could go the whole race without needing to fill up or change tyres. They had Englebert tyres, which were very hard, and could cover the 310 miles of the race without any difficulty. We were relying on Pirellis. These were softer, but provided better grip. The Maserati could put up a very good show with those tyres, as it was well balanced and very manageable, but the trouble was that the tyres wouldn't last the race. So the mechanics did some trial runs, and in thirty seconds were able both to change the two rear wheels and put in more fuel. The man who was then chief mechanic, Guerrino Bertocchi, said to me, "If you take off thirty seconds halfway through the race, we'll change your tyres in thirty seconds."'

In practice, Fangio broke the record with a time that bettered by 24.5 seconds the time he had done in the Mercedes-Benz, and that done in the Lancia-Ferrari by 25.6 seconds. At his side at the start were Hawthorn (Ferrari), Behra (Maserati), and Collins (Ferrari). His ex-scuderia team-mates were driving the 801 model, derived from the 1956 Lancia-Ferrari. It had a shorter wheelbase and was very manoeuvrable, a rival to be taken seriously, although he had bettered Hawthorn's practice time by nearly three seconds under identical conditions, with both cars carrying little fuel.

'From the start', Juan recalls, 'the two Ferraris took the lead. I let them do so, and in fact I was surprised at the way they kept passing each other instead of working together as a team. Instead of thinking about how to get out in front together, they were playing around for the lead. I kept behind for the first two laps, and that allowed me to study their style of racing. On the third lap, I took advantage of the fact that they had stopped dicing with each other, and challenged and overtook both.'

Fangio was going ten seconds faster than he had done the year before in the Lancia-Ferrari, and by the middle of the race he had a twenty-eight-second advantage. On the following lap, the twelfth, he went into the pits twenty-eight seconds ahead:

'I stopped the car and got out. While I was having a drink, Bertocchi and Ugolini were putting me in the picture about the state of the race. My mechanics were working away, but they weren't doing a good job. I don't know whether they were nervous or what, but the fact is that I lost all the advantage I had gained, plus another forty-eight seconds. While they were working, I heard the two Ferraris pass, one very close to the other . . . When the mechanics finally lowered the jack, they had taken much longer than they had first allowed for. There were ten laps left of the twenty-two-lap race. When I set out again I felt quite disappointed, as I was losing a race that could win me the championship.

'I had to get the tyres bedded in, so on the next lap I was fifty-one seconds behind. After that, the car really began to perform to my liking. I knew the Nürburgring very well. It's one of those tracks where you lose touch with things; you think you're going fast and you're not going fast at all. I began to use higher gears. I had learnt from experience that if you left the car in a higher gear for some of the faster curves, and as long as you went in at the correct angle, you came out with the engine revving at a faster rate on the following straight, which made a difference in terms of time. It wasn't very comfortable, feeling the lack of grip as the car went round, but after all, I had to win. I began to take nearly all the bends in a higher gear than I would have normally used. That's how I was driving when I came to the dip below the bridge, where I had passed Froilán in 1954 in order to gain the lead in the first lap. This time, I didn't lift my foot off the accelerator. Normally, we took that curve in fifth, trying to skim rather than jump, so as not to jolt the car and allow a margin for error when it landed. This time I took it without slackening at all, with my foot down. I tried to stick well to the inside above the dip, where the car "took off", and I touched the ground again on the opposite side of the track, uncomfortably close to the wire fence . . . There were no guard-rails in those days. In my mirror I saw the cloud of dust I'd raised at the edge of the track. I'd done it right. It was a risk worth taking. The curve linked two straight stretches, and I had treated it as if it were just one straight. I knew I'd make up some seconds there.

'They told me afterwards that there had been quite a stir in the Ferrari pits. As I seemed at first to be losing rather than gaining after my pit-stop, they had told their drivers to reduce their pace. But when they looked at their stopwatches after the first lap in which I used higher gears, they couldn't believe their eyes. I had made up ten seconds!'

Of course, it was not only the Ferrari team's stopwatches that had registered the difference. So had those of other teams and of the race organizers. The loudspeakers round the track announced the feat, and the public broke into loud applause. On the sixteenth lap, Fangio came very near to the fastest lap he had done the fifth time round, but it was on the next lap that the real battle against the clock began, as he chased the Ferraris. What follows is a breakdown of how the times for fastest laps improved. The twelfth alone was not done by Fangio but by Peter Collins. That was the lap when Fangio stopped in the pits to refuel and change the rear tyres:

LAP	MINUTES	SECONDS	KPH
2nd	9	34.6	142.8
3rd	9	33.4	143.2
5th	9	33.0	143.3
6th	9	32.5	143.4
8th	9	30.8	143.8
10th	9	29.5	144.0
12th	9	28.9	144.4
17th	9	28.5	144.5
18th	9	25.3	145.3
19th	9	23.4	145.7
20th	9	17.4	147.8

When Hawthorn had completed his twentieth lap and had two laps to go, he had a lead of one second over Collins and three over Fangio:

'On that lap, I saw a red blur disappearing round a bend, among the trees, and I said to myself: "I'll certainly catch that Ferrari." The pits had signalled to me that there were not two cars in front of me, but only one. I had no idea that the other was only a few metres in front of the one I had seen. On the Adenau descent, I saw the two red cars, one behind the other. I knew I was going to catch them. By the time we passed the pits, I was tailing them. We came into the second to last lap, passed the semi-circle, onto the straight behind the pits, and on the way into the left-hand North curve, I got on the inside of Collins. I had pressed the Maserati a bit too hard, and it was too far over coming out of the curve. Collins gained some yards on me and overtook me again, and placed himself strategically for the next curve.

'I didn't want him to think he had got the better of me, I stuck to his tail through a series of bends until we reached a short straight that led upwards to a bridge. I got alongside him. At the speed we were going, it seemed that there wouldn't be room for two cars. I had overtaken him before, and Collins gave way, I got in front of him at the little bridge and went down the "toboggan run" that followed it. And there was Hawthorn's Ferrari, right in front of me, going down into a right-hand bend.

'I accelerated through the various bends that followed. I started tailing him, and was beginning to work out how many chances I had left to overtake him, when the opportunity suddenly presented itself. After that series of curves came a short straight, which ended in a ninety-degree turn to the left, followed by an equally sharp turn to the right. On the straight stretch, Hawthorn pulled to the right to get his angle. I saw my chance, and cut in on his inside. Hawthorn must have suddenly seen a red blur to his left, because he suddenly pulled over as if startled. The Englishman collected his wits again, but not enough to press me hard. I made a point of getting away from him before reaching the straight, because there he might have taken advantage of my slipstream and passed me. My lead was sufficient for him not to be able to stick close to me. I kept it up for the whole of the last lap, and won the race.

'What a celebration there was! I was carried here, there and everywhere on people's shoulders. When I managed to get to the podium, Hawthorn and Collins were ecstatic, as if they had been the winners. They never stopped congratulating me and shaking me by the hand, even though my car had thrown up a stone and broken one of the lenses of Peter's goggles. They were both very good lads. Both truly appreciated me, and their congratulations were sincere. I was already sure that this was so in the case of Collins, who had shown his respect for me the year before, at Monza, when he gave up his car to me . . . The proof that I had gained the respect of Hawthorn came some months later, at Reims, my last race.'

From *Fangio: My Racing Life* by Juan-Manuel Fangio with Roberto Carozzo
(Patrick Stephens Limited, 1986)

The Le Mans Story

Georges Fraichard

The annual 24-hour race, run on roads just outside the town of Le Mans, began in 1923 and quickly became world famous.

C.H.

The motor car had already done much to spread the name of Le Mans before 1923. In 1873, Amedée Bollée was making a vehicle which 'could move without horses, at a rapid walking pace' in his small workshop in Le Mans. The cars which for so long carried his name, illustrious among the pioneers, have disappeared from the roads like so many others. But the works still exist, and you can see them on the outskirts of the town on the left, coming from Paris.

Old timers remember the first Grand Prix of the Automobile Club of France, organized in his locality in 1900 by the young men who were then the guiding spirits of the Automobile Club de l'Ouest. It was a typical Grand Prix of the period: 770.499 miles had to be covered in two days on a circuit measuring 64.113 miles. I was much too young then and I do not regret missing this race, however exciting it may have been, which was won by Pierre Szisz driving a powerful Renault at an average of just over 63 m.p.h. The new circuit, used in 1911 and 1913, measured only 33.554 to the lap.

In 1921, a new request by the Automobile Club de France to hold its annual Grand Prix made Georges Durand and his friends think in less grandiose terms.

The proposed circuit measured only 10.726 to the lap. It had been laid out so close to the town that its nearest point was at Pontlieue, a suburb of Le Mans, at the intersection of the Tours and Laigné roads.

The American racing driver Jim Murphy won this race at an average of just over 77.5 m.p.h., driving his big Duesenberg, despite the tricky bits through Pontlieue. This proved that the circuit was suitable for high speeds. By carrying out modifications to meet its special requirements this could become the ideal circuit for the twenty-four-hour race.

And, of course, it was here that it did take place, on 26 May 1923, before a great crowd. The organizers had chosen this spring date in the hope that the first race would be favoured by good weather. But squalls of wind and rain followed each other throughout the night, making a fantastic and unprecedented scene. The cars sped by with all their lights blazing, past the grandstands and pits, which were also lit up by current supplied by the town grid. France had never before seen motor racing like this.

In the event of an electrical breakdown (not unusual in those days), there were two sets of field generators, while dangerous corners and difficult sections of the course were marked by acetylene lamps.

The general organization may have been somewhat primitive by our standards, but the race organization proved to be perfect. The timekeepers could easily read the numbers of the passing cars and, all round the circuit, observers watched to see that the race was run according to the rules and regulations. They also saw to the information service, helped by Victor Hémery, the driver of the only private car to be allowed on the circuit during the race. This car was at the complete disposal of Charles Faroux, but on his instructions it could also take round members of what is now known as 'Crowd Control', or of the medical services if this became necessary.

Victor Hémery, who unfortunately died recently, was in later races replaced by another driver, the worthy Walter Sleator, but there is always one car which has the privilege of going round the circuit among the competing cars. For this very first race the start took place at four in the afternoon, and the tradition thus set has been observed ever since.

As laid down by the regulations, there were no final placings, but, except for the S.A.R.A., the Berliet and the Lorraine, which retired after covering respectively 139.439, 461.221 and 525.578 miles, all the other competitors qualified for the second round of the first triennial Rudge Whitworth Cup.

The two Chenard et Walcker cars covered the greatest distance in the twenty-four hours: car No. 9 – 1371.939 miles (57.206 m.p.h. average) and car No. 10 – 1330.035 miles (55.418 m.p.h. average). The two Bignan cars came next, while the Bentley which followed them put in the fastest lap of 66.690 m.p.h.

At the finish a spectacular accident took place: Paul Gros was crossing the track to shake hands with a friend when Bachmann arrived, going flat out in his Chenard. Gros was shot some twenty feet into the air, and was very lucky not to have been killed outright.

This first event had provided much valuable experience. The competing manufacturers, and particularly those who had come to watch, immediately recognized the value and importance of such a display; the drivers, too, had learnt much; but it was the organizers who benefited most by the lessons of this race.

Even before the start, the road surface had not been perfect. It was definitely bad after so many cars had gone over it repeatedly at high speed, totalling some 31,000 miles, without counting the mileage put in during practice!

Georges Durand is reputed to have ordered: 'This is a very serious problem, Le Tyneves, and one which you must solve.' The Civil Engineer raised his arms to Heaven in a gesture of despair.

From *The Le Mans Story* by Georges Fraichard
(The Sportsmans Book Club, 1956)

Le Mans 1955 – the most tragic race of all

L'EQUIPE

Jacques Ickx

The landscape of Le Mans, normally such a happy place, is coloured only grey. A curtain of fine rain obscures it. The weather itself seems to want to be unified with the sombre thoughts which have weighed so heavily on everyone since Saturday.

In their Jaguar number 6, Hawthorn – open faced and curly blond hair – and Bueb get ready to welcome a victory without joy. They have won as decisively as they could after the retirement of their main opposition.

Their average speed eclipsed the existing record despite twelve hours in the rain on slippery tyres in a demoralizing atmosphere. The record lap by Hawthorn passed all imagination . . .

But a victory in mourning cannot satisfy anyone, and there will always remain doubt about what actually happened.

The 'race of three' (Jaguar, Mercedes and Ferrari) so eagerly anticipated never happened. The monster cars of Ferrari collapsed from the start, proving once again that at Le Mans sheer brutal engine power means nothing without meticulous preparation. The Mercedes, on the other hand, held the advantage until an order from their headquarters in Stuttgart made them withdraw; but you cannot, viewing the Mercedes, talk of domination.

These 24 hours of Le Mans were cut in two by the appalling tragedy which struck so hard that the organizers, the ACO – without doubt the most conscientious organizers of all – were completely overtaken by the course of events.

I was in the pits, specifically standing on the pit lane counter. I wasn't due to take over from Fangio just yet. I saw it happen, although when you're just watching the cars go past, you don't get a replay so I didn't say at the time, 'That looked a dodgy move'. You have to put the bits together in hindsight to work out why it happened. Mike pulled over in front of Macklin, and if he'd been thinking about it he'd probably have given it another thirty feet. But don't forget this was a battle and they were *racing*.

S.M.

On the evening of Sunday 12 June, seventy-eight spectators lay dead after a crash at Le Mans which is still a subject of profound controversy. Dramatis personae: Mike Hawthorn and Ivor Bueb in a Jaguar; Juan-Manuel Fangio and Moss in a Mercedes; veteran Frenchman Pierre Levegh in another Mercedes; Lance Macklin in an Austin Healey. In the third hour of the race Hawthorn, preparing to pit, pulled in front of Macklin who braked and skidded. Levegh, coming hard behind, struck the Austin Healey and ploughed into the crowd.

C.H

Before that, the race was a frenzied sprint whose pointlessness still unleashed enormous enthusiasm. It was profoundly beautiful to see, for two hours, the drivers refusing to accept realistic objectives [running at an even pace to complete the 24 hours] and wanting instead – at any price and for the love of glory – to put their mark on the fantastic initial stages.

In this dog fight Eugenio Castelotti [Ferrari], well placed at the start, had to achieve miracles for an hour before being caught as much by Hawthorn (Jaguar) as by Fangio (Mercedes), come from a long way back after being lost in the middle of the pack. He broke and re-broke the track record.

The second hour belonged to Fangio; the third to Hawthorn who'd been passed by Fangio but re-passed him quickly and set lap records of such speed that nobody could threaten them. Then came the drama which it is useless to return to today because everything that can be said about it has been said.

It was total disarray among the competitors. Hawthorn and Karl Kling [Mercedes] stopped for a long time. When they went back out Fangio had escaped their clutches; and the pit stops, Moss taking over from Fangio and Bueb from Hawthorn, accentuated the advantage of the Mercedes number 19.

At the ninth hour, at one o'clock in the morning, the two Mercedes held a substantial lead. People no longer spoke of the Ferraris, of which the last retired after 109 laps. At this moment Fangio and Moss could count a lead of almost two laps but nothing is certain in a 24-hour race with only half the night gone and anything can still happen . . .

In fact events were already moving. Since the catastrophe of the third hour the Mercedes officials in their pit had vainly tried to telephone the senior management in Stuttgart, who alone could decide if their drivers would continue the struggle or be stopped as a sign of mourning. At last Stuttgart replied: 'Stop immediately.' The silver-coloured cars returned to their pits, leaving the track to the Jaguars.

It was no small task which faced Hawthorn, nerve shaken by having been cruelly mixed up in the drama of the day before, and the newcomer Bueb. They were alone out there, alone with the rain.

From *L'Equipe*, 13 June 1955

I was not in agreement with the decision to withdraw. None of us were. I can see why it was done but it was of no benefit. Obviously there was a big problem in that if Mercedes had withdrawn immediately after the accident a lot of people would have left the circuit, causing chaos on the roads which the ambulances had to use. That would have been terrible. The decision was taken later — out of respect, I suppose — because they had to get hold of the directors in Germany and that wasn't easy to do. Fangio and I weren't happy about it because we were in the lead and the decision didn't really do anything. We felt it wouldn't bring back the dead — even if there was never another motor race ever anywhere in the world. We felt people had gone for a race and we were making a race. It was an easier decision to take when you're in Stuttgart than when you're at the circuit in the middle of the race because you haven't got the passion of the moment.

S. M.

Pierre Lalanne

We have succeeded in meeting Lance Macklin, the driver of the Austin Healey which was hit by the Mercedes of Levegh. The Englishman told us of the profound sadness which the fantastical allegations from certain of our fellow journalists have caused him.

'People maintain I lost my head after the accident, and that I set off like a madman in my car through the crowd. It's absolutely false. On the contrary, I was very calm, perfectly in control of myself and I stayed for more than half an hour in my pit. After that I stayed for at least two hours at the circuit. It was only then that, with my brother-in-law, I returned to the town to telephone and reassure my family, which had been impossible at the circuit because the lines were blocked.'

The question which is still on the tip of our tongues is the centre of the drama. How did it happen? Lance Macklin, better placed than anyone to see and understand, replied simply and frankly.

'I had just been passed by the Jaguar which Mike Hawthorn drove. I couldn't exceed a speed of 180/190 k.p.h. while Hawthorn ran at around 260. He undoubtedly wanted to pass me to gain one or two seconds and then get back over to the right in order to stop at his pit for refuelling. [The pits were on the right.] Maybe he miscalculated his distance. He moved back over too abruptly, and above all he braked with equal abruptness.

'The brakes of the Jaguar are much more powerful than those of the Austin Healey and for my part I had to brake for dear life – my wheels locked – to avoid wiping myself out against the rear of my fellow driver's car. This extremely powerful braking was the cause of the drama. What I didn't want to do to Hawthorn, Levegh couldn't avoid doing to me.

'At the instant my wheels locked, my car swerved slightly and began a skid. I succeeded in regaining control over the car and, just as I gave a sigh of relief, a shattering blow at the back of the car made it pirouette. My left rear wheel was torn off and I was projected at more than a hundred k.p.h. backwards towards the railing without being able to control anything.

'When I got back to my pit Hawthorn sent one of his mechanics to me saying that he [Hawthorn] wanted to speak to me. I replied that I had nothing to say to him. Then he came himself. I was perfectly calm: he was like a madman, in an extreme state of hyper-excitement. He'd realized at that moment the appalling consequences of his manoeuvre. He'd realized and wanted to speak to me, as if he could draw comfort from that.'

From *L'Equipe*, 13 June 1955

My first taste of Le Mans [1972] was a pretty stark experience, a bit like viewing the world through a black and white filter. In contrast to those wonderfully colourful, sunlit days driving the Formula One Ferrari, Le Mans seemed drab and full of foreboding.
Derek Bell, four times winner

You don't feel the speed unless you look sideways.
Alain de Cadenet, private entrant

I don't think the race is dangerous from a fatigue point of view but I think it's too long: 24-hour racing is a bore to the drivers, the managers, the mechanics, nobody enjoys it at all except the spectators, but they are the most important people.
Mike Hailwood, 1974

What's it like at 230 m.p.h. down the Mulsanne Straight?
The cars are so stable that it gives you a chance to relax.
Derek Bell

Casablanca 1958

Mike Hawthorn

Looking back on Casablanca, Mike did the biggest favour he could have done for me! He repaid me for giving evidence on his behalf after the Portuguese Grand Prix, two races before Morocco, where he went up the escape road and had to be push-started – which was outside assistance and therefore meant disqualification. When I gave evidence I said, 'Look, Mike wasn't actually on the circuit so that, although it's almost a technical point, the push start wasn't illegal.' Mike was reprieved – he finished second to me in the race. I didn't want to win the Championship by default, as it were. The favour? Being the name of a chap who won the title a certain year is less important to me than being the chap who many say should have won it but never did – it gives me a sort of uniqueness the others haven't got! Look at Greta Garbo. If you study it, she never made successful films but everybody remembers her...

S.M.

Mike Hawthorn went to the final round of the World Championship in Morocco knowing that unless Moss won, set the fastest lap and he – Hawthorn – came no higher than third, he had the Championship, the first Briton to achieve it.

C.H.

1957 was the first time the Moroccan race had been run and the trip out had not been too good with a cramped and most uncomfortable flight by Air France to Casablanca with no food on board but cheese sandwiches. I had been wondering what to do about getting there this year when David Yorke, the Vanwall team manager, telephoned me to say that Tony Vandervell had chartered a Viscount from BEA for the trip and would I like a seat? I jumped at the chance. Such was the interest that the race had caused that there was another charter flight going out on a DC-6, but I thought the Viscount would be more comfortable. Lofty England also came out with me. He had telephoned me a week or two before to tell me that by some strange coincidence he found it necessary to go out to Casablanca and have a look at the Jaguar sales organization there and found that it coincided with the Grand Prix. I said that it reminded me of that other classic case of coincidence: the football enthusiast whose grandmother used to die regularly every year and was always buried on the day of the Cup Final at Wembley! I was very happy about this because Lofty is one of the greatest team managers in racing and the thought of having him in the pit for this vital race was a most comforting one. Although Tavoni, too, is a very good team manager, it would mean a lot to me to have Lofty standing by.

Rodney Walkerley came out with us as well, forsaking for the first time his usual stately form of progress to and from the Grands Prix. Another friend of mine, Mary Taylor Young, flew out with us, as her parents, Mr and Mrs Martineau, having set out to drive to

Casablanca in their 3.4 Jaguar, had had an accident near Barcelona – the car had been damaged quite badly and Rosemary Martineau had had her left arm broken. However, as soon as it was put into plaster she insisted on going on to Casablanca for the race and so Mary came out to look after her mother. We found them already installed in the Maharba Hotel, which was very modern and American in style, like most of the hotels there.

We arrived on the Thursday and were all dining in the hotel that evening when Tavoni came in and gave me the entry list to look at. The sight of it really upset me for I had been given the number 2. Phil Hill had 4 and Gendebien 6. No doubt it was partly due to nerves, but as Peter [Collins] and Luigi [Musso] had both been killed with the number 2 on the car I asked Tavoni to have it altered. He soothed me down and said I could have 6, and he would ask the organizers to give Gendebien a number at the other end. However, Olivier Gendebien agreed to take my 2 as he said he wasn't superstitious.

Next morning we went out to our garage to look at the cars. I had my Italian Grand Prix car as before with the Dunlop disc brakes and Phil's car was the lighter Formula Two chassis with the normal Dino 246 engine and the diagonally finned front brake drums. Gendebien's car was the Monza 500 car, but it was now being tried out with Girling disc brakes. As we went in I could see Phil's car with 4 on it, and Gendebien's with 6, but there was a cover over mine. Oh hell, I thought, number 2 is on it and I just daren't look. Once again Tavoni calmed me down saying it was quite all right because no number had been painted on my car at all. I must admit that I was behaving more like an Italian than an Englishman, and Tavoni was being the calm, phlegmatic type, soothing his temperamental driver!

Ranged against us for this final and decisive event were three Vanwalls with Tony Brooks and Lewis-Evans backing up Stirling, while BRM had no less than four cars, two for Behra and Schell as usual, a third car for Ron Flockhart, now recovered from his accident at Rouen, and a fourth car for the Swedish driver, Bonnier. In all there were twenty-five starters as the organizers were running a Formula Two race in conjunction with the Grand Prix. This helps to make up a good field, but many of the Grand Prix car drivers were not too happy about the mixture, and I was one of them. I just do not agree that one can mix fast cars and much slower ones. The line you take on a fast bend is the same for both Formula One and Two cars, but the latter are doing anything up to 30 m.p.h. less and it is asking for trouble to come up behind one with such a speed differential.

The Ain Diab circuit measures 4.7 miles and is a pretty fast circuit. The start and pits, like Portugal, are opposite the Atlantic Ocean; from there one goes round a right-hand corner which winds inland and uphill to another right-hander on to the back straight, which like every straight past the pits, is very fast. This leads on to a vicious right-hander, quite fast and very nasty late in the day as the sun sinks and shines straight into your eyes; then there are a left- and right-hander, both of them fast, bringing you back along the straight parallel with the seashore.

The first day's practice was on Friday afternoon in hot sunshine, and I went out fairly quickly to get acclimatized, trying both the disc-braked cars; I preferred my own Dunlops as the Girlings were a little disappointing. They had not got the ratio quite right and the back was tending to lock up quite badly. This was fixed before the race and Gendebien told me that they were very good indeed. Behra set fastest time with the BRM in 2 m. 25.2 s., then Tony was next fastest, then me, then Stirling – nobody was really belting round, but just getting used to things again. The sun was very tricky as also was the sea mist which would suddenly envelop the circuit. It didn't make the circuit dangerous, but it was a little difficult to see at times and the salt tended to stick on my visor. To counteract the glare of the sun we had the Perspex air-intake covers painted a matt black and also the top of the cockpit inside the wrap-round windscreen. I had a dark visor made as well to fight the glare and this worked very well.

Tavoni was delighted to have Lofty in the pit to help. The race was going to need the most accurate timekeeping and signalling so that I could be informed exactly where everyone was. If I was second, I wanted to know how far ahead the first car was and how far back the third; I also wanted to know if anybody was coming up through the field quickly. I was going to drive for second place, which was what I needed to win, whereas Stirling would have to go all out to win and make fastest lap.

Saturday's session once again took place in the afternoon, but a sea mist had reduced visibility enormously, though the dampness was assisting carburation; lap times came down quite a lot and I set fastest time with 2 m . 23.1 s., just a tenth of a second quicker than

Stirling. Lewis-Evans was not much slower, but Tony was in the third row, Stirling having taken over his car in preference to the much-lightened machine that had been specially prepared for him. Between the two sessions I had had my axle-ratio lowered and this gave me much better acceleration out of the corners; I felt much more confident for the following day. At one time on the Saturday, Phil and Gendebien had both set better times than me, but I finally got my time down all right. Marie-Claire, Olivier Gendebien's wife, who had come over to watch, suggested that I should take the Ferrari mascot out for a lap or two to bring me luck. She had found a chameleon; it was an odd little creature, and had a pair of beady eyes which could look in different directions at once which was a little disconcerting but very useful for watching motor races. It was quite tame and Gendebien had had it in the car with him when he put up his fastest lap. I thought it would be better for the chameleon not to come round with me as he might get car sickness and turn a very peculiar colour.

The night before the race I really meant to go to bed early. Although the past five weeks of waiting had been quite a strain I found it was all gone, instead of getting worse as I had thought it would. I had worried over little things like catching a cold and once I had got a pain in my stomach and thought it might be appendicitis. The night before a big race is always a bit twitch-making; you lie in bed thinking of what might happen, but this night I went straight to sleep with the sound of fog horns blowing. Fortunately by the morning the fog had cleared. Thinking back I realize that I could not have got to bed terribly early as it was about eleven-thirty when, with Mary Taylor Young and Jean Howarth, who had come out on the other charter flight, I returned from a party given for the British contingent by the Ambassador, Sir Charles Duke, and Lady Duke, at the Consul's residence. But I was in bed earlier than some of the drivers who went on to another party! The hospitality we were shown was terrific.

The next morning when I awoke I was delighted to see that it was cloudy, but the clouds cleared; by lunch-time the sun was shining and it was very hot. The Moroccan Grand Prix is the main social occasion in the country and, as in the previous year, King Mohammed V and his entourage were present. It was a most colourful sight with the King's bodyguard mounted on white BMW motor bikes and massed bands and soldiers in bright uniforms. I noticed that the royal cars were German too, nearly all Mercedes. We were all introduced to the King and then he took his place in the Royal Box in the grandstand.

The start was a bit of an anti-climax after all this pageantry. 'Toto' Roche from Rheims was the starter, and a quarter of an hour after the appointed time we were still not in our cars. When we were all settled in Roche held things up because one of the Coopers would not start; we were all getting a bit edgy. Then Roche waved the Cooper off the grid and we took this as the starting flag. Everyone moved off leaving Roche to scramble out of the way as best he could. Although I had much stronger clutch linings I took the start easily and Stirling shot away with Phil chasing him; then came Lewis-Evans, Bonnier and me.

At the end of the first lap Phil was still on Stirling's tail doing his appointed job wonderfully well and I was behind him in third place. On the third lap Phil tried braking with Stirling on the right-hander after the pits, but his drum brakes could not compete with the Vanwall discs and he had to take the escape road; so I moved up to second with Bonnier third. By the sixth lap Phil caught me up again so I waved him through to have another go at Stirling. Round about the twelfth lap Tony, who is a rather slow starter, got wound up and after a real ding-dong he took me on the nineteenth lap. I found that I had the speed on the straights, but out of the corners the Vanwall was quicker. If I passed him all he had to do was to get into my slipstream along the straights and then he would nip past me out of the corners. The Vanwall plan was obviously for Tony to keep me out of second place; if Stirling then won and made fastest lap, he would be Champion.

At one point Tony got a lead of about three seconds, but I got it back and as we swapped places every now and then I noticed there was a little stream of smoke from the engine compartment by the exhausts and occasionally Tony would have to wipe his windscreen and his goggles. Well, he's not going to last very long, I thought, nothing to worry about there.

As it turned out I was wrong; it was the breather which was deflecting the fumes onto the exhaust pipe; a little oil would collect there and it was this which was burning and giving off the smoke. I would not have been quite so happy if I had known this at the time.

With Tony in the race my title was anything but secure; once he went out there would be no opposition to my plan of finishing second.

By lap 30 I had gone ahead of Tony again and then the Vanwall blew up, a valve dropped in, broke a piston and the rod came through the side. Oil streamed on to Tony's rear tyre causing him quite a moment before he brought it safely to rest by the side of the road.

Twenty-three laps of the race remained and I was back in third place, with Stirling well out in front with no worries at all, although he had had a little shunt with Seidel's Maserati early on in the race. He had bashed the front, closing up the air intake a bit, but the water temperature was not affected. Tony's blow-up spilled oil on to the circuit and unfortunately Gendebien spun on it; Picard, who was behind him, could not avoid him. The Cooper went off the road on the left and the Ferrari went off to the right, hitting a rock which completely sliced the back off the car from just behind the seat. There were many conflicting rumours about this accident, too, and Olivier was variously reported to be either perfectly all right, or alternatively seriously hurt with a broken back. The truth of it was that he was suffering from bruises and shock; he was able to go home to Belgium a couple of days later. It was his wife who returned home in plaster! Poor Marie-Claire slipped on the hotel steps a day or so after the race, fell and fractured her elbow.

Another Cooper also crashed at about this stage in the race: it was driven by Bridger and he too escaped more or less unhurt. Phil now lay second, nearly half a minute behind Stirling who had set the fastest lap in 2 m. 22.5 s. on his twenty-fourth circuit. Tavoni signalled Phil to slow down and let me up to second place and I went into this position on lap 39.

In effect the race now became two races; no one opposed Stirling in his efforts to get the maximum of nine points for a win and fastest lap, while I had things my own way in my race for the second place and the Championship. The only possible danger to me was Bonnier who was going very well indeed with the BRM in fourth place. Phil tucked in behind me and so we drove on. Although Bonnier picked up on us we were both aware of it and were able to put on speed if he came up too close.

With just about ten laps to go I came along the top straight and I was appalled to see a huge column of black smoke rising up. When I got to the end of the straight and to one of the corners leading down to the sea there was oil on the road and a car burning fiercely on the inside of the circuit. I could just see part of the bonnet hanging from the car with *Vanwall* written on it. I could see no number on the car.

As I passed the pits I realized that it must have been Lewis-Evans' car, for had it been Moss, Tavoni would have signalled that I was now first. The car had blown up, as Tony's had, but unhappily for Stuart the car had caught fire. He scrambled out, burned and dazed by the shock, and ran clear. But he ran in the opposite direction to the people who could help him, people with fire extinguishers and blankets. It took that much longer to reach him, and poor Stuart was badly burned. He had been lying fifth in the race at the time.

The last laps ran out with Stirling way out in front, neither of us able to do anything about the other. The Ferrari was going well and everything was normal. I realized that, barring a stroke of a real misfortune, I was all right, as I was lapping seconds within the capabilities of the car.

Three laps to go and Phil toured gently round behind me, a loyal and brilliant driver, who at both Monza and Casablanca had done his best to help me. Two laps to go . . . one lap . . . and then there it was; the chequered flag. As I passed it *The Autocar* said I gave a great wave; *Autosport* said I gave myself a boxer's salute. I don't know what I did; all I knew was that I had just become the Champion Driver of the World, the first Englishman to achieve the title.

All I can remember of my lap of honour was that when I was about a hundred yards or so from my pit it dawned on me that I had not really savoured it to the full, for it was the last time that I would drive a Grand Prix car in a race. I suddenly felt sorry that I had not been more conscious of the fact and enjoyed the feeling of exhilaration that comes from being the sole master of a single-seater Grand Prix racing car and which forms the main excitement and satisfaction of racing driving. The death of Peter Collins had made up my mind for me – at the end of the season I would retire.

I switched off at the pits and got out of my car. I was practically mobbed by the Ferrari mechanics, who were off their heads with delight. People patted me and crowds milled around the car in a scene reminiscent of Piccadilly Underground station during rush hour. Lofty shook hands with me, David Yorke of Vanwall was one of the next to do so. Tavoni was wonderfully happy, clapping me on the back as I got out of the car.

'Next year,' he said, 'we will do it again.'

I shook my head at him. 'I won't be racing next year,' I said. 'I'm going to retire.'

He laughed and patted me on the back. 'Of course you'll be racing.'

Then came the presentation, laurel wreaths and cups and Stirling came up and congratulated me: 'You did it, you old so and so.'

He had driven an absolutely magnificent race, perhaps the best he has ever driven. He had known that he had to win and make fastest lap, and to do just that very thing called for the highest skill and courage. Stirling has both those qualities and sportsmanship as well; if he had not given evidence on my behalf after the Portuguese Grand Prix I might have been congratulating him as Champion. Although this was the fourth time he finished runner-up to the Champion, some of his disappointment must have been offset by the fact that it was to a great extent his driving that gave Vanwall the Constructor's Championship, the first time that that award has ever gone to a British car.

From *Champion Year* by Mike Hawthorn (William Kimber, 1959)

Sixteen on the Grid – the hours before the Monaco Grand Prix 1963

Peter Garnier

When I first met Peter he was editor of *Autocar* but he also became secretary of the Grand Prix Drivers' Association, of which I was one of the founders. My view, incidentally, was that if you didn't like a circuit you didn't have to go to it – but certainly you didn't try and ruin it for everybody else. My whole philosophy was to accept the challenge of a circuit and beat it – not say, let's re-design it. We set up the GPDA but initially called it by a French name, UPPI [Union des Pilotes Internationaux]. People didn't like the 'union', which had a different meaning in Britain and conjured up images of strikes, so we became the GPDA. Peter went to all the races for *Autocar* and we asked him to be secretary. I understand he sometimes found himself in tricky situations after our meetings because he was sworn to secrecy and when his fellow journalists questioned him he couldn't comment!

S.M.

Sunday morning at last, with the clear, cool, early brilliance of a perfect day filtering through the slits in a venetian blind and lying in stripes across the floor. I wondered in how many similar hotel bedrooms throughout the town people were lying awake, mentally checking – checking over details in the cars in their charge perhaps, or the lap-scoring and time-keeping equipment they were to use – stopwatches, charts, pencils – or broadcasting equipment and time-tables, or publicity arrangements after the race, if there was anything to publicize; or, in the case of the Press, telephone bookings to get the story through to newspapers all over the world; or the fuelling arrangements, not easy in Monte Carlo – unique among GP circuits in not having a pad-dock; and the drivers, with more on their minds than most people: gear-change points, gear ratios, too late to do anything about those now, helmet, spare goggles, clean underclothes, yes, you never know; or perhaps something much more down to earth, like the speech that had to be made as guest of honour at some dinner, somewhere, soon (if anyone was worrying about that it would be Phil Hill).

I have often wondered, and never liked to ask, whether in his heart of hearts, on leaving his hotel room on the morning of race day and closing the door, anyone pauses to wonder whether he will ever open that door again. This, if it were me, would be the moment to think about giving it up. I do not know of a driver who is completely unmoved before the start of a big race; if he were, he would not then give of his best when the time came. It is the same in any field in which the participants depend for their success on their own particular skill or ability, '. . . the readiness is all', as Shakespeare said in *Hamlet*.

I believe – through an almost unnatural control which through the years he developed – Moss was almost impervious to pre-race nerves. When driving his Lotus through the tunnel at the Nürburgring, on the way to the starting grid before the 1961 German Grand Prix (which he won), he called out to a friend, 'Hey, can you remember the name of that firm in London that makes water-softeners?'

With steady inevitability through the forenoon, the climax to the weeks of work and the days of practice and preparation approached. In the town the hotels served their 'Grand Prix Luncheon', which differed from any other in that it was earlier, and more expensive. Since few drivers eat lunch before a race, there were not many among the customers. Down at the pits the rate of build-up of tension increased suddenly as, at around 1 p.m., the cars began to appear in the area, some driven raucously through the streets – now closed to normal traffic – and some arriving quietly on the ends of tow ropes, like animals being led into the prize ring.

The sun blazed down; and the crowds packed the stands, or perched like roosting birds along every available balcony, every window, every terrace – backwards and upwards towards the Alpes Maritimes which prevent winter from reaching the Principality. And the expensive yachts, with bow-lines ashore to the Quai Albert Premier, hauled their sterns out towards moorings in the harbour, the rules forbidding any craft to remain alongside during the race.

Around the pits the mechanics put final touches to their charges – so soon to be removed from their care – and wondered what they had forgotten, and how the picture would look in three hours or so, when the whole thing would be over. Then the drivers, forsaking the peace and privacy of their hotels for the full brilliance and publicity of the sunshine and the blaring clamour of the public address loud-speakers, began to appear like Roman gladiators in the arena, the property now of the paying public who had come to see them perform.

Carried by a dozen open sports cars provided by the British

Motor Corporation, racing drivers of past years made a lap of honour of the circuit which for some of them had been the scene of '... battles long ago' – Chiron, Etancelin, de Graffenreid, Giraud-Cabantous, Villoresi, Farina, Taruffi, Manzon and others. The Royal Party, arriving in sombre black sedans and escorted by a posse of motor-cycle policemen, drew up on the threshold of the red-velvet Royal Box and took their seats, with the exception of Prince Rainier. In a convertible Porsche Super 90 with the roof down, he drove Louis Chiron round the circuit, officially closing 1.9 miles of the streets of his Principality and handing them over to the drivers, free of charge, speed limits and conditions, to use as they cared for the next 2¾ hours or so.

Not only were the drivers, as the principal actors, preparing themselves. All round the circuit the flag marshals were checking their flags, and the curious new electrical signal boxes that the organizers had introduced; the Press, sitting row upon row in the Press Tribune, was ready with notebooks, stopwatches, lap-charts where necessary and poised pencils; the official timekeepers sat quietly, fingers on chronometers ready to set their department in action as soon as Chiron dropped the starter's flag; broadcasters of many nations sat in sweltering little glass boxes, wet through to the skin, either painting the scene for a listening audience, or explaining to viewers what they saw on the screen; Boissy was standing by in his rescue boat on the harbour's blue waters; individual timekeepers and lap-scorers in each pit were settling down to 2¾ hours of the most intense concentration imaginable, in sweltering heat and hideous noise.

Everywhere there was last minute preparation, quietly waiting for Chiron to drop the Monégasque flag and set it all in motion.

The cars were wheeled out to their grid positions – seven rows of two cars each with Brabham's car (the Team Lotus Lotus 25 with carburettor engine) on its own, on the eighth row – while Louis Chiron, race director and Clerk of the Course, and one of the *anciens pilotes* who had not only raced, but actually won, on the little circuit through the streets of his home town, addressed the drivers some-what excitedly on what was expected of them. For a brief moment the blaring loudspeakers were silent; and the howling rescue and television helicopters took themselves out over the harbour, leaving Chiron's voice temporarily in charge.

Then, the 'headmaster's' meeting over, the drivers shuffled off to their cars, standing waiting on the still-crowded grid, some preferring to chat in an effort to take their minds off their 'butterflies' and others slipping down into the confined, narrow cockpits.

Once in the cars they were able to see for the first time their positions relative to other drivers 'in the metal', as it were, and to make plans for the start. 'Old So-and-so's certain to stall it, or mess things up somehow, better try to slip through between him and the pits', or, 'So-and-So usually gets away like a rocket, no harm in tucking in behind him and getting a clear run'. Then came the 'Two Minutes' signal, everyone now in his car. Suddenly there was uncontrolled pandemonium as a couple of vee-6s and thirteen vee-8s burst into life, the noise boxed in by the tall buildings on the landward side and echoing and reverberating out across the blue harbour – two Ferrari engines, eight Coventry Climaxes and five BRMs breaking into song.

From this moment, until the glorious relief of the drop of the starter's flag, come the tensest and most important moments of the race, moments during which, if things go wrong, the months of preparation, the training, the mechanics' hours of work and perhaps even the World Championship itself, can be thrown away. The combination of ear-plugs and the deafening uproar going on all around is such as to make one's own engine note completely inaudible, or indistinguishable, from the others. A bit of vibration, but more particularly the rev-counter, are the only indications that it is running at all, but neither can tell the driver *how* it is running, nor whether all plugs are firing properly.

At the 'One Minute' signal comes a reassuring 'thumbs-up' from the mechanics, and they and the great assembly of people leave you on the grid. It's up to you from now on, and in your hands lie all the hopes and fears of the many people who have done so much and spent so much to make this moment possible. As the last few seconds tick by, you pull your goggles into position, poke the gear lever into first, and then worry whether you've mistakenly pushed it into second, or reverse, so you check it again. You check the instruments, the temperatures; and you keep 'blipping' the throttle to make certain that you don't oil a plug, or plugs; that is if you haven't oiled any already; you can't hear that you're blipping it, but you can see that you are on the rev-counter. And all the time you're keeping your eye on the starter's rostrum to make certain you see when the flag is raised – so that you can get some idea of when it is going to drop, and you have another surreptitious check to see that it really *is* in first. The seconds seem like hours, then suddenly, up goes the flag.

Up comes the clutch until it is just beginning to bite, but not enough to move the car forward, and up go the revs until the rev-counter is reading perhaps between four and five thousand. The flag should be up for around five seconds, Chiron, at Monte Carlo, and a few other experienced starters, counting off the seconds with the fingers of the other hand, so that the drivers can see their passing. Then down goes the flag, and, if you have managed to keep one eye on the starter and the other on the rev-counter, the clutch will bite, the wheels will start spinning and, controlling the spin on the throttle, you will get away to a clean start. If you have been too mesmerized by the starter's antics, and have allowed your attention to wander from the rev-counter, you may let the clutch up with too low an engine speed – in which case you will probably stall the engine and be rammed from astern.

In fact, nothing went wrong at Monte Carlo, and the fifteen cars got off to a perfect start.

From *16 On the Grid* by Peter Garnier (Cassell and Company Limited, 1964)

There ought to have been sixteen of them, but Chris Amon (Lola) didn't start.
C.H.

Clark Wins '500' at 150.966
Rookies Snare 5 Of Top 10 Places
First Foreigner to Score Since '16;
Parnelli 2d

Dave Overpeck

Scotsman Jimmy Clark became the first foreigner to win the 500-Mile Race since 1916 yesterday as he guided his Lotus-Ford to a record-breaking triumph before a record crowd of more than 250,000 fans.

The little Scotsman finished the 500 miles in 3 hours 19 minutes and 5.34 seconds for an average speed of 150.686 miles an hour. Clark's average speed surpassed the old record of 147.350 miles an hour, set last year by A. J. Foyt.

Clark was 1 minute 58.97 seconds — almost two laps — ahead of second place Parnelli Jones in the Agajanian-Hurst Lotus-Ford.

The last foreigner to win the race was Dario Resta in 1916 when the race was scheduled for 300 miles. The last foreign winner of a 500-miler at the Speedway was Rene Thomas in 1914.

Clark's victory was the first ever by a rear-engine car. The triumph of Ford's 485 horsepower V8 engine broke the eighteen-year-old stranglehold of the Offenhauser in this race.

I didn't ever drive in the Indy 500 because I couldn't. I was already racing every weekend. But it is something I missed and I'm sorry I did. However my father raced there in the 1920s where he was known as the Duke of Moss or the Earl of Moss! My father did a lot of funny things. He was a dentist and he conned my grandfather. Dad said, 'The finest dentistry is taught at the University of Indianapolis,' so grandfather said, 'OK, we'll send you there.' That's how Dad got to Indy. In 1965 I went over to cover the race for *Life* magazine and spoke to Jimmy afterwards. I don't think he liked the place too much because of the razzmatazz.

S.M.

The Indianapolis 500 is arguably the greatest race in the world. In 1965 a quiet chap called Jim Clark went there in a Lotus to try and beat the Americans in their own Brickyard — as the track was known. The headlines above are from the *Indianapolis Star*, and just as they were writ.

C.H.

Clark probably will pick up almost $200,000 including $28,500 in lap prizes out of a prospective purse of $600,000 at tonight's Victory Dinner in the Egyptian Room of the Murat Temple.

From the *Indianapolis Star*, 1 June 1965

Carolyn Pickering

They didn't take a stitch at the track hospital yesterday.

And, for the first time in anyone's memory, including that of head physician Dr Thomas A. Hanna, not a single driver required even a check-up during the 500-mile race.

So, all the news was the happy kind at the tiny field hospital where men and women in white yearly toil to save lives without getting so much as a glimpse of the classic.

Doctor Hanna, overjoyed 'at the safest race we've had', said the day's successful running was mute evidence of the advantage of rear-engine cars which, he feels, 'are safer than the heavier equipment.'

Head nurse Barbara Webb said even the entourage of drunken customers who normally file into the hospital after being involved in fights was down to a new low.

She said a 'portable' jail – a big bus manned by deputy sheriffs – had taken several loads of potential patients to jail before the race got underway.

While there were no big tragedies at the hospital, the staff was anything but idle.

A 235-pound woman with a sick stomach was brought in and it took three men to carry her to a waiting cot. [Bed if you're British.]

The height of audacity was expressed by an enterprising pair of teenagers who strolled in – not for any treatment – but to inquire of Miss Webb whether they could cabbage onto tickets for seats vacated by ailing spectators.

From the *Indianapolis Star*, 1 June 1965

It will take more than the biggest payday of his life to bring Jimmy Clark back to the Indianapolis 500-Mile Race.

The wiry little guy with the steady nerves of a bomb demolition expert admitted quite frankly yesterday that he'll return to the Speedway next May only if he's sitting in pretty good shape in the race towards the world's driving Championship [the Formula One Championship].

'I just can't say right now whether I'll be back,' said the man who won in what looked like a one-man trophy dash as the rest of the field sort of melted away before the onslaught of the blazing sun and Clark's Lotus-powered-by-Ford screamer.

'It does take a bit of the edge off by winning this race,' he said. 'The challenge was here for me – not to prove anything to myself, but to a lot of other people. There's so much said out here in the month of May.

'Now that I've won the thing, the race has lost something, I'll admit. I almost wasn't coming back this year [he'd competed in 1963 and 1964]. First I wasn't going to, then I decided to come.

'I don't like the length of it – not the 500 miles but the entire month. It would be much better if it were set up like grand prix racing, where you'd come in and practise a couple of days and then run the thing. That's the way the rest of the championship races are won over there, anyway. Why not this one?

'This will be the biggest payday of my life if Colin [Chapman, boss of Lotus] will give me some of it. At least I got a $20 allowance for today. We'll be at the Victory Dinner to accept our money.'

'Yes, we will,' chimed in Chapman. 'We had to win this race to stay in business. It's unbelievable what it costs to build a car for a race like this and bring all your people over and keep them for a month.'

From the *Indianapolis Star*, 1 June 1965

I remember when we used to talk about Indianapolis. Jimmy said he didn't like it and needed room for four or five laps until his eyes and brain and everything adjusted, and then he completely put out of his mind the speed he was doing, let everything come back to what he knew.

Andrew Cowan, rally driver

Driving round Indianapolis is reasonably straightforward. I would go up through the gears but once in top I'd leave it in top and then give the brakes a dab coming into the corners. The big difficulty was judging the braking points, or the apex of a corner, as the track is quite featureless.

Jim Clark

I always had the feeling that, in the early days, Jimmy was ill at ease in the United States. He would come back confused, feeling that the Americans didn't really want to know about Europeans, for the plain and simple reason that they had their own forms of racing and their attitudes were so different.

Graham Gauld, Clark's biographer

Hill Wins Disputed '500'
Sponsor Claims Clark Victor; 7 Running At End

Dave Overpeck

Graham Hill evidently won the most fantastically confused and incredible 500-Mile Race in the fifty-year history of the event yesterday, finishing 41.13 seconds ahead of defending champion Jimmy Clark.

Hill's victory was strongly disputed by Clark's car owner, Colin Chapman, and sponsor Andy Granatelli, who maintained that Jimmy should be credited with the victory.

The contested finish was in keeping with the tenor of a race that simply defies description. Eleven of thirty-three starters were wiped out in a thundering crash that stopped the race before the leaders could get through the first turn of the first lap.

Miraculously, no driver was injured in the pile-up which involved sixteen cars, nor in any of the five accidents that followed.

The ending was just as incredible as the start as both Hill, a Londoner who gained his ride in the American Red Ball Express after Walt Hansgen was killed in an April crash at Le Mans, and Clark headed for Victory Lane.

Just ten laps from the finish, both looked like also-rans as Hill's team-mate, Jackie Stewart, in the Bowes Seal Fast Special, led by more than half a lap.

Then Stewart's engine – which had been laboring for seventeen laps with failing oil pressure – gave up the ghost in the third turn with victory just twenty-five miles away.

Clark twice spun his STP Gasoline Treatment Lotus-Ford while leading the race. The first time came on the sixty-second lap when he had a lead of more than half a lap over Lloyd Ruby.

He looped coming out of the fourth turn but regained control and came on around to the pits.

Then, on the eighty-fourth lap, when he held a lead of approximately twenty seconds on Ruby, he did a complete spin in the third turn, but again he regained control. But the ensuing pit stop cost him dearly in time and most certainly victory if Hill, indeed, won.

All positions are unofficial until the final timing tape can be checked. The official finish will be posted at 8 o'clock this morning. Crews then will have half an hour to lodge an official protest.

The crux of the argument on whether Hill or Clark won was the 175th lap. Hill passed Clark on the front stretch of that circuit, but the dispute concerns whether Hill was taking over second place or simply unlapping himself at the time.

As far as George Bignotti, who saddled his third winner as a chief mechanic with Hill, is concerned, the 1962 world road racing champion was moving into second place behind Stewart.

In fact his crew showed Hill a board reading 'P 1–2' indicating that he was running second behind Stewart.

But Chapman and Granatelli were just as certain that Clark won. Chapman said 'we think that they (the scorers) gave Hill an extra lap some place. There is no question of an official protest at this time. We want to see the timing tapes. If they showed that Hill completed his 220 laps before Jimmy did, then he won the race.'

Granatelli was in a much less compromising mood than the calm (under the circumstances) Chapman. 'How could Hill win when they were announcing and showing on the scoreboard that Stewart and Clark were running 1–2 and Hill was half a lap away on the backstretch? If that was the case, Hill had been leading all the time and Stewart was never in front.

'We lapped Hill on the 47th lap and we were running faster than him the rest of the way. Now where did he pass Clark?' he added.

Neither Hill or Clark knew any more than what their pit crews told them. Hill said 'I haven't a clear view' while Clark ventured 'I'm just the driver.'

From the *Indianapolis Star*, 30 May 1966

Graham Hill was confirmed as winner of the 50th Indianapolis 500-Mile Race today in official standings released by timers and scorers.

And, after checking the scoring records, Jimmy Clark's crew, which yesterday said it would lodge a protest, changed its mind and decided to be satisfied with the 2nd-place finish.

'We did not lodge an official protest,' said Andy Granatelli, sponsors of Clark's car. 'All we asked was the cooperation of United States Auto Club officials in looking at the official scoring. It showed that the scorers were equally as confused as we were.

'On the 47th lap we lapped Graham Hill. On the 50th it was announced that we had lapped all but the first five and that Hill was running 9th. But when Clark spun on the 67th lap, Hill got by. We didn't see him do it and assumed Clark was still in front. On the 109th lap, we just assumed that when Hill passed Clark, he was just unlapping himself. So, from the 120th to the 180th lap we were confused on what we thought.'

From the *Indianapolis Star*, 31 May, 1966

We'd better have a prize for the first American home.
Graham Hill, Indianapolis, 1966

[Clark had been involved in controversy in 1963, finishing second, but many felt the winner, Parnelli Jones, should have been disqualified for dropping oil.] The day after the race at a luncheon Eddie Sachs [a driver who'd spun on the oil] expressed his views a bit too forcefully. Parnelli Jones decked him with a right cross.
The *Indianapolis Star*

They're not supposed to do that!
Mansell, after being overtaken by two cars near the end of the Indy 500, 1993

It's official title was STP Oil Treatment Special. Some called it the 'Silent Screamer'. Some referred to it as the 'Whooshmobile'. To still others it was the 'Pregnant Porpoise'.

The *Indianapolis Star* on Parnelli Jones's turbine-powered, four-wheel drive car, 1967

Imagine being paid that amount of money for turning left eight hundred times.

Jim Clark

The Indianapolis 500 is tremendously promoted, but it's a long-winded affair and goes on and on for more or less the whole month of May. They have a slightly funny way of qualifying: all the cars which qualify on the first day fill up the first rows of the starting grid; the cars which qualify on the second day might be faster than those which qualified on the first, but they don't get to go to the front row of the grid.

Graham Hill

Graham enjoyed Indy because he enjoyed all the American hype. He loved Americans. That was the fun side of Graham, you see.

Bette Hill

Mirage at the Masta?

Mark Kahn

'Slowly and with gentle care, the nuns began to dress me. At least, I think they were nuns. And I think they were dressing me. If, that is, they were there at all. You see, I cannot be sure.'

That uncertain ghost of a memory comes from none other than the brilliant and normally assured Jackie Stewart, three times world champion racing driver, with more Grand Prix victories to his credit than anyone else in history. And it concerns a climactic experience on what was probably the fastest and most dangerous circuit in the world: Spa in Belgium. So dangerous, indeed, that the 1969 Grand Prix to have been held there was called off because the drivers refused to race under the prevailing conditions.

That was three years after Stewart's nebulous encounter with the nuns.

Nuns? Dressing him? On the track at Spa? What have we here? Certainly no joke.

But first, to get this matter in perspective, it is necessary to look at Jackie Stewart – and then at Spa.

John Young Stewart is perhaps the man above all whom the older generation of racing drivers have in mind when they say they 'don't understand' the men who have succeeded them.

He's all mod. Placing him by appearance (a dangerous game with anyone, I agree, but one we all play with people) you would be forgiven for imagining at a quick estimate that here was someone strictly from the pop scene. That shoulder-length hair seems to attest it. So does the often flamboyant gear topped by that absurd peaked cap which he has made famous. He likes kipper

I'd classify Mark Kahn as a populist writer – he worked for the *Sunday Mirror* – who gained general acceptance in motor sport. This extract is about the Belgian Grand Prix at Spa in 1966, and Spa was more daunting than the Nürburgring. You had, you see, a hairpin [La Source] which meant bottom gear and yet you were still averaging 130 m.p.h. per lap. That equalled enormous speed and you very rarely dropped below 140 to 150 m.p.h. When you're travelling at that rate, things get very delicate. The Ring was more fun because on an awful lot of it you'd go through the gears and find a wonderful rhythm. Spa was as challenging as The Ring but in a different way. The Ring gave pleasure, Spa gave exhilaration. Both were dangerous – I had a front wheel come off at Spa...

S.M.

In his office, Moss has two steering wheels, both horribly twisted: one from Goodwood, 1962, and the other from Spa, 1960, when the wheel came off and he smashed into the banking. These two artefacts of a life, so stilled and silent, are extremely eloquent. They chart the dangers of another age and demonstrate how survival was essentially luck if something did go wrong. If you point to them, Moss discusses them dispassionately.

C.H.

ties. He has been known to wear shocking pink trousers and peacock shirts. He once arrived in London from his home in Geneva wearing a purple blazer and lilac trousers. (He had to dash out and acquire an off-the-peg conventional suit to attend a function for which even he considered they would not have been quite proper.) A singer, you'd guess. Guitarist. Drummer. Perhaps a songwriter. Or manager of an avante garde pop group.

But you would look again, of course. The eyes are piercing, the nose strong, the mouth and chin powerful. The face is hawkish. The face of a *competitor*. (That function for which he bought the suit was to present the Jim Clark commemorative medals.)

The Stewart story begins in Scotland thirty-three years ago. What makes for brilliance, for a talent that distinguishes its possessor from the ordinary ruck of mediocrity? If only we knew the answer! Certainly there is no clue in the Stewart background.

He left school at fifteen and went to work in his father's garage in Dumbarton at three pounds twelve shillings a week. Money and the things you could do with it, the things it could do for you, was something he was keenly aware of even before then. He tells how when he was a child a family friend used to visit his parents. The man would leave half a crown for the boy after Jackie had gone to bed. Religiously he saved it. When he began work in the garage, on the petrol pumps, he says he angled for tips – and saved those. He wanted to buy an old car, an Austin A30, and this was the way to do it.

In his younger days his sport was clay-pigeon shooting. Perhaps this needs essentially the same qualities that go into the making of a world-class racing driver. Steadiness and lightning reflexes, superb vision, a flowing smoothness of action. He was a magnificent shot. Just how good, you can gauge from the fact that at twenty-one he was in the clay-pigeon shooting teams of both Scotland and Britain.

His brother Jimmy, eight years older, was the racing Stewart.

It was Jimmy Stewart who got Jackie into racing. Jackie went to circuits with him. But Jimmy had a series of crashes. At Le Mans he was hurled out of the car and his elbow was crushed. In his next race after that injury had healed, his D-type Jaguar turned over at Silverstone; and in the race after *that*, at the Nürburgring, he found himself under his car with the fuel tanks burst. It was then that Jimmy felt it was time to call it a day . . . to the relief of his parents.

Jackie began to race in 1960. His mother wasn't too pleased, but he used to get up very early, before she was awake and so couldn't say no, and go racing in a sports car lent to him by a garage customer. The famous Scottish team, Ecurie Ecosse, offered him a place in 1963. He won his first race for them. In fact, in twenty-three events he won fourteen races, was second once and third twice.

Ken Tyrrell, needing a driver for his Formula Three team, gave young Stewart a trial. He had never driven a single-seater before (he thought them dangerous). Bruce McLaren was doing some testing as Jackie was having his try-out. He bettered Bruce's times. McLaren went out again. Faster. Jackie bettered those times too. His first drive for Tyrrell was in March 1964 at Snetterton, Norfolk. He won the race. He won eleven out of thirteen races in Tyrrell's Cooper. (A little over five years later he became world champion, driving for Tyrrell.)

The big works teams were taking notice. Stewart went to BRM where the No 1 driver was Graham Hill. He was reaching the big time. He was sixth in his first Grand Prix – in South Africa in 1965. At Monaco he was third. Second in Belgium. Fifth in the British Grand Prix. Second again in the Dutch. He didn't finish in the German Grand Prix, but he won the Italian. And he won the International Trophy race at Silverstone. A convincing demonstration of quality.

The boy who had always wanted money, who had saved his half crowns and angled for tips at the petrol pumps, had come from retainers 'amounting to perhaps a fiver and fifty quid in the bank' to earning around £10,000 in 1964. That was more money than it would be today, but even so, is less than chicken-feed compared to the sums he commanded later. And very properly commanded. Those who really understand what is involved in driving on the limit, the very edge of controllability, something as sensitive, as 'nervous' as a Formula One car, know that here indeed was a rare talent, master of his machine by a remarkable empathy, and of himself by continuous, ruthlessly honest assessment.

Jackie Stewart was also probably the most safety-conscious of all the top racing drivers. He was, for example, the first racing driver to use safety harness. It needs, he says, someone to speak out about safety who is too fast to be accused of cowardice.

Are you surprised that talent and success of Stewart's order have not endeared him to *everyone* in motor sport? It is seldom indeed that such spectacular triumphs – in any field – do not breed resentment somewhere. Even his concern for safety is attacked as somehow out of keeping with the traditions of motor racing. I remember expounding to one former world class racing driver Stewart's argument. 'Take Tom Jones, the singer,' I said. 'He must earn at least as much as any of the top drivers. Probably more. Stewart would say that nobody therefore expected Jones to risk his life every time he appeared on stage. Or Jack Nicklaus. He makes £100,000 or so a year out of swinging a golf club. And the worst that can happen to him is that he might fall into a bunker.' My friend regarded me unmoved. 'If Stewart feels that way,' he said, 'let him go and sing or play golf instead of motor racing.' The very unreasonableness of this retort made a rational reply difficult. You cannot reason with prejudice.

And now to Spa.

Just how fast this track is, you can gather from the fact that lap speeds are over 150 m.p.h. It is a long circuit, and it curls through the Ardennes Forest. If a car goes off, the chances are that it will hit a house or crash into the trees. Rain has a habit of descending there in sudden drenching torrents with no warning at all. What is worse, the length of the circuit means that it can be dry at one side and almost awash on the other. Cars can find themselves going into a deluge at nearly 200 m.p.h. on 'dry' tyres. And back in 1966 not so much was known about aquaplaning as today. The wet weather tyres were rudimentary.

On the first lap of the Belgian Grand Prix at Spa in 1966 it happened in just that way. The cars tore into a downpour that the drivers never knew was there until they hit it.

Eight of the world's finest drivers went hurtling off the track in one of the most astonishing and dramatic scenes ever witnessed in a Grand Prix. It was on a long right-hand bend. Stewart was immediately behind Jack Brabham. Jack 'lost it' and went heading in the general direction of a farmhouse – without too drastic consequences. 'I just missed Jack,' Stewart told me. 'I got through by a miracle. I remember giving a slight sigh of relief that I was clear. And then, suddenly, in the Masta kink, I hit a wave of water which flooded across the road. Jochen Rindt went spinning right through the Masta. My car just aquaplaned.'

Jackie Stewart went off the circuit at 150 m.p.h.

'All I remember clearly at that moment is spinning,' he said. 'I hit a metal railing affair and demolished a couple of walls and part of a house. I don't remember the bumps.'

He was injured, of course. Broken ribs, broken collar bone, a dislocated shoulder, and he was more or less concussed. But all this was not the worst part of the situation. The injuries could reasonably be considered light in the circumstances. The real trouble was in what had happened to the car. The monocoque of the two-litre BRM was bent ('like a banana,' said Stewart). The fuel tanks had split and the cockpit was filled with something over thirty gallons of petrol. The fuel pumps were working away and the dashboard, with its switches, had gone. So there was no way he could turn the pumps off. The steering wheel was buckled and trapped him in the car — even if he could have moved he wouldn't have been able to free himself. The fire risk was horrifying.

To appreciate fully the magnitude of this risk, you must realize that the modern Formula One car is little short of a mobile incendiary bomb. There is the fuel, of course. And there are components made of magnesium. This is used for lightness and strength. So far technology has not come up with anything else so good. It is true that solid magnesium, unlike the powdered variety, does not easily catch fire. It can even be oxy-acetylene welded. But when it *does* ignite, as through gallons of blazing petrol, it burns with a ferocious white hot intensity that is almost impossible to quench. One thinks of Lorenzo Bandini dying in his blazing car at the Monaco tunnel in '67. Of Piers Courage in the Dutch Grand Prix at Zandvoort in '70. And — a tragedy that was brought into millions of homes by television — of Roger Williamson trapped in his March last year, also at Zandvoort, while another British driver, David Purley, frantically braved the flames alone in an, alas, unsuccessful effort to save him. Just three of many.

So there was Stewart trapped in his car with the imminent extreme likelihood of it exploding into flames. Fumes from the petrol were sending him drifting over the edge of unconsciousness. And the petrol was adding its own agony to his injuries. It had soaked through his racing overalls, and his underwear (the thermataugic material worn by racing drivers) was soaking it up like a sponge. It was setting up a dreadful irritation. It was *burning* him.

Jackie's team-mate, Graham Hill, and the American driver, Bob Bondurant, had also spun off the waterlogged track. They were able to climb out of their own cars, and staggered across to investigate.

The semi-conscious Stewart looked up at the American. 'Bob had blood coming from his lips. I wondered why he looked so sorry for himself. After all, it was I who had crashed.'

Hill and Bondurant saw that they couldn't release him with nothing but their hands. There were no marshals or other officials around, so they went in search of help. They (and Stewart) were lucky. They discovered a spectator with a car in which he had a set of spanners. Back they came with them. The luck held. One of the spanners fitted the locking nut on Stewart's steering wheel. They were able to get it off, which made it possible for them to free him. It took almost half an hour to get him out. All the while the pumps were working with the likelihood of an inferno, the petrol was burning him, and the fumes were sending him towards unconsciousness.

No ambulance had come up. A helicopter appeared and stayed droning overhead. Stewart got the idea it was for him. It wasn't. It was taking film shots.

Stewart remembers desperately asking Hill to take off those petrol-soaked clothes, and that is all he remembers with clarity of the next bizarre episode in these events. He believes that Hill and Bondurant did, in fact, undress him. Or was that merely the beginning of a strange fantasy?

Hill and Bondurant went off to organize help. That much is certain. Stewart lay on the ground. Naked – if his memories are real.

Enter the nuns.

There were three of them. Or were there? 'To this day,' says Stewart, 'I can't make up my mind whether they were really there, whether they were just part of a semi-delirium.'

They looked down at him. What on earth would they make of the situation? A nude racing driver must have been outside their experience. At any rate, gently and with delicacy, they began to dress him . . .

It was ten or fifteen minutes before an ambulance came – a vehicle that had been a bus. In it were Jackie's wife, Helen, Jim Clark and Louis Stanley, the BRM chief.

Jackie was put on the floor of the bus. Somebody was making

signs to him that he should not upset Helen. 'I remember saying very seriously, "Helen, this is very good experience for you."'

As the ambulance got under way, Jackie began to talk to Louis Stanley. And then found that he had a problem. What on earth to call him? 'It seemed too formal to call him Mr Stanley. I thought, I can't call the man Stanley. I'd better call him Lewis. That was how I pronounced it. Lewis. Finally, he looked at me and said, "Stewart, if you are going to call me by my first name, I'd prefer you to call me Louis."'

Stewart was taken to St Thomas's Hospital, London, where they have repaired many top drivers. His skin where the petrol had seared it was blackened and peeled. But the crash did not keep him from racing for long. He was lucky and he knows it.

He has had other close shaves. In 1970 when the cars of Jackie Oliver and Jacky Ickx collided and burst into flames, Stewart came on them as he rounded a corner. There was nothing he could do but bury his foot on the throttle and drive through a wall of fire. He came through unscathed – and went on to win the race. And in practice for last year's South African Grand Prix the brakes on his Tyrrell-Ford failed at 180 m.p.h. near the end of the straight at Kyalami. He went down through the gears like lightning to reduce speed, then spun the car into a barrier. He was saved by three wire-linked fences that had been put on this part of the circuit as an extra safety measure. He stepped out of the car unhurt. And in the car of his ill-fated team-mate François Cevert (killed at Watkins Glen last year) Jackie went on to win that race too. 'That crash was the hairiest moment of my life,' he said.

The hairiest *moment*. But those long minutes at Spa with the pain and the danger must have been worse. That accident and the ride with Louis Stanley led, incidentally to Mr Stanley establishing his famous Grand Prix ambulance unit, magnificently equipped and staffed, so that at least injuries can be properly treated on the spot.

Spa, in Stewart's view, is not really up to the demands of modern Grand Prix racing. Four years after his accident, there he was writing: 'I want Spa stopped.' He doesn't go quite as far as that these days because some improvements have been made, but still feels that it is dangerous, with no spectator protection. The 'purists' may argue that spectators as well as drivers are warned that motor racing is dangerous, but Stewart understands the anti-motor-sport climate that exists in many places. A big crowd disaster – apart from being tragic in itself – could lead to motor racing being banned in more than one country.

Last year's Belgian Grand Prix was held at Zolder. The circuit was in poor condition. The drivers protested. Some improvements were made, and a threat that the race might not be run was averted. And the Belgian Grand Prix, run on a crumbling track, was won by Jackie Stewart.

Who better to talk about safety? Nobody when he was driving. Nobody now he has retired from the Grand Prix circuit with a record total of twenty-seven wins behind him.

There is one aspect of the story of Jackie Stewart and Spa that may raise a question. Would it not have been possible for him – or the author for that matter – to have probed the reality or otherwise of those three nuns?

Perhaps. Perhaps. But Stewart hasn't done so. And nor have I. After all, there are some things it is more intriguing not to know.

From *The Day I Died* by Mark Kahn (Gentry Books, 1974)

Six Days in August

Michael Cooper-Evans

John Surtees has invited all his mechanics, from both the Formula One and Formula Two teams, to join him for dinner in the Christophorus Restaurant after the race. He was the only driver to make this gesture towards his mechanics, although other teams had far more to celebrate than either Honda or Lola Racing. But it was not a gay party; conversation around the large table was stilted, for Surtees was still disappointed and frustrated by the performance of the Honda, and his guests took their cue from him.

Surtees had encountered a number of problems during the race, some of which were all too familiar. As at Spa earlier in the season, the power curve of the Honda engine had proved, under the added burden of full fuel tanks, to be totally unsuited to the gear ratios required on a circuit which demanded maximum speeds in the 170–180 m.p.h. range on the straight. There was no real acceleration. 'The main problem was that it just stood still coming out of the corners with a full tank load.' Two other factors combined to aggravate this problem of the limited range of engine speed at which power is available: firstly, the day was hot – hot enough to aerate the fuel in the low pressure lines despite the revised exhaust system – so that the engine suffered from fuel starvation on the slow and medium speed corners which abound at the Nürburgring, and already poor acceleration became even worse. Secondly, the Honda mechanics had taken it upon themselves to assume that the day would be cold – as witness their attempts to blank off a part of the radiator before the start – and had in consequence increased the richness of the mixture in order to compensate for the low temperature they had expected. Thus, in the the heat of the day, the engine was running too rich, even with the manual mixture control on the instrument panel turned by Surtees to the fully weak position. (Because of this rich

John Surtees is an extremely intelligent man who is always good value.

S.M.

Honda entered Grand Prix racing in 1964 with their own car. For 1967 they hired John Surtees to drive it. Cooper-Evans, a perceptive writer, had served in the XIth Hussars, taking part in anti-terrorist operations in Malaya, before working in a London advertising agency. This extract covers the aftermath of the German Grand Prix.

C.H.

mixture setting the car had used nearly forty-six gallons of fuel, to return a fuel consumption figure of only just over 4.54 m.p.g.; for once the Japanese safety margins had been necessary.) At the post-mortem Nakamura had had the good grace to acknowledge full responsibility for this error, but Surtees, while kicking himself for not having guessed what was afoot before the race, was none the less irritated by the fact that it should have occurred at all; depressed that the lesson had still not been learned that no changes to the car – however logical they might seem, or however trivial – should be made without everyone being aware of them.

As if all of this had not been enough, the new differential, although an infinite improvement on previous units, had begun to deteriorate as the race progressed, creating problems in transmitting power to the road, and further affecting acceleration. And, in addition, the car had been handling badly. 'When we tried to motor on over the bumps, we just were not managing it.' With full tanks it had been bottoming and grinding on the bumps, despite the raised suspension and the extra packing pieces, and Surtees had had great difficulty in keeping it going in a straight line over the rougher sections of the circuit. One aspect of the car's performance had been new to him; 'It's a little weird with a very heavy car quite how it does react in places. When you dive into some of those hollows' – at 140 m.p.h. or more – 'you feel for a moment that it's never going to stop going down through the earth. You seem to stop for a moment at the bottom, just as if it's dug in – it really is strange, something I've never encountered before.' All in all, it had been an unusually harrowing experience.

Later in the race – as fuel was consumed and the tanks emptied – the lightening fuel load had improved handling and acceleration, and at the same time clouds began to obscure the sun so that the water temperature gauge on the instrument panel, which had been indicating nearly 105° centigrade, dropped to 90° centigrade. Almost at once, as the fuel had stopped bubbling in the lines and the temperature had become more appropriate to the rich mixture setting, the engine had become cleaner. But these improvements had come too late for John Surtees to make much use of them. 'The people in front of me had got away to such a distance that without taking a hellish chance I couldn't honestly have caught them. It takes an awful personal effort to do a really quick lap in the Honda because you're scratching about at the limit of the car's performance, and I doubt whether I could have kept it up without going off. If it had been a question of taking a chance for first place it would have been a different matter, but as it was there wasn't any point.'

David Hobbs, on the other hand, was quite pleased with his performance, more because his lap times had been faster in the race than in practice, and in slower conditions, than because he had finished third by virtue mainly of the fact that his car had outlasted the opposition. Had he not lost so much time in the pits he might well have won the Formula Two race, for his lap times had been consistently faster than those of the actual winner, Jackie Oliver, and he had, in fact, made the second fastest race lap. 'That was a shame about David, wasn't it? I'm only sorry that we couldn't have given him a car that didn't suffer from those early problems. It would have been nice for him to come home – it would have given him a nice encouragement.' But then, motor racing is full of ifs and buts. 'Let's face it, if we'd been lapping fifteen seconds a lap faster, we would have come home!' One thing that gave Hobbs particular satisfaction – and no little amusement – was Steinmetz' effusive change of attitude towards him; he now behaved as if David was a long lost friend and God's greatest gift to motor racing. [Steinmetz, BMW team manager, objected to Hobbs being in the race on the grounds of inexperience.]

As a result of his pit stops, David had had a lonely race. One of the few other drivers he had seen was John in the Honda ('I practically drove off the road to let him by!') hotly pursued by Jacky Ickx in the Tyrrell Matra-Ford. Hobbs was one of those who had been rather less than impressed by the performance of the young Belgian driver and offered as his opinion that his dinner with Ferrari had probably had less effect on his stomach than on other parts of his anatomy. John was much more vehement; 'It was stupid – he had that race in the bag and he just threw it away. He was all over the place, jumping banks *that* big!' – he indicated with his hands – 'I've seen blokes trying, yes, but never anything like that.' It seemed that if Ickx had been hoping to impress people, he had succeeded only in doing exactly the opposite.

Service in the Christophorus Restaurant was slow that night, and John Surtees arrived late for the prize-giving ceremony in the Martini International tent, a curious plastic balloon structure with no visible means of support. It was decorated for the occasion with huge framed photographs of the best known Grand Prix drivers, among whom, apparently, Denny Hulme was not numbered by the Germans; his picture, unmounted and rather smaller than the others, had been hastily sellotaped to a wall behind the bar which dispensed free drinks to all comers. Late though he was, Surtees arrived before Prince Metternich, the President of the AvD, had completed the presentation of prizes to the winners and runners up of the supporting races; the Formula One prize giving was the last item on the agenda, the climax to the evening.

As he waited, sipping a glass of ginger ale in the hot, crowded room, buzzing with conversation and thick with cigarette smoke, Surtees' thoughts dwelt on the future. The German Grand Prix was over, the cup he would receive for his fourth place, the cheque, the handshake, the applause, belonged, like the blisters on his hands and the aching fatigue in his muscles, to the past. Ahead there were plans to be made for new races, new problems to be solved, new challenges to be met, greater hope of success. 'This is all very quiet and hush-hush at the moment, but just before we came out here we got the OK to build a lighter chassis for the car. One of the reasons for this decision is that although the present chassis is immensely stiff it does have some localized weaknesses and now that it's all getting very tired, things are beginning to move on it. This showed up when we weighed the car and in all that trouble we were having with the ride heights; it flexes just enough to adjust itself to the surface. Jimmy Potton swears he could hear it creaking every time he put a jack under it! The other thing is that in the race it could only have bottomed through things whipping, because the car was at a point where it could not have bottomed purely with the suspension being up, because we had solid clearance even with the tyres flattening out.' Old age – what one of the mechanics had described as 'a severe attack of anno domini' – had probably been responsible, too, for the high frequency vibration which Surtees had experienced again in the race.

'So we're going to get cracking back at Honda Racing in Slough, because naturally it can be done very much quicker there, and we hope to get it ready for Monza; we've got our original chassis engineer coming over from Tokyo and we've taken over three people from Lola on the production side. It's being built by Honda, though, with the assistance of Lola production facilities, because naturally they haven't got enough facilities of their own over here. It won't be a really pukka car, but it will be a step in the right direction, a general experimental car from which we can get all the data we need to build a completely new car for next year. We'll never get it down to the minimum weight while we've got this engine and gearbox because they weigh far too much – the engine weighs 500 lb as against the Ford's 358, which is out of this world. But we should be able to get a bit of weight off it and it should be quite a lot quicker, especially if we get the modified engine we should have had earlier in the season, with more power at the top and a slightly better curve. And also, of course, we can outbuild the suspension geometry problems we have had – I reckon we can tweak the suspension by a second a lap, so I think that with a bit of luck we might shake a few people.'

From *Six Days In August* by Michael Cooper-Evans (Pelham Books, 1968)

Fuji 1976

Niki Lauda

Lauda was such a mixture and it's difficult to forgive him for some of the things he said about the sport. There were times when he drove like a racer and there were other times when he didn't want to drive at all. I find that difficult to understand. I respect his right to withdraw from the Japanese Grand Prix but somehow I feel that if you are defending World Champion, as Lauda was, it's not correct to scale that height and suddenly turn round and say, 'It's too dangerous'. Motor racing hadn't got more dangerous. It had always been dangerous. I felt he did the sport a disservice, particularly as he had the privileges which come with being World Champion. In mitigation, however, I'm sure the crash at the Nürburgring and the burns he received in that must have played a major part in his decision and that perhaps makes it more understandable.

S.M.

Niki Lauda, recovered from an horrific crash at the Nürburgring in 1976, went to Japan for the final round of the Formula One Championship. James Hunt (Marlboro McLaren) trailed him by three points. In a downpour Lauda retired – voluntarily – on lap 3 and drove to the airport with Ferrari team manager Mauro Forghieri.

C.H.

We have to go off early to catch our aircraft. Marlene, Forghieri and I are in the car. If Hunt is fifth or worse, I am still World Champion. When we drove away Hunt was in the lead, but with tyre change nothing is yet settled. From the car radio we gather that Hunt has fallen behind. After that, nothing more about the Grand Prix. A quarter of an hour later the race result is announced and at that very moment our car goes into the underpass near the airport and we can't hear.

Only at the airport the Ferrari man gives the news: Hunt is World Champion. I'd had bad luck. At the moment I hardly minded. I can't begin to cry because the rain happened to stop.

Forghieri and I rang up the Old Man from Tokyo airport. I told him my feelings, my reasons, I told him it would have been madness to go on. He was very realistic, said aha, yes, yes, hm, yes yes, goodbye; he said not a word against me or against my decision, but he also gave not a grain of comfort or the slightest help. He never said, 'Don't worry.' And it would have been marvellous if he had.

I could just about guess what it was like when Ferrari laid down the receiver. The usual storm.

I only got the tip of it; officially the Old Man stood firm behind my decision, but that didn't help me really. After all those days and weeks of recovery after the accident my firm was blowing hot and cold, though it was all wrapped up in pretence and the show was not the reality.

Naturally in their heart of hearts they didn't agree with my decision. Even good friends like Luca Montezemolo thought Lauda is finished, he can't do it any more, he's too cowardly, he's had too much of a shock. My decision didn't fit the notion: win races or give up racing. Not to drive, to think it over and give up, that was too much for them.

The Ferrari underground simmered.

I couldn't worry about it too much because the operation on my right eye couldn't be put off any longer. While I was still in the St Gallen clinic, Luca Montezemolo told me from which direction the danger threatened: they want to make you team manager. And Luca – so serious was the situation – was even himself a little bit sold on this plan; he was wavering. The idea was adventurous, because it would solve all Ferrari's worries at my expense. They were afraid I wasn't as good as I had been, and therefore they preferred to get another driver, but they were also afraid of the opposite, and that in another team I should be a dangerous opponent. As team manager I could perhaps be used for testing, they would have me under their control, and I would not be dangerous.

It was the worst time. The pressure from Japan was still upon me, I was worried about my eye, I didn't know what the result of the operation would be. And on top of everything, this hit below the belt. I said to Luca: 'If you don't want me to drive for you, let me free at once from my contract, and I'll leave immediately. There's no question of me being team manager.'

Luca no longer wavered; he was once more on my side, told the 'underground' my answer – and with this the case was settled. Not, though, the attitude of Ferrari towards me.

Hardly were my eye bandages off, hardly could I see again, than I flew to Bologna, to present myself and to discuss the future. It was obvious that we should have to test, test and test again, if we were going to catch up with the arrears of our car. I was up and about, the world championship was over and done with as far as I went; for me what counted was the coming season and getting ready for it.

When I asked for the programme, I got the answer that Reutemann was to test during the coming week at Paul Ricard. Fine, I said, I'll be there. Then they drew back and twisted and turned and finally said unfortunately there's only one car. Carlos should drive on the first and second days, I on the third day. Nothing was said against this.

I had another press conference about my show, and I told among other things that we were off again, and about Paul ricard and so on. When I got back to Salzburg there was a telegram in the office from Ferrari, with more or less this text: 'We learn from the newspapers that you are planning to test at Paul Ricard. This does not conform with our test programme. You must be that day at Fiorano.' There was not even a personal signature, only 'race section'.

It couldn't have been made more obvious to a driver that he had been pushed down to second place, and must knuckle under. Impossible to treat someone who has just got over an operation and is ready to begin again, in a more brutal way. I was crazy: it couldn't be true. While the great Reutemann did great work at Ricard, I was to go round and round Fiorano.

I telephoned Enzo Ferrari and had the most decisive talk that I had in all my four years with Ferrari. What did this mean? I asked. Well, he said, since I (Lauda) had made a wrong decision, all decisions henceforward were to come from him, he would take it in hand himself. Wrong decision, what did he mean? Monza, he said; I shouldn't have raced at Monza. If I had missed the race because of my accident we should have lost the world championship in a way that would have looked better. I was utterly furious and shouted at him that perhaps for an Italian it would be all right to lie in bed and in bed to lose in a way that looked well, but when I fight I fight, and I don't lie in bed. If I lose the world championship on the road, well I accept it. Thanks, goodbye, I slammed the receiver down.

A little latter Ghedini rang up, full of complaints, the Old Man is raging, everything is finished, he's chucking you out. Telephone at once and apologize. No question of that, I say, I'm not going to apologize.

I was all in, depressed and furious. Why had I been through hell, got myself out of hospital, worked every minute on my body to recover, given everything I had to it, just to be treated in this way at the end of it all. Naturally when the Old Man said Monza he meant Fuji. If at Fuji I had driven like an angel through the water, everything would have been grand. I tried to put myself in his shoes. OK, he pays for Ferrari to race and Ferrari to win. He pays for the world championship, and then all of a sudden the fool won't drive because it's too dangerous for him. But when I go on thinking as Ferrari must be thinking, I can't help coming to the human situation, for after all he's got a man under contract, not an ape. He can give the ape a kick up the arse and order him to drive, but a man must be expected to think. And if he didn't consider me an idiot before, then he must accept the result of my thoughts. When I think over the whole picture, including the Nürburgring, and when I add the quite special pressures on Niki Lauda in that autumn of 1976 and look back on it all, I can't see one iota of a possibility of it being fair to punish me for Fuji.

From *For The Record* by Niki Lauda (William Kimber, 1978)

The Tragedy of Ronnie Peterson, 1978

Fredrik Petersens

An extremely experienced Swedish journalist, Petersens was a close friend of Peterson and Gunnar Nilsson. The book he wrote on them – Nilsson died of cancer in October 1978, a month after Peterson died at Monza – remains a haunting and emotional account of human sadness.

C.H.

It was a happy and relaxed Ronnie who went down to Monza. He was just twelve points behind his team-mate Mario [Andretti], and there were three more races to go. He had signed a new contract with McLaren and, as he said himself, one of the best he ever signed.

But everything went wrong from the start in Monza. After a few laps' practice Ronnie came back and rolled slowly into the pits. The engine was blown in a big way. He jumped out of the car looking very disappointed and studied Mario's time, which was quick, very quick. The Lotus team had brought only three 79s as Mario had wrecked the fourth in his first lap accident in Austria and there had been no time to build a new one. Ronnie's second car was a faithful old 78 in which he won the South African Grand Prix and was rolled out for the second session.

After a few laps he was back in the pits again.

'No use driving this old machine. It is too slow and it's a waste of time to set it up as I'm driving my racing car tomorrow.'

A fresh engine was installed and Ronnie was in a good mood when he drove out in the hectic traffic on Saturday morning. But this was one of these weekends when everything went wrong. A few laps later he was back in the pits and he didn't look too happy under his helmet. There was something wrong with the brakes.

'There must be a valve sticking somewhere in the system,' he told Nigel Bennett.

There was more trouble to come an by the end of the session he was back again. A gearbox oil seal had failed and the lubricant was leaking down on to the clutch. The 79 was taken back to the garage and Ronnie sat down waiting. He was upset and didn't want to talk to anybody and after a while he went down to the mechanics to have a look.

With just ten minutes to go the mechanics ran into the pits with the car and Ronnie was strapped in and with a terrible wheel speed he drove out on to the circuit to try to improve his time.

About five laps later practice was over, and Ronnie had not improved. His time, 1 min. 38.256 seconds, was only good for a fifth place overall and in the pole position was his rival Mario.

'Everything went wrong but I never give up and the race is not over until the man jumps up and down with the chequered flag and I will drive flat out till I see him.'

Early on Sunday morning the roads to Monza were blocked by thousands of Italians. When the traffic did not move they opened their wine bottles and had a bit of their salami sausage and everybody was in a good mood.

The drivers, the team managers, the mechanics were sitting in the shade and just waited for the race. In the background they could hear the crowd scream 'Ferrari! Ferrari!' and wave their red flags with the black horse on its hind legs.

The drivers came out slowly from their mobile homes and went to the pits for the warm-up laps.

'I don't think much can happen on these few laps,' Ronnie said just before he started the engine and joined the others in the queue waiting for the green light. After a few laps the black car number six was missing. In the distance you could see a tall, fair-haired man with his helmet in his hand walking back to the pits.

'When I came to the second chicane the brakes didn't work and I went straight on. I don't know how many layers of cat fencing I went through before the car stopped. The catch is rather badly smashed and I guess I'll have to drive the old one in the race.'

He fled into the mobile home to escape everybody and to have a look at his slightly bruised legs. I went down to see what was left of the car and about fifteen minutes later Ronnie joined me. We sat there in silence just looking at the car and didn't say a word. Finally, Ronnie broke the silence.

'Someone made a mistake with the brakes. There was a split pin missing but don't tell anybody.'

He jumped into the 78 to fit in the pedals and to see that he was sitting comfortably. A couple of hours later he was out on the circuit again, determined as usual to do a good race and stay close behind Mario. When the twenty-four cars came back after the warm-up lap the starter, who must have been very nervous, switched the light from red to green too early. The last cars were still in second or third gear when the first row stood still.

Villeneuve, who shared the first row with Andretti, made a perfect start and led the field when they approached the first chicane. One driver went on the outside of the field where the road is wider, overtook a couple of cars and, where the starting-line narrows, it suddenly all happened.

Ronnie, who had made a bad start, why nobody knows, was hit. One car, probably Hunt's McLaren, was hit by another car and slid into Ronnie's.

The black Lotus crashed into the guard-rail and the car exploded. The burning wreck, as if shot from a catapult, flew out on the circuit again and was hit by another car. It bounced on a guard-rail on the left-hand side and came to a halt in the middle of the road. The race came to a chaotic halt. There were cars everywhere – Hunt's McLaren, Reutemann's Ferrari, Daly's Ensign, Lunger's McLaren, the two Shadow cars of Stuck and Regazzoni, the Tyrrells of Depailler and Pironi, and a Surtees with an unconscious Brambilla at the steering-wheel.

I was sitting among the other radio commentators and we just looked at each other. We stared at our TV monitors and everybody was silent. Then finally after minutes that seemed to be as long as hours we saw that it was car number six. James Hunt, without thinking of himself, rushed into the flames and tried to help Ronnie out of the wreck. Patrick Depailler kicked the steering-wheel and a lonely brave marshal doused the flames as best he could. Seconds later came Clay Regazzoni, and together they managed to pull Ronnie out. James just shook his head when he went back to the pits and a policeman who wanted his autograph was pushed aside.

After a long delay an ambulance drove Ronnie to the waiting helicopter, which flew him to the Niguarda hospital in Milan. The first report said that he had broken both his legs but there was no danger for his life.

No one wanted to drive the race, but were more or less forced to by the police who could not guarantee safety if the race was called off. Everybody was shocked.

'I didn't want to drive in the restart,' Patrick Depailler said. 'I understood how badly injured Ronnie was, thinking of his pain. A couple of years ago I broke a leg myself and I know it is terrible. I was not driving the car in the race. I was just sitting there like a robot and could not think, just could not understand what I was doing in the car. There were others who were not capable of driving either and we did some crazy things, so crazy that I can't talk about them.'

When Mario Andretti heard the early news from the hospital that Ronnie would survive, he said with relief, 'Thank God.' This should have been the happiest day of his life. He thought he had won the race, but both he and Villeneuve who was second were penalized for jumping the start and Niki Lauda won the race with his team-mate John Watson second; Mario was sixth but that was enough to clinch the title. Two months later James was awarded a gold medal for his heroic achievement by the Royal Swedish Automobile Club.

Later that evening three of us went to the hospital, and because of the first report we were so optimistic that we thought we could see Ronnie that night. We had a new shock when we came to the hospital. It was dirty and all over the floor were cigarettes. You had absolutely no feeling of being in a hospital and everywhere were photographers waiting for The Picture. In a way it was like a night-mare and you just wanted to wake up.

We talked to one doctor who gave us his version, but we did not like what he said, so in the middle of the night Ronnie's old mech-anic, Ake Strandberg, phoned Colin Chapman and Staffan Svenby [Peterson's manager]. They told us that Ronnie was being taken care of very well and there was nothing to worry about.

We went back early on Monday morning and when we saw Staffan we realized that something had happened during the night.

'Only a miracle will save him. He is in a deep coma and there's nothing we can do but pray and hope.'

Ronnie's circulation was becoming impaired as bone marrow embolisms got to his bloodstream and a couple of hours later that Monday morning Super-Swede died.

I wanted to be alone and needed some fresh air and went for a walk and met Mario when he came to see Ronnie. He did not know what had happened. When I broke the sad news he just looked straight ahead and said, 'Oh no. I wanted that title so badly but I did not want to win it like this. What the hell shall I do with it now? I don't feel anything for it. One of my best friends is gone and motor racing will never be the same again. I was really looking forward to next year, he in the McLaren and me in the Lotus and we would have a good fight and afterwards sit down to have a beer and a good laugh about it.'

Ronnie's old friends Emerson Fittipaldi and his wife came to the hospital very early on Monday morning and Staffan told them what had happened.

'I just can't believe it. We have been friends for so many years and now he is gone. Racing will change a lot for me. He was one of the greatest drivers and no one will be able to replace him,' Emerson said.

Four days later, Ronnie Super-Swede Peterson was buried in his home town Orebro and the coffin was carried by Emerson Fittipaldi, James Hunt, John Watson, Niki Lauda, Jody Scheckter, Ake Strandberg and, behind, Gunner Nilsson who was too weak to carry it; seven of Ronnie's best and oldest friends.

Once, many years ago, when Ronnie came back to the pits after another of his spectacular crashes he said, 'Someone up there must like me.'

Someone was not watching this Sunday, 10 September 1978.

From *The Viking Drivers* by Fredrik Petersens (William Kimber, 1979)

CHAPTER THREE

THE MIND OF THE DRIVER

My Philosophy

Jim Clark

You need more than your fair share of luck to make a successful career out of motor racing. You need luck in finding the right car to drive at the right time, the right people to encourage and advise you, and luck in your early races to give you confidence. Every year, hundreds of people come into racing. Most do so in a small way – just as I started. They are not in there to become World Champions, but just to try and capture the thrill of racing. This thrill occurs at all levels, and you can get just as much excitement driving a small family saloon as driving a Grand Prix car. The main thing is that you are taking part.

I feel sorry for people who are obviously keen on racing but who don't race because they can't afford to, or feel they do not have the ability. Anyone who is really interested in racing deserves to have the chance at least to try driving a car round a circuit as quickly as he can, if only to put his ability into perspective. It is true that many people become completely disillusioned with their first attempts at racing. I know exactly how they feel, for I went through these spells to begin with, and the only difference was that I had at least two people behind me pushing me on when I began to lose interest and faith.

My feelings about Jim Clark were summed up in a conversation I had with Rob Walker, for whom I drove in Formula One, when Jim started Grand Prix racing in 1960. I said, 'We're going to need this year's car, not last year's if we're going to beat this bloke.' (Walker, as a Lotus privateer, couldn't always command the latest equipment whereas Clark, a works driver, automatically got it.) You could see the qualities that Jimmy had even then. And, you know, in the end we always did have last year's car. I think that what Jimmy had he was absolutely born with. It's like some people can sing. OK, they train their voices but they already have a great voice to train. Jimmy was very lucky in that he met Colin Chapman, a highly intelligent man and a brilliant engineer. Jimmy couldn't explain technically how the car performed – 'when I go into the corners it's a bit funny, it does this' – but Chapman could interpret that. Together they made a most powerful partnership.   S.M.

Clark, from the Scottish Borders, drove in 72 Grands Prix between 1960 and 1968, taking thirty-three pole positions and winning twenty-five times. He was World Champion in 1963 and 1965. He died in a crash during a Formula Two race at Hockenheim on 7 April 1968.   C.H.

People who race are motivated by many things. Some race because they feel that they can make easy money at it, but if they have no latent ability they are soon disillusioned. Others race because it is the 'done thing' or because it might make them more attractive to girls. This sort of thing is no more than comic book fiction, but the idea still exists today and there are quite a number of drivers who come into racing because of the 'glamour' of it all. Some of these drivers even progress through influence or private capital to fairly high places. There were drivers who were competing in top-line motor races a few years ago who used to buy up bundles of race programmes if their photographs appeared in them and sent off copies to their friends. Few exhibitionists like that reach the top today because there are too many good drivers with ability who are filling up the entry lists.

Lastly, there is the driver who has a natural liking for racing, and a curiosity for what racing can offer him. I think I fall into this category for curiosity has pushed me on right from the start. I used to wonder what it would be like to drive in a race like my friends. Then I raced and my curiosity turned to the types of car or the circuits. As long as I remained curious, I was interested in racing and this curiosity still remains.

How do you go about learning to race once you have the opportunity? Well, certainly there is a lot to learn and many ways of learning. Some people say that if you arrive at a new circuit you should go round it in a saloon car and see where the corners are. In an earlier chapter I talked about my first visit to Spa and how Jack Fairman took me round in a Volkswagen to show me where to brake. If I learned anything by that trip it was very little indeed. I like to go out in the car I'm going to race and find my own way around. In this way you don't have any false values.

Learning a circuit is very much up to the individual, and practice alone makes perfect. But you find that everyone wants you to go round with someone first of all. Over in America, you get a kind of complex about this. You arrive at a new circuit and are showered with advice. Drivers come up and advise you that there is a little bit of reverse camber on the first part of turn six and you have to take it in a certain way. They go to great lengths to say that this is the only way round the track and then you go out and take a completely different line from everyone else and they don't understand it.

This indeed is a very interesting point. You can go to any circuit and find that some drivers take a completely different approach from others and also drive their cars differently through the corners. To illustrate this, I remember that Bruce McLaren – writing in his *Autosport* column just after the American Grand Prix in 1963 at Watkins Glen – described how he walked to one corner during practice and studied both Graham Hill and me taking this corner. According to him, my technique was to come bombing into the corner and put power on in the middle holding the car with the power on through the rest of it. Graham, on the other hand, did all his braking well before the corner, had the power on before he actually arrived in the corner itself, and was using power throughout. After weighing up this, Bruce concluded that my style was better for this corner and adopted it in the race. But, in fact, Graham's style probably suited the handling characteristics of the BRM.

Even experienced drivers are sometimes perplexed at the way in which another driver will line up his car for a given bend on a given circuit. I remember testing the Lotus Cortina at Silverstone in the wet. Colin Chapman, who has probably done more racing on Silverstone than I have, wanted to see what happened to the handling if we added some weight at the back over the back axle. The best way to find out was for Colin to go round the circuit with me at racing speeds so he climbed into the back and braced himself as well as he could spreadeagled across the car. Naturally I tried hard and was really enjoying myself with the car throwing it about in the way in which you can throw Lotus Cortinas about and get away with it. After a couple of laps of this Colin shouted from the back that he thought I took some very odd lines round Silverstone so I asked him what he meant, as this was my normal way of driving the car. He then explained that he went into the corners much later than I did and took a completely different line. Half the time he expected me to go through the walls or hit the banking on the outside. This shows you how two drivers can have different ideas on how to drive any particular car. Whereas there may be a theoretically correct line through every corner, it depends on what kind of car you are driving whether you take this line or something more suited to the handling of the car which may not be theoretically true.

There may be some truth in Colin's comments though, for I know I am inclined to go into a corner earlier than most people. By that I mean that with today's cars most people run deep into a corner before turning the wheels to go round. In this way you can complete all your braking in a straight line, as everyone recommends you do, before setting the car up for the corner; but I prefer to cut into the corner early and even with my brakes still on to set up the car earlier. In this way I almost make a false apex because I get the power on early and try to drift the car through the true apex and continue with this sliding until I am set up for the next bit of straight.

This brings me to what I think is the most important thing you can learn in racing – how to brake. It comes as a great shock to find that you can brake much later than you ever thought was possible and all through racing in its every form braking is more important than most people think. It is considered that leaving your braking to the very last minute is important and I would agree; but I would also say that where you take the brakes off again also matters. It depends very much on how the car you are driving handles. Often, if I want to go through a given corner quicker I don't necessarily put the brakes on any later than usual, but I might not put them on very hard and take them off earlier. Where you are led into the trap is leaving your braking too late and having to run deep into the corner and brake at the last moment. You might certainly arrive at the corner quicker, but there is a psychological tendency then to brake much harder than you need to and therefore overbrake.

It often happens that a driver will be in the heat of a race and set up a fast lap. Then his pit will tell him to ease off and the driver will be surprised to find that he is lapping just as quickly. In other words when he was really trying he was actually braking too hard and slowing himself down more than he needed.

All this is part of getting used to the car. Some drivers take a long time getting into the swing of a new car, or maybe driving a vehicle which has been rebuilt after an accident, or one with a different suspension. They go out and do about twenty or thirty laps and then come in and prepare to go out again and do some really quick laps. I find that if I have been out in the car and them come into the pits and hang about for ten minutes or so I can usually set up a fast time on my third, fourth or fifth laps on going out again. If I don't and a really fast time is needed for a good starting position I then take one slow lap to relax my mind and then have another go for a fast lap. Normally, I never like to stay out for more than about five laps at a time, for this gives me plenty of time to discuss with the mechanics how the car is behaving and carry out any adjustments well within the time of the practising period, apart from the obvious fact of wearing out the car.

Racing cars change year by year, sometimes more frequently, to keep up with new technical and design developments. This is progress. A new alloy, a new rubber, a fresh engine design or a more refined application of aerodynamic principles may shave a vital tenth of a second off a lap time. World reputations are built and smashed on these margins, and the Lotus 25, which carried me to the World Championship, is no exception.

But some changes are more fundamental, and yet attract less attention. Take the drivers, for instance. In the last twenty years we have seen in motor racing, as in every aspect of our lives, a growing trend towards specialization. The racing driver today is in most cases a full professional. The playboys and the talented amateurs have almost disappeared from the world's circuits – certainly in Grand Prix racing. I would not like to say whether this is a good or a bad thing in the long run, but it has led to an intensification in competition, to higher standards of driving, and to remarkable departures from established practice.

An example of this is the way the technical boys tinkered about with engines and chassis for decades before it occurred to them to alter one factor which they had considered as almost constant until then – the position of the driver! Certainly we had watched drivers settle themselves more comfortably in the seat over the years, slumping back a few centimetres each season. When I began racing in 1958, the usual position was a far cry from the days when the great drivers would huddle forward over the controls, with their noses resting on the top of the wheel.

But it came as a shock to me when, one day early in 1962, Colin Chapman led me over to see the new design of his world-beating Lotus 25. It was practically a bed on wheels! I suppose I should have seen it coming when Colin first started toying with the idea in the Lotus 21, but I never expected it to go as far as this!

In the Lotus 21, Colin had a beautiful low-slung car, with a really sleek profile. But he was faced with the problem that the driver was sitting much too high, and was thereby increasing the frontal area and wind resistance by an excessive amount.

Colin tipped the seat back and, hey presto! the problem was solved. All very well for the designers, but what about the driver? I remember, the first time we tested the car at Goodwood, having great difficulty adjusting myself to that position. The front wheels seemed much higher than eye level, and the fact that now my weight, more than ever before, was distributed up my back, meant that the theory of driving by the seat of one's pants had to be extended. Still, I accepted gracefully, as I could clearly see the aerodynamic advantages, and in time I became accustomed to the position in the 21.

The 25 however, took the principle a good deal further and I had a lot more adjusting to do. If you have ever stepped from say a truck into a sports car, you will have noticed the strange sensation of a new eye level. Your whole perspective is altered. Imagine what such a process does to you at 150 m.p.h. With the Lotus 25, I literally had a worm's eye view of the track. Taking the correct line through a corner became much more difficult, and each one had to be reassessed in the light of the near-supine driving position. Indeed, some corners on a track which one used to be able to see round now became 'blind'.

Although, once again, I could see the tremendous aerodynamic advantages of this position, I must say I was glad that there are limits to which the lying-down principle can be taken. There are two main factors in this limitation. One is that the driver's shoulders must be high enough to allow his arms to move freely without his legs and the rest of his body getting in the way. The second is the tremendous muscular strain which comes from having to keep your chin jammed down on to your chest in order to see where you are going. On a long race this position, combined with the heavy G-forces which come into play at high speeds, is likely to cause a very stiff neck.

Now that I have become accustomed to this position, I feel quite at home, however, and I feel uncomfortable sitting too erect in a saloon car. But in the back of my mind is the nagging suspicion that one day these design people are going to ditch the driver altogether in order to produce a perfectly flat racing car!

There are other changes taking place all the time in various aspects of racing. Take team tactics, for instance. A lot has been talked about team tactics in motor racing and to a minor degree they do affect the results of races. There were occasions in 1963 for instance when the finishing positions might have been different if some of the pit crews had been on their toes. But generally, the real days of strict pit control went out with the 2½-litre formula and probably with Alfred Neubauer of Mercedes-Benz.

Neubauer virtually dominated his drivers, and they ran to his orders. This situation prevailed in a number of other teams but at Mercedes Neubauer made a fetish out of it. Today things are different. At least they are different at Lotus. Colin Chapman lays down few team tactics and I run my own race. This is certainly true of Grand Prix racing but there have been occasions when our team has been superior, such as in South Africa in 1961, when Trevor Taylor and I set out to be one, two and played the race that way. In modern Grand Prix racing, where every team is entered, you don't get a chance to play team tactics – the competition is too great. For one reason or another I have rarely had a Team Lotus car in a Grand Prix playing team tactics successfully.

I am not controlled from the pits in any way, and Colin has never told me to speed up and only once told me to slow down – and we lost the race! All Colin does is try to give me information as to what is going on in the race. I pay close attention to his pit signals as to my nearest opponents, and I plan out my own races. Usually, I have a basic plan which I have prepared in practice by watching the other drivers and trying to take advantage of their mistakes. I have always told Colin what I intend to do, so that if I suddenly ease off and hold station, he knows that I am probably conserving my engine and playing a waiting game.

From *Jim Clark at the Wheel* by Jim Clark (Arthur Barker, 1964)

Mind and Body

Richard Garrett

A psychologist, Mrs Berenice Krikler, did fascinating research into the mentality of racing drivers, something extremely unusual twenty years ago. Even in those days most motor racing coverage concentrated on what happened in the races. She interviewed a whole lot of drivers because of me. After my crash at Goodwood in 1962, she came and interviewed me but she had no rules to go by, no way of setting what I'd told her into context because there had been no research. When she'd assessed me she said, 'Well, all this doesn't really mean much,' so she went on to the other drivers. It was a fascinating exercise in its time and perhaps fascinating now because drivers' minds don't really change. S.M.

After Moss's crash Mrs Krikler was asked by a neurosurgeon treating him if she'd carry out an assessment to see if – mentally – he could make a complete recovery. Her initial problem was that she hadn't known Moss before, and therefore found it difficult to know how much damage had been done. To compound that, she had no experience of the thought-processes of racing drivers. Hence she extended her field of research. She discovered that all the drivers were intelligent; she also discovered they were capable of thinking in the abstract but almost never did so. Their lives were locked entirely into the racing. She'd heard people say that drivers had a death wish – but speaking to them she discovered the exact opposite. 'They accept the challenge of the danger in order to beat it, in order to prove they are immortal.' Although not fully recovered, Moss took Mrs Krikler for a lap of a circuit. 'I knew that he wouldn't take risks and I treasure the memory of that lap still.' C.H.

When one questions a Grand Prix driver about the role of a team manager in his life, he readily agrees that it is an important one. However, it soon becomes clear that the importance is confined to practical matters. The manager provides all the facilities which are necessary to go motor racing and he handles a great many details which, to the driver, would be tedious. If one hopes for any such answer as 'he's a father figure', or 'he's rather like the captain of a Rugby XV – he holds the team together and gives it morale', one will be disappointed.

Grand Prix drivers do not need father figures. Nor, nowadays, do they pay very much attention to the idea of a team in the sense that other sports use this word. They are essentially loners: men who need nobody to boost their morales or to listen to their troubles.

This streak of independence may have become more pronounced in recent years. In the late 1920s, W. O. Bentley took a collection of his cars and drivers to Le Mans for the 24-hour races. They won the event five times, and became a legend. The drivers, who included at least three exceptionally wealthy men, and a doctor and a journalist, were all of them tremendous individualists away from the circuit. At Le Mans, however, they did exactly what Bentley told them to do. They were under orders to work as a team, and they never questioned his instructions.

When I once asked what, in his opinion, was the greatest difference between a racing driver of those days, and a contemporary member of the profession, Mr Bentley told me, 'It used to be a question of one make of car competing against another. Nowadays, it is one driver competing against all the others.'

It may seem strange, this unusually high degree of emotional independence. They are, after all, living lives under a great deal of tension. What is more, they sometimes have to make decisions which are, literally, a matter of life and death. These decisions, of course, occur in such minute particles of time, that it would be quite impossible to turn to a co-driver (assuming there was one), and to say, 'Something awful's coming up. Let's talk this thing through.'

Most people, when they are in a state of tension, smoke rather more heavily, possibly drink more than usual, and nearly always turn to other people for some kind of comfort. Grand Prix drivers, in contrast to the majority, seem to live rather ascetic lives — if not downright puritanical. Few of them smoke; they consume large quantities of soft drinks but rarely touch alcohol; and mostly lead remarkably blameless married lives. They are good fathers; take a pride in their homes; and may fairly be regarded as excellent examples of middle-class respectability.

I once discussed this with a psychologist, who pointed out that riotous living is not the only way in which people find distraction from problems. Another way is to indulge in activity: to drive a car, go for a long walk, take a trip to somewhere. The drivers have opportunities for this kind of thing in a very high degree. Consequently, other ways of finding relief become unnecessary.

Danger features large in a driver's life. A normal person's reaction to it is fear. When the hazard is still some distance away, it may only take the form of apprehension. When it is imminent, however, this can quickly be transformed into terror.

The only time I saw Stirling Moss before a race was at Goodwood on Easter Monday, 1962. It was a few minutes before the Formula One event. Before the afternoon was over, he had crashed and been most terribly injured. But there were no omens of disaster in the cool spring sunshine. I was drinking coffee at a snack bar in the paddock. Moss was a few yards away with a group of friends. He, too, was drinking coffee. They were all talking volubly, and he was laughing a lot. He showed no signs of nerves or apprehension.

I asked Rob Walker, for whom Moss drove on a good many

occasions, about this. He told me, 'I only once saw Stirling nervous, and that was before the Grand Prix of Portugal at Oporto in August, 1960, after his very bad accident at Spa. I do not know whether he himself knew that he was nervous, and it was only very slightly obvious to me because I knew him and his habits so well. After the race, however, he had such a reaction that he was physically sick the whole night. But, when he recovered from this, and I am sure it was only caused by nerves, I never saw any further signs of it.

'With Siffert, who drives for me now, I have never seen him nervous in any way at all, though he did tell me that he was rather excited before the 1968 British Grand Prix, which he won. Perhaps it was because he realized that he was in with a good chance.

'Fangio had the reputation of being able to take a quick nap on the pit counter up to ten minutes before a race, I believe.'

During the race itself, a driver's life may be in jeopardy. Between the instant of losing control of the car and the moment of impact, there is a brief period of time. It is the type of situation in which drowning men are reputed to see their entire lives passing before their eyes, as if projected by some souped-up cinema device. Newspapermen have written a good deal of rubbish about how the drivers think of their widowed wives and orphaned children on these occasions – a fact which they vigorously deny. Indeed, they dislike being questioned too much about such matters. They might point out that a painter prefers to discuss his masterpieces, and not describe what happens when he spills paint on the studio floor. A racing driver's art is to control a car as near perfectly as can be. Survival is only a part of the art.

In the race which nearly cost Vic Elford his life at Nürburgring, Piers Courage was also involved in an accident. It happened on the second lap. He was driving with about forty gallons of petrol on board as he took off on one of the humps.

'I jumped a considerable distance,' he told me. 'When the car came down, instead of just landing and going on down the hill, it hit the ground very hard on the chassis. There was a lot of right hand lock on, and a chassis doesn't have so much adhesion as the tyres. Consequently, it just slid sideways. The moment this happened, I knew that I was in for trouble, because the hedge was very, very close. So I put on opposite lock and I had the brakes on. But my left hand rear wheel was too close to the hedge, which was a fairly stiff one. It knocked the wheel off. I had my foot hard down on the brake but nothing happened. Luckily the car just slid down the road as I watched the bank coming up. Normally, you can judge your speed of impact, and I thought, "Ah – obviously the car is going to reach the bank, but it won't be going very fast." It all happened very quickly but your brain accelerates enormously. In fact, the car landed up just against the bank. The nose was damaged but it didn't bend the radiator or anything.'

Courage walked away from the smash. The jolt of impact had set off the fire extinguishers, and the gas from them 'made me feel very fuzzy. I sat down and I felt, well, not quite dizzy exactly, though I did feel rather groggy for a few moments. I think that as the accident's happening your brain is working overtime, trying to cope with the situation. When it all stops and your brain relaxes, there is a sort of reaction: you're a bit shaky for perhaps thirty seconds.'

I asked him whether, just before the moment of impact, he had felt scared.

'You feel slightly apprehensive,' he said. 'I don't think you really feel scared, because there is absolutely nothing you can do about it. The actual accident is sort of continuous, you know – and so you are working all the time. It is not something you are waiting for, but something you are trying to prevent.'

Another driver also referred to this question of the brain accelerating. 'I have never felt fear in a race,' he said. 'Just before a shunt, it's quite entertaining. You feel it must be possible to recover. It's all happening in such slow motion. I've never heard anyone speak of fear, no matter what the consequences may have been. You know that if you're not under control you're in for big time bother – and I am a big coward. It is only under these circumstances that I think this way. You imagine it probably won't be too bad. There's a lack of realization. When you're heading straight for a big tree at 150 m.p.h., the truth doesn't register. There's just going to be big bump. But you always feel you can get the car back. It's all in such slow motion that it seems to take hours and hours.

'Everything becomes so concentrated on what you are doing, that you have a different perspective of time. I think that, if you're cramming more thinking into a given amount of time, then the time seems longer.'

One person who has studied the mentality of Grand Prix drivers in some detail is Berenice Krikler. Mrs Krikler is a psychologist, who used to be employed at St George's Hospital in London. Her interest in the matter was occasioned by the clinical investigation of a driver who had suffered a severe head injury. There had to be some way of assessing his condition and the likelihood, or lack of it, of his returning to the track.

Since racing drivers are uncommon people, it was necessary to judge his performance against that of a group of men with similar skills. She asked five star performers from the Grand Prix circus to come to the hospital for a number of tests. Later, five ordinary motorists were also examined. The work took place at the height of the racing season, when all the aces were extremely busy. Nevertheless, they all agreed.

On the face of it, the main sacrifice demanded by the assignment was that of giving up valuable time. But, as Mrs Krikler explained to me, this was by no means the only one. Tests such as these can be disturbing experiences. There is always the risk that one may not show up so well as one had imagined. There is the chance that, being tested, one will be found wanting. One has to admit the possibility that one's image of oneself may not come out entirely unscathed.

'But they accepted this,' Mrs Krikler said. 'They took it all very seriously, for they are serious people. When they are skylarking, it is almost done deliberately – as if they feel they ought to be doing it, that it's expected of them.'

The first test was simply to find out something about them. One at a time, the drivers were interviewed and given a verbal intelligence test. They all came out of it very well indeed. Their IQs were well above average – 'at university level', Mrs Krikler said. In this respect, they corresponded with the ordinary motorists, all of whom were graduates.

If one assumes that a driver's co-ordination of his eyes and hands are adequate, there needs to be some way of measuring his powers of concentration. For this purpose, Mrs Krikler found a piece of apparatus which had been built for some research several years earlier and called 'track tracer'. A twisty route was drawn on a drum, which revolved. Using a stylo, the subject had to trace the course of the moving track without, as one might say, running out of road. Every time he came off, a mark was chalked up against him.

As in most other activities, the subject's performance improved with practice. Each of the drivers did this test forty times. At the end, their average marks were worked out.

In fact, it was more than simply a test of concentration. It also assessed the subject's powers of judgement and the level of his aspirations. Before each run, the drivers were asked, 'How well do you think you will do this time?' And, after it, 'How many marks do you think you've run up?'

The ordinary motorists also did this test. Their actual judgement turned out to be less stable than that of the drivers. Sometimes they were accurate, and sometimes they were not. The drivers knew their own capabilities much more clearly, and, afterwards, they had a better knowledge of what they had done.

To judge their mental speed, a series of sequence tests was arranged. You probably know the kind of thing. Something such as 'aaa, bbb, ccc, ccc, ddd' is written down. The idea is to work out what comes next. Unlike the track tracers, it is a standard test that is comparatively widely used.

For the first attempt, the drivers were allowed to work quietly. They could do it at whatever pace suited them best, and their performances were not timed. After that, however, Mrs Krikler turned on the pressure. 'Work as fast as you can,' she told them. She flourished her stopwatch; breathed down their necks; banged on a desk at twenty-second intervals to make them aware of the passage of time.

Apart from certain types of neurotic, anybody's performance tends to improve under pressure. When they were doing the test at their own rate, the drivers were below average in ability. But once they were under pressure, they speeded up to a degree which was considerably better than normal.

A similar result was revealed by a session on apparatus provided by the Royal Society for the Prevention of Accidents. On RoSPA's reaction-tester, which involved them in a series of steering wheel and brake tests, they showed greater variability than the ordinary drivers. Sometimes their reactions were very quick indeed: at others, less so. On average, however, there was little to choose between the results of the two groups.

Using a Miles Trainer driving simulator, they were then put through two more tests. On the first, they were told to drive norm- ally: on the second, they were instructed to go as fast as possible, as if they were on the track. Their reaction times were measured in each. In the first test, there was little to choose between the two samples. In the second, when they were driving under stress, the racing drivers tended to do very much better. Indeed, under these conditions, the reaction times of the ordinary motorists tended to slow down.

It was also necessary to assess the drivers' personalities. Were they, for example, impulsive? To discover the answer, Mrs Krikler used a simple device which is known as a Porteus Maze. It is exactly what its name suggests, and the idea is to see how people approach the problem. Do they blind off without any thought at all, and end up in one of the wrong alleyways? Or, do they consider it carefully before taking any action?

The results were to rip into shreds any ideas people may have had about drivers being rake-hell creatures of impulse. They looked at the puzzle studiously; they thought about it; they considered this and that possibility; and then they applied their thoughts.

During this period, Mrs Krikler had many conversations with the drivers, and formed some strong impressions about them. As the tests had revealed, they are miles removed from the wild ones, the devil-may-care desperadoes of the track, that fiction suggests. They are responsible people, who think carefully; have above average intelligence: and have a very controlled approach to life. They are introverts rather than extroverts, are highly competitive, and seem to experience a need to be constantly testing themselves. They not only compete against one another: they are also competing against their own selves, trying to match up to their personal criteria by doing something supremely well.

This may explain why, even if a driver has obviously no chance of winning a race, and is lying at the back of the field, he will continue to do each lap as well as he and his machine are able.

I asked her about danger. 'The drivers cut off about death and injury,' Mrs Krikler told me. 'They have the ability to switch off. On the other hand, they are very safety conscious. They go over their cars very carefully with the mechanics before a race. They certainly aren't daredevils and they don't take chances. They don't look for accidents and their attitude to death shows no suicidal tendencies.'

Writing about this work in an article printed in *The British Journal of Psychiatry*, Mrs Krikler observed: 'The reasons why they [the drivers] do choose their profession give rise to interesting speculation. Most have shown an interest in cars and their mechanical organization from childhood, but so do the majority of boys. None interviewed had had the ambition to be racing drivers as children.

'If one considers what is involved in driving in general, control is an important aspect and this seems to be a considerable personality need in motor racing drivers. The need to feel in control is satisfied by handling a machine delicately and skilfully at high speeds. Driving at these speeds and performing a task which is quite obviously highly dangerous, at the limits of one's ability and the limits of the car's capacity, gives rise to a particular exhilaration and feeling of successful control of objects and oneself.'

I asked Mrs Krikler about those of us who go to watch them. She told me that we seldom feel omnipotent and completely in control of things. Those who are, or who appear to be, reassure us. As we see them driving right up to the limits, we ourselves experience a feeling of power – almost of invulnerability.

'The crowd gets a kick out of seeing people go to the limits,' she said. 'There's tremendous reassurance in observing that someone can risk so much and not be overcome. And, of course, there's a great deal of excitement in seeing a great skill being demonstrated.'

From time to time, Grand Prix drivers, or some of them, are connected to ingenious pieces of apparatus, which measure their heartbeats during a race. It is, perhaps, worth noting that, when Armstrong stepped out of the lunar module and became the first man to tread the moon's surface, his heart was beating at the rate of ninety-four to the minute. In comparison, racing drivers' hearts may beat at over 150 to the minute during the fifteen minutes before an event and at something between 180 and 210 during the race itself. This does not suggest that the astronauts are calmer people than racing drivers. On one occasion, when a capsule was going into the re-entry phase, a light which should have indicated that the retro-rockets had fired, failed to come on. For a few seconds, one of the crew went through an experience known as 'heart block'. His heart actually stopped its normal beat, and blipped away at the rate of ten to a minute.

A doctor who has carried out an investigation into the heart rates of racing drivers is Peter Taggart, of the Middlesex Hospital. Dr

Taggart is, himself, a driver. He competes in sports car events to such an extent that, he agrees, he might be said to have two professions.

Similarly high heart rates in excess of 190–200 had been recorded in young athletes. This is understandable. At the time, they were taking violent exercise. The drivers, on the other hand, were sitting down and driving. Dr Taggart wanted to discover why this apparently sedentary task should produce an effect similar to that experienced by a fully stretched runner. It had, he knew, to do with the secretion of adrenalin but he wished to be more precise. 'It was an assumption,' he told me, 'and one never likes assumptions.'

Adrenalin is a hormone which is excreted by the adrenal gland under emergency conditions. It is said to cause either fight or fright. One either becomes hopping mad, or else one turns tail and flees. It causes the hair of cats to stand on end: in human beings, it makes the heart beat faster and more strongly and generally brings the body's performance up to a higher pitch.

The only way in which to measure the amount of adrenalin in the blood is to take a sample. This is a great deal more easily said than done, for the hormone has a very short life. Within about half a minute of being secreted, it is almost undetectable.

However, with considerable patience, Dr Taggart at last managed to take blood samples from seven racing drivers within one minute of their races coming to an end. 'In every case', he said, 'the level of adrenalin was quite astronomical. It was the kind of figure you might get if a tumour were present in the adrenal gland. It was quite extraordinary, and certainly explained the high heart-beat rate.'

Since the technique of measuring adrenalin has only recently been a practical proposition little is known about it. Nevertheless, Dr Taggart's research may, one day, benefit medicine. 'It's a series of steps,' he told me. 'First, we have demonstrated the fact that emotional stimulation, such as one gets in a racing car, is just as powerful as – if not more than – the effect of hard exercise on athletes. Then we discover a very, very high level of adrenalin in the blood. We can assume that adrenalin is probably causing the high heart beat, and thus that the hazards of coronary complaints may be increased by anxiety. Certain patterns are forming, though there are still a number of assumptions. We are almost certain we're right, but we can't prove it yet.'

If Dr Taggart finds his proof, it may very well be good news for heart cases. There are already tablets available which block the access of adrenalin to the heart and yet retain the remainder of its twenty actions, all of which make various other parts of the anatomy function better.

Considering a Grand Prix driver from these twin aspects of mind and matter, one comes to the disturbing conclusion that he may indeed be some sort f super man. Every doctor who has ever examined one of them seems to be agreed that they are excellent specimens physically. Mrs Krikler's research has shown that they have a much more controlled and considered approach to life than many of us enjoy.

The last of the characteristics that I can find accredited to racing drivers is exceptionally good eyesight.

In his book *The Racing Driver*, Denis Jenkinson recounted the story of how he once showed some exceptionally small print to Stirling Moss (it was a tiny photostat, about one inch high, of an article he had written). 'Even though I knew the article well, I could not read the small type without the aid of a magnifying glass,' Jenkinson related. 'Imagine my amazement when he took it from me and read it aloud without the slightest hesitation. I was so incredulous that I suggested he must know the opening lines from memory, having seen the original, but to convince me he read, just as easily, a paragraph half way down in the page. I tried as hard as I could, even with my supposedly corrective spectacles, but I was quite unable to read a word.'

From *Anatomy of a Grand Prix Driver* by Richard Garrett (Arthur Baker, 1970)

The Basic Principles

Jackie Stewart

Jackie was the first of the modern-style drivers, a man who drove fast enough to win but at the slowest possible speed. That's not a contradiction because he did the professional thing and won with the least effort. He'd never drive harder than necessary. I'd rather lose a race driving fast enough to win it than win it by driving slow enough to lose it. That's my philosophy and it may be entirely wrong! Jackie was a pathfinder, what I call the true professional, where winning is what matters, not racing. To me, the racing mattered. But he's a tremendous guy and I respect what he did.

S.M.

However much a technocrat, Stewart takes his place in history as a great driver. Between 1965 and 1973 he competed in ninety-nine Grands Prix and won twenty-seven times. Subsequently he became a businessman and television commentator as well as helping his son Paul run a team in lesser formulae. He's as restless and active as Moss!

C.H.

If you are convinced mentally about your own superiority, you are disregarding the most serious threat, namely the competitive element of your adversary.

If you are so dogmatic as to believe in yourself to that extent, you clearly do not respect the level of your competition. I would far rather put my opposition up on a pedestal and be satisfied when I have shot at them successfully.

How can anybody start strutting around saying that they are the best? I mean, what a wonderful platform to be knocked off. It's silly. Why put yourself in a position where, if you are beaten, you have to start making excuses? Why not acknowledge the fact that somebody else might be faster on a particular day? I know of several out-of-work racing drivers today who are entirely under the misapprehension that they were great and never given the right chance. Somehow or other racing dealt them an unfair blow. They remain convinced that they could have been the best.

As for those drivers who think they are so extraordinary – I have never seen one of them make it. And if they haven't made it, that factor has probably been the reason for their failure – it may not have had anything to do with their natural talent. That cup might have been brimming over, but this mental attitude, this dogmatic over-confidence has probably not helped them.

I'm always fearful when I hear people say, 'You've got to believe in yourself, you've got to believe you're the best, in order to win.' I think for me it's quite the reverse. When you believe you're the best you then take liberties with the opposition, you're always under-estimating them, because you don't believe they're as good as you.

When I go to a test track and drive a car, I never want to tell a test driver/engineer that I'm going to be better or faster than him because I've won three World Championships and twenty-seven Grands Prix. It's crazy! This guy could go on to win fifty Grands Prix! So what sort of a fool am I putting myself up for? There's no point to it. It has no benefit at all for you to be under any false impression of your own talent. You can kid a lot of people, but you can't kid yourself. People turn round and say, 'Jackie, you've been successful.' And that's true, up to a point. But am I as successful as I could have been? I'm really not sure. I think I could have done a lot better.

Being successful is one thing, but reaching your true, ultimate potential is entirely another. A lot of people accept less than their real potential can deliver. They gain some success, but is this in fact just a stepping-stone? Go back to some of my earlier examples. Would Tony O'Reilly not have been perfectly satisfied with being a top-line rugby player? I might have been equally satisfied with being a top-line clay-pigeon shooter and a top-line racing driver. But I like to think that I've achieved almost as much in my later life in the area of business and some of my consultancy agreements as I did on the race track. But am I reaching my true potential in what I'm doing today? Am I really as good as I should be? I'm not sure of that. I'm still striving to improve in so many different ways.

I appreciate what my shortcomings are. Perhaps I made some poor decisions – and I don't mean just about driving, I mean in general. I'm sitting here in very comfortable circumstances, but it doesn't prove that I've done everything right.

The other thing is that you must never, ever, go beyond the limits of your own ability. You must absolutely discipline yourself never to go beyond that point. That's where the 'clinical' criticism comes in. People say, 'Why didn't he go for it?' When I went off the road early in 1985 in the new four-wheel drive Ford RS200 prototype I was testing on the Boreham Special Stage, I should probably have stopped one lap before I went off. I had it in my mind to do it, but I made the wrong decision. I was doing that last lap because I wanted to learn more about the car's behaviour, but if, in fact, I'd been a little brighter I'd have realized that I wasn't going to make any more progress. The tyres had already 'gone off', so the chassis was no longer giving me good information.

I didn't live with my own judgement, and I know it. It reminded me of a good lesson. One of the reasons I'm sitting here today is that I generally lived well by my own initiative, by my own judgement, about stopping before I did something silly. Or before elements or circumstances caused something untoward to occur. Sometimes it's difficult to take the bull by the horns and make a good clear judgement. You'll be given more credit for stopping early than stopping late. And when you are driving over your limits, something will happen.

I can't remember ever having broken my own rule like that when I was in Formula One. I remember stopping more often than I remember continuing. I never did, for example, one more lap than I needed to do at the old Nürburgring in Germany. It's 14 miles (23 km) round, has about 180 corners per lap and was the world's most difficult and most dangerous track. There were so many occasions when I was over the limit because it required a commitment early on in a sequence of corners. Once you got started into them at that pace, that trajectory, you didn't stop halfway through. From Brunchen there was a section like that; the descent to Adenau; the Foxhole and up through the left- and right-hander at the end of it; the Hatzenbach section. There were so many sections of the Nürburgring where you were just a passenger, although perhaps I was slightly less of a passenger than some other people. I knew that I was going at a speed that if anything ever so slightly went wrong there was no space to get out of the trouble; I mean I was going to have a mammoth accident. I never did a single lap more at the Nürburgring than I had to, never. I never enjoyed it when I was there; I enjoyed it in January or February in front of a log fire, or talking about how I did it. But, no, I didn't enjoy the place when I was there.

OK, so you ask, 'What about your win in 1968?' I had tyres which were a great help to me that day, but so did Piers Courage and one or two other drivers. But that wasn't the point. That day I drove well, took the advantage at the right time, even though I didn't start from the front of the grid. But don't make any mistakes about the fact that I wouldn't have wanted to do one more lap. You've got to know where to stop. Never drive outside your limitations.

From *Principles of Performance Driving* by Jackie Stewart
(Hazleton Publishing, second edition, 1992)

*I don't know if dyslexia spurred me on. I think all it did was
depress me. School was the unhappiest days of my life.*
Jackie Stewart

*Getting your bum into a car and driving a car are two very
different things. Before you can drive a car you have to have
one. To have one requires ducking and diving; it takes
wheeling and dealing and conniving. And that part of motor
racing is the bigger part. It's like the bottom six-sevenths of an
iceberg — nobody who hasn't hit one knows what it's like.*
Alan Jones, World Champion 1980

*As a youngster I adored cars, although that scarcely
distinguished me from other little boys. The engines revved,
which meant speed. It was fascinating.*
Jacques Laffite, French driver

*For me a race is extremely tiring, exhausting. During the race
it is thirst above all which torments you — a terrible thirst,
which some men must quench, thus forfeiting the race.*
Alberto Ascari

*At the time, I didn't try to analyse all this, but I knew one
thing for certain: those few minutes on the track had been
magic. Somehow, out there, you could express yourself, you
could let your instincts take over, you could compete. You could
live.*
Alain Prost on first trying a kart at fifteen

The Pride Factor

Keke Rosberg

Keke, World Champion in 1982, always came out with terrific quotes. He was an absolute star and never afraid to say what he believed. Even in this extract you'll see that.

S.M.

I'm no more proud of what I do than I would be in any other profession. I'm proud of having found a job I like and I'm proud that I do it well. But I don't think of it as being better than what someone else does. I make a better living than most, but that doesn't entitle me to look down on other people. There is a difference between being pleased and expressing that pleasure, and being proud and expressing that pride by looking down on others.

I was proud when I won the world championship. Yes. That was a job well done. Only thirty people a year in the whole world do the particular job I do. That's what it's all about, and you can be satisfied if you are one of those thirty.

There are teams which deny you even that. They don't think Formula One is special because of the drivers. Formula One is special because it's a platform for the most sophisticated techniques of motor sport, because it is extreme, at the far edge of innovation. Drivers are not that important: after all, they don't exist unless they have something to drive around. I don't think the public buys that. It buys one individual racing against another. The public does not follow the constructors' championship; it follows the drivers' world championship.

But for Frank Williams, the constructors' championship is a matter of pride. Ferrari rates it pretty evenly; if anything, Ferrari exalts the drivers a bit. That is odd, when you think about it, for they use their championship for marketing purposes, like Lotus. But nothing more. I don't see where the pride lies in that. I understand that it's better than winning nothing, but I'm always surprised that Frank doesn't see that the drivers' championship is the heart of the matter. I would be proud if I had created a car and found and sustained the driver who won the world championship.

Pride is inner satisfaction. In what you do, you are good, very good or the best. There is no championship quite like the Formula One drivers' championship: not in its imponderables, not in its variety, not in the things that can go wrong, nor in the things that can come right; not in the consistency required to become champion; not in the determination, the stamina required. In no other form of sport do you have to race sixteen races in a frail machine, a machine that can betray you at any time, against a number of other people who are so nearly your equals that there's practically no difference between the top six or seven. In no other sport do you race on four continents under every kind of climate, in sun and in rain, on streets and on circuits. Just being a part of that calls for pride.

Sex

Q. Alan Jones said driving a car competitively was in some way connected to sex and power.
A. No.
Q. Don't you feel more powerful in a car? Isn't a car an extension of masculinity?
A. All competition, if you're successful, adds to power. You derive power from competing against others and if you beat them, yes, you feel more powerful.

From *Keke: An Autobiography* by Keke Rosberg and Keith Botsford
(Stanley Paul, 1985)

You have one disadvantage with high natural talent and that is you are not used to working hard. And then you go to a level where you're going to fight with Senna – a level where you meet people with very high natural talent who also spent twenty-four hours a day working on it.
Gerhard Berger

I was attached to it [the six-wheel Tyrrell F1 car] as if it was my own child in spite of its faults, in spite of its caprices – because it was the expression of a big idea.
Patrick Depailler

What is it that drivers such as Senna have? A very special gift of speed and car control so they can operate where others cannot, that little extra – plus a good intellect and a good control over that intellect. These drivers have a supernatural gift in the cockpit.

Frank Williams

The drivers often say that we ask stupid questions, but I often think that I am wasting my life asking some stupid driver normal questions to which they don't want to reply.

Pino Allievi

I think I'm only not *nervous because I keep active before a race. The most nervous time for me is two minutes before the start. You're sat there in the car with a little bit of a wobble going, invariably wanting a pee, and wishing you'd had one ten and not fifteen minutes ago.*

Derek Warwick

You keep your emotions under lock and key. When the race stops or I've retired from the race, as soon as I get out of the car the pent-up emotions are ready to leap out. In the car they're kept under control. I think it's a normal and human way to behave, and if it upsets anyone that's unfortunate.

James Hunt, 1976

When I decide to do something I don't like to change. I go straight for that one thing. Even if I have a lot of difficulties I try to overcome them. Only when I'm really beaten, and I know it, do I stop completely. If I can't win at that particular thing I recognize it quickly and cut it out of my life.

Emerson Fittipaldi

When Senna took a swing at me [in Japan, 1993] I thought, 'Here's a few quid coming.'

Eddie Irvine

What did Jimmy Clark have? All the ingredients plus a burning desire which never showed except, funnily enough, off the track. I remember a party we had at Colin Chapman's house. It all got a bit out of hand and people had had a lot to drink. Bets were laid on who could get up the stairs on a pogo stick. People tried – they were jumping and falling. When Jimmy got onto the pogo stick he went bomp-bomp-bomp straight up the middle to the landing.

Peter Warr

Alberto Ascari was just the opposite of what is generally the case: usually it is the driver in the lead who is worried – he is harassed, he wonders whether or not he can hang on to first place – but Alberto felt sure of himself when he was acting as the hare.

Enzo Ferrari

Don't talk to me about Communism. I'm not saying that as one of those people who see Reds everywhere. I've been there! It was because of Communism that my family moved to the States. Before the war, the family lived in Montona, near Trieste. It was in Italy but the whole area is now part of Yugoslavia. Suddenly Communism arrives . . . everybody's equal, right? Too damn right everybody's equal. We all had nothing.

Mario Andretti

Alain Prost: The Believer

Pino Allievi

Prost is a Frenchman with a British sense of humour and an enormous, reasoning talent in a racing car. His career is interesting because it proves that you never level out on the way to the top, you keep going upwards. You might have one bad year because you've a bad car, but that's about all. I can't think of any driver who has levelled out for a considerable time and then gone on towards the top. You take Prost, Senna, Clark, Stewart, all of them. You thought, 'Who the hell is this young guy Clark?' and then suddenly he's World Champion; same thing all through history, same with Prost.

S.M.

Quiet, scholarly, restrained, Allievi has reported on motor sport – bikes and cars – for a couple of decades. He heads the Grand Prix reporting team of the national sports daily *La Gazzetta Dello Sport*, based in Milan. While Alain Prost was at Ferrari, Allievi deliberately conducted an interview with him about everything except Formula One, although, of course, Formula One did obtrude. Small wonder. Between 1980 and 1993 Prost drove in 199 Grands Prix, taking the World Championship in 1985, 1986, 1989 and 1993. He won fifty-one races and his career points total (798½) was an absolute record.

C.H.

ALLIEVI: You were born in 1955, the year of the Warsaw Pact, the death of James Dean and the Afro-Asian conference on anti-racism and atomic weapons. What sort of relationship do you have with history?

PROST: I didn't know that the Warsaw Pact was signed in '55. I knew about James Dean though. History? It's like a river carrying along lots of events which I follow, or at least try to follow, even though things flow past so quickly these days. I can tell you the dates of things that happened in the last thirty years. Even though I'm the type of person who takes an interest in everything, someone in a job like mine has a chance to catch only a glimpse of events. I'd be lost without the news but when you try to get more information the event is already over. Take what happened in Eastern Europe, for instance. It's the biggest change to happen this century yet today it already seems to be taken for granted, consolidated, almost in the past.

ALLIEVI: What do you feel about the fact that your name will, in the future, appear in the encyclopaedia alongside other great people such as Julius Caesar, Roosevelt, Kennedy, Churchill?

PROST: I think the entry will be brief. Alain Prost, born 1955, racing driver, winner of three, four or five world championships. However, so many important people will be listed before me that no one will notice my name.

ALLIEVI: Drugs are one of the scourges of this century. The more we battle against them on a worldwide level the more the average person becomes convinced that it's a battle that is doomed to failure from the outset.

PROST: Just like all battles. The one against drugs reminds me of the one against road accidents or the one to ban smoking. Fortunately everyone can see the problem and has to face it, but there is so much hypocrisy because there is so much financial interest hidden behind it all. I see a willingness to reduce the phenomenon but not to get rid of it completely. It's like smoking. It's all very well to suppress advertising but if smoking is really harmful why not ban cigarettes? I think that if countries such as Colombia, Bolivia and so on have been tolerated up until now it's because there are other problems that we don't know about.

ALLIEVI: In your opinion, is the world getting slowly better or worse? Or do you think things simply appear worse because things seem to happen all at once thanks to modern communications and news reporting in the media?

PROST: I don't think the world is improving. In fact I think it's getting worse, but only slightly. It's not happening at any great speed. Many people say that things were better in the old days but who can prove that to us?

ALLIEVI: Italy is unfortunately a country in which kidnappings continue to be commonplace. In other parts of the world the same thing happens on a smaller scale and for different reasons. Have you ever been frightened for yourself or for your son Nicolas?

PROST: This is an embarrassing thing to answer. These things do frighten me. They frighten everyone, don't they?

ALLIEVI: A world-famous sportsman such as yourself must often meet other equally famous people. Which of these meetings has affected you the most?

PROST: The Pope. He's the person who's made most impression on me. To a Catholic the Pope represents something very special but it's difficult to assess the sensations that one feels. On meeting Pope Wojtyla [John Paul II] I immediately appreciated his greatness. We talked of many things even though I felt a bit confused. He even told me that he occasionally watches the Grand Prix on TV. One thing in particular struck me, however. It was the end of 1985 and the question of whether or not we should race in South Africa was being discussed. His Holiness broached the subject of apartheid and told me that in his opinion I should have gone to Kyalami so as not to lose touch with this nation which was troubled by so many doubts.

ALLIEVI: What are your views on apartheid? It is a much-talked-about problem in Italy with a subtle difference. We define the many young people who come from Africa to look for work as 'non-EEC citizens' rather than 'negroes' as they are called in America.

PROST: It's a plague. Just like the drugs problem we discussed before it is full of hypocrisy. Only a madman could declare himself in favour of racial segregation. But, to be honest, I must say that when I have visited South Africa I have never seen the things that are so often reported in the newspapers, probably because I usually experience life in the hotel and at the racing track and not much else. I am, however, against any sporting boycott whatsoever. What sense is there in refusing to compete or to race in South Africa when the multinationals continue to trade there all the time? On the other hand, sportsmen who go there should perhaps do more or say more about the situation. As it is, in Formula One we end up discussing oversteering and understeering and that's it. The opinions of people like us who are far removed from politics could be useful. Then there is the problem of immigration into Europe of people from places like Tunisia, Mali and Senegal who come to seek a better life. It's not so much a question of immigration as integration. Often people do not integrate into the host country and that can give rise to racial 'incidents', above all in countries where there is high unemployment.

ALLIEVI: What about Eastern Europe? Did you foresee the upsets brought about by Gorbachev?

PROST: Yes. Gorbachev is a man I have faith in, but in such a short space of time the face of Eastern Europe changed completely. The speed of it all was completely unexpected.

ALLIEVI: How about terrorism? It was presented to us as the evil of a society that was bound by the most exasperating form of wealth and consumerism – leading inevitably to pockets of alienated people who were often the weakest members of society. In the economic renaissance that is happening in Europe, is it a phenomenon which will disappear altogether or flare up again?

PROST: I've read a lot about this subject and I've reached the conclusion that it's less serious than it seems. There are too many conflicting scientific reports. I find the problem of continued pollution over the whole planet much more worrying. It's easy to forget all about it: the problem is not as serious for us as it will be for our children.

ALLIEVI: Have you ever taken part in any ecological campaign?

PROST: No.

ALLIEVI: The newspaper *Le Figaro* has reported that almost all French people keep a secret diary of their lives. Do you?

PROST: I read that, too, and I don't believe it. The French are too lazy to do such a thing.

ALLIEVI: In France, as in Italy, there is an ever-increasing number of sexual crimes committed against women and children.

PROST: There are more and more people who can't integrate into society and who do totally incomprehensible things.

ALLIEVI: The roads have become one huge cemetery. How could the number of road accidents be reduced?

PROST: Road safety is something we have to face up to. Deaths caused by road accidents are something which affect me deeply. In France, for example, there are double the number of deaths that there are in England and, I believe, one and a half times as many as in Italy. The problem is that people are not valued. They are treated like children. For example, I think it's an insult to people's intelligence when we see flimsy tinny cars on the road when we know that technology in this field is sophisticated enough nowadays to produce something much stronger. On the one hand people are allowed to build cars that are unsafe, on the other hand cars that are safer and built to the highest standard must not exceed certain speed limits. This is real hypocrisy. Take Formula One. You see the most awful accidents but cars hardly ever burst into flames, whereas on the motorways you only need an accident between two old bangers and the people inside are burned to death. If our safer petrol tanks were fitted to mass-produced cars, hundreds of thousands of lives could be saved.

ALLIEVI: Are strikes the only way to achieve anything?

PROST: To strike is the reaction of someone who feels and is in fact weak, someone who sees no other way of obtaining what he regards as rightfully his. Whatever the relationship between ownership and staff, it should always be remembered that a strike could plunge a whole nation into difficulty and can cause harm to those who have nothing to do with it. It only takes the immigration officers of one country to stop working and half of Europe comes to a halt.

ALLIEVI: Is it easy living in Switzerland?

PROST: It's easier than in other places.

ALLIEVI: Are you still totally opposed to the socialist government of France?

PROST: The political scene has changed a lot. In France old stereotypes such as right wing, socialist and communist mean nothing. It's the same everywhere. Nowadays I am disappointed at the way certain individuals practise politics.

ALLIEVI: Are you still criticized in France for choosing to live in Switzerland?

PROST: No. Their mentality has changed over the past few years.

ALLIEVI: You have a six-year-old son. What influence does TV have on children?

PROST: In normal doses TV can be stimulating. But I see the most incredible things in Japanese cartoons: death, massacres, killings. Nicolas is a very sensitive child and gets upset by them. At the same time I suppose he can begin to get an idea of what the world is like. I myself was speechless when I saw *Akira*, the latest cartoon to hit Europe. It's incredible.

ALLIEVI: What are you views on abortion?

PROST: In the twentieth century it's quite a normal thing. I am a practising Catholic. It happened to me once and I was badly affected by it. I had no choice. I was eighteen years old and I hadn't been involved with Anne-Marie [now Prost's wife] long.

ALLIEVI: Are you afraid of illness?

PROST: Yes, very. I'm afraid of sickness and of old age. Old age, after a full sporting life lived in good health, is difficult to come to terms with. Since the death of my brother from a terminal disease I am petrified by illness. I never take medicine. I'm scared to go to the doctor. I do, however, have two complete check-ups per year.

ALLIEVI: What type of student were you?

PROST: I worked hard at practical things, subjects I could see an immediate practical application for – languages and geography. I had long hair. I protested.

ALLIEVI: What do you think about when you are driving on the roads?

PROST: Lots of things. Whatever's going on at the time. Music quite relaxes me. I like all sorts of music but I can never tell you who sings what song.

ALLIEVI: Do you like the cinema?

PROST: Yes, I go a lot. It's a bit annoying when people turn to look at me instead of the film. Being well known stops me enjoying lots of little things. For example I love wandering around the shops, buying things like toys for my son or even just window shopping, but in some places I can't walk around at all. It's not easy looking like Alain Prost.

From *La Gazzetta Dello Sport,* 1990

In Islam, for someone about to die death is a game. The problem here [the Japanese Grand Prix, 1990] is that we have seen Senna ready to take all risks to win the Championship.
Alain Prost

Prost is always trying to destroy people. He tried to destroy me in the past on different occasions and he hasn't managed.
Ayrton Senna

In a Different Dimension

Gerald Donaldson

Ayrton Senna was to my mind the only driver who could be spoken of in the same breath as Fangio and Clark. I might even have put him above Jimmy. I'd say Fangio number one, then Senna and Jimmy. Senna did create genuinely incredible racing laps, like at Donington in the wet during the European Grand Prix, 1993. Of course, I accept that this is all debatable — hotly debatable! — but that is one of the attractions of motor racing.

S.M.

Donaldson, based in Toronto, has written extensively on motor sport, including a celebrated biography of Gilles Villeneuve of which there is an extract later in this book. He reports for the *Toronto Star*, the magazine *Formula* and CBC TV. A studious and fastidious man, he spent a year in pit and paddock talking to a broad spectrum of people involved in Grand Prix racing. This is what he found when he reached Ayrton Senna.

C.H.

He is undoubtedly one of the greatest racing drivers in history, and one of the most controversial. Everybody has an opinion about him, invariably a very strong one. Yet the man himself remains an enigma. He's the subject of endless speculation and, it would seem, considerable misunderstanding. This is mainly because he seldom speaks publicly, which is a great pity, for Ayrton Senna has a great deal to say.

He is a complex man – intense, introspective, sensitive, private – and very intelligent. He is probably the most intellectual of all the drivers and, if Alain Prost is The Professor, Ayrton Senna should be The Philosopher. Noted for his fierce commitment to racing, and his penchant for taking risks, it may really be his intellect that most sets Senna apart from his peers.

He is remarkably articulate (even in English, a language far removed from his native Portuguese), though talking about any superior talents he might have makes him uncomfortable. 'To say that I am better than most drivers is something you have to discuss, to see if it is really true. If it is true, it is for me an uncomfortable feeling. It is in a way pleasant, of course, but talking about it publicly, just being open and natural about the subject, is difficult for me.

'I do try very hard to understand everything and anything that happens around me. Not only in the car, but in my behaviour as a professional on the circuit, outside, in the garage, and so on, and it takes a lot of energy. At the end of every day I feel very tired, because I just give everything I have. It drains me completely.

'Sometimes I think I know some of the reasons why I do the things the way I do in the car. And sometimes I think I don't know why. There are some moments that seem to be only the natural instinct that is in me. Whether I have been born with it, or whether this feeling has grown in me more than other people, I don't know. But it is inside me and it takes over with a great amount of space and intensity.'

Behind the wheel he constantly strives to combine his metaphysical inquiries with his natural instincts to make a supreme effort. But sometimes he finds himself in the grip of an unknown superior force and Senna becomes a passenger on a surreal ride into unexplored nether regions – beyond his normal limits, beyond his understanding. It's an experience that can be frightening.

'When I am competing against the watch and against other competitors, the feeling of expectation, of getting it done and doing the best and being the best, gives me a kind of power that, some moments when I am driving, actually detaches me completely from anything else as I am doing it . . . corner after corner, lap after lap. I can give you a true example I experienced and can relate it.

'Monte Carlo, '88, the last qualifying session. I was already on pole and I was going faster and faster. One lap after the other, quicker, and quicker, and quicker. I was at one stage just on pole, then by half a second, and then one second . . . and I kept going. Suddenly, I was nearly two seconds faster than anybody else, including my team-mate with the same car. And I suddenly realized that I was no longer driving the car consciously.

'I was kind of driving it by instinct, only I was in a different dimension. It was like I was in a tunnel, not only the tunnel under the hotel, but the whole circuit for me was a tunnel. I was just going, going – more, and more, and more, and more. I was way over the limit, but still able to find even more. Then, suddenly, something just kicked me. I kind of woke up and I realized that I was in a different atmosphere from what you normally are. Immediately my reaction was to back off, slow down. I drove back slowly to the pits and I didn't want to go out any more that day.

'It frightened me because I realized I was well beyond my conscious understanding. It happens rarely, but I keep these experiences very much alive in me because it is something that is important for self-preservation.'

In that 1988 Monaco Grand Prix Senna was leading his team-mate by nearly fifty seconds when he crashed – inexplicably. While

Prost went on to win, Senna did not return to the McLaren pit. He walked the short distance to his flat and promptly went to sleep. He later acknowledged that he lost concentration when his pit ordered him to slow down. The accident was a major turning-point in his inner life.

'I am religious. I believe in God, through Jesus. I was brought up that way, was maybe drifting away from it, but suddenly turned the other way. Things that have happened in my racing career contributed a lot to my change of direction. It was a build-up of things that reached a peak, and then I had a kind of crisis. Monaco was the peak and it made me realize a lot of things.

'It is something that is difficult to talk about, very touching for me. But it is something unique in life, something that can hold you, can support you, when you are most vulnerable. It has made me a better man. I am a better human being now than I was before this. I am better in everything I am and everything I do.'

There have been other changes in his attitude towards life. Much has been made of Senna's absolute single-mindedness, how he divorced his wife because he was so consumed by his racing passion. He has always been deeply devoted to his family, but now he feels the need for a more balanced life, and to share it with another person.

'Time shows us, as we progress, different perspectives of life. And a few years ago I had no time for anybody or anything other than racing. Today I not only have the time, but I *need* the time for my family, my friends, and particularly for my girlfriend. And it is something that I fight for and I organize my life in order that I can get the right balance between the private life, the personal life and the professional life. Because only that way, having the equilibrium between both sides of myself, can I perform to my best.

'Now, even when I am doing my job, the need for somebody to be by my side is great. It gives me something I don't get in any other activity in life. You know, I think when you love a woman you feel more human. You feel stronger, a better man, more macho, and at the same time you feel inner peace because it fulfils the empty space that you have, that we all have in us, and that only love can fulfil.'

Little Ayrton Senna was only four years old when he first drove a go-kart, and as a schoolboy his head was filled with heroic visions of the exploits of Stewart, Lauda, Villeneuve. The highlights of his life were Grand Prix mornings in São Paolo when he awoke, trembling with anticipation at the prospect of watching his heroes in action on television. He remembers that just before the start of the race the palms of his hands were wet.

'Now, before the start of the race, I have still a lot of expectation – tension – when I am waiting. My hands still perspire a bit, but I have other feelings. Like an empty space in my stomach, a feeling of wanting to sleep . . . there are several conflicting emotions.'

Senna admits he brings a high degree of emotional intensity to his racing, but it goes beyond his profession. 'I am intense about everything I do. I have an attitude about life that I go deeply into it and concentrate, and try to do everything properly. It's a part of my personality.'

His public personality has been called remote, ruthless and arrogant, accusations that began shortly after Ayrton Senna da Silva came to England at the age of twenty, following several successful years in kart racing. He soon shortened his name (in the interests of brevity and clarity for journalists), and his reputation for a willing-ness to sacrifice anything on the altar of motor racing began with his divorce in 1982.

When he came into Formula One with Toleman, in 1984, appreciation of his obviously superlative skills were leavened by those detractors who maintained he was prepared to win at any cost. He was accused of reneging on his Toleman deal (he bought out his contract) to join Lotus, where he refused Derek Warwick as a team-mate, but accepted Johnny Dumfries because, the cynics said, he was worried about Warwick's competition. (Senna's reasoning was that Lotus couldn't field two equally competitive cars.) Certain of his peers joined in the disparagement: Mansell attacked him physically after one on-track encounter, Piquet did it verbally, and the word along the pit lane was that Senna was dangerous and not to be trusted in close racing situations. More recently there was the trouble with his McLaren team-mate Prost, which caused Prost to leave the team.

These conflicts have contributed to what for Senna is the worst part of his profession. 'The most difficult time is when you have to put up with people that you don't really enjoy. When you have to live with people that you cannot trust, or people who you know by previous experience are just waiting for a small mistake from you, to beat you. That is the worst, that is the most difficult time.'

Here, Senna is not speaking just of those drivers with whom he has had much publicized feuds, but of others within the Formula One environment with whom he finds himself at odds. When his public criticism of FISA and Jean-Marie Balestre in late 1989 led to a demand for an apology, or the governing body would take away his licence, it caused him to come within a phone call of retiring from the sport. He returned out of a sense of loyalty to his team, particularly his mechanics, and those at McLaren who depend on Senna to earn their living.

'If I had pushed for what I think was right, and what I thought was true, I would have created a major problem with everybody on the team. I practically gave up racing. Then I had to face up to it and give in, not for myself, but in the interest of a whole group of people, particularly those who really work, day after day. They need their work, so I gave in. But for no other reason than the responsibility I felt to those people who gave me the chance to win races. It was the least I could do for them.'

From *Grand Prix People* by Gerald Donaldson (MRP, 1990)

CHAPTER FOUR

THE SKILL OF THE DRIVER

The Car Game

Ted Macauley

With the wrong toe-in or toe-out, the car veered wildly from side to side and was virtually impossible to handle with any safety. It used to take me two or three hours' training merely to sort out these 'minor' problems. Then, having got the car in some sort of order, I had to concentrate on getting round the circuit in a decent time, against the world's best drivers, often in a car that was still unstable despite all my struggles. I must have been a hair-raising sight to some of the more experienced drivers.

The troubles I was having must have been obvious to the others, because they were constantly offering me help. The snag was that I *knew* what was wrong with the car. I knew the feel and the balance were wrong somewhere – but I couldn't explain the trouble. It was frustrating knowing that the car wasn't right but not being able to do anything about it other than complain.

Short of driving the car themselves, which of course was out of the question, the other drivers could get no idea of what I was talking about and when I tried to explain I got tongue-tied. Consequently, I was too often struggling to compensate with my driving for the car's erratic behaviour.

I knew Mike Hailwood fairly well and in fact we did a book together, *Racing and All That* (Pelham, 1980). He was an artist on two wheels, like Geoff Duke and John Surtees. The way he tried to make the transition to racing cars was interesting to watch. He had learnt half the trade. He came into racing unequalled in his field – bikes – and he knew certain tricks of the trade, he knew about racing. His problem was that his career was based on two wheels, so he'd built a different kind of foundation from the one he now needed on four. He knew racing tactics but didn't necessarily know about cars, about slipstreaming and so on. A lot of situations arise with four wheels which don't arise with two and vice versa. This extract charts graphically the difficulties Mike faced.

S.M.

Many claim to have been close to Mike Hailwood. Few were, but Macauley – who covered Hailwood's career from 1961 for the *Daily Mirror* – certainly was. They became friends and constant travelling companions and Macauley wrote two books with him; and a third, on him, after his death in a road accident in 1981. Between 1959 and 1967 Hailwood won nine World Championships. His Grand Prix car career unfolded in two segments – from 1962 to 1965, then from 1971 to a crash at the Nürburgring in 1974. He drove in fifty Formula One races with a highest place of second in the Italian Grand Prix, 1972.

C.H.

I'm well aware that every driver has to go through all this at some time; and I know that it would all have come clear to me eventually. I understand, too, that disappointment in car racing may stem from over-anxiety and lack of experience; but I was desperate to do well, and to do well quickly. I was downhearted because, hard as I strove, I couldn't achieve any measure of success.

I must have covered miles in the paddock, running about looking for somebody to help me out of my dilemmas. Graham Hill was my chief target. I never left him alone, but he was as patient and understanding as always. I can't remember a time when he showed even the slightest resentment. He's one of my happier memories of motor racing.

Over the years Graham has jotted all the problems he has encountered into a little black notebook. When he goes to a circuit he simply flips the pages and finds out what problems to expect and how the car should be set up to beat them; this way his motors are always in perfect order.

Each time I approached him with my troubles he used to thumb through the book and ask, 'Do you think this is what's wrong? Or is it that?' He would, in his unruffled way, go through the book until I thought I recognized the ailment. Too often, however, the rules for his car didn't apply to mine.

But there was a lot more behind my flop in car racing than just the baffling technical setbacks. Many people, I know, have since laughed up their sleeves because I didn't have the triumph I would have liked.

I suppose there are always know-alls around to say, 'Well, old son, I did tell you, you know.' They get some sort of pleasure out of the accuracy of their forecasts. And that was just the sort of response I didn't want. I'm afraid that those who were unwise enough to pass remarks received some cutting replies.

It's one thing to realize you've made a mistake, and another to be regularly reminded of it. Patience, in the light of such arrant and stupid advice, is not one of my strong points. I fully realized my own mistakes, without any outsiders having to emphasize them.

I certainly don't want to make any excuses for my failure in cars — but there were *reasons*.

I'd hovered on the brink of a switch from two wheels to four for ages; I'd secretly nursed the ambition to change without really making an attempt to do anything about it. For a long time I was in a muddle of advice. There were people who said, 'Have a go.' There were others who advised, 'Stay where you are, on bikes.' And there were more who said that they thought I could mix the two.

I'd had a tiny taste, enough to whet my appetite for car racing, one wet, cold and windy morning at Silverstone in 1960.

The UDT Laystall team was there; Ken Gregory and a couple of drivers. They invited me along for a try-out to see if I would be of any use to them. I was flattered by the offer.

I'd never even sat in a racing car before. I used to rush round in my own 3.8 Jaguar, but of course there was a world of difference, and the margin soon dawned on me.

I was loosed off in a Lotus 4 Climax. The idea, it seemed, was to throw me in at the deep end to see if I came up again. I had no sensation of danger, no worries. I had no idea that in the rain – and there was plenty of it about – these cars can be extremely dodgy.

After a lap or two I began to get the feel of the Lotus, to get the hang of its power. My confidence welled up and I decided that I'd try to get round Maggot's Corner flat out. The fact that the rain was bouncing about a foot high off the track didn't worry me. The road was wet and shiny as a mirror, but I was in a mood of sheer delight, bordering on hysteria. I was like a kid with a new toy. But the Lotus was anything but that.

I steered towards Maggot's yelling 'Whoopee!' foot pressed hard to the floor and totally unaware of the threat of any danger. I was hard into the bend when I lost control completely, the car ran away with me and clouted the banking with considerable force.

Whatever cockiness I had in me was knocked out there and then. A great scarlet blush took the place of the excited look on my face as I motored, with a good deal of embarrassment, back towards the pits in the bent and battered car.

They were quite kind to me, really. I think they'd half expected this to happen, just from watching me going round the circuit. Nobody rebuked me, there was no criticism, at least not while I was still there. They said they'd let me know, and I'm still waiting. . . .

Before I'd spun off I'd just managed to get round at two minutes for the lap. Innes Ireland had been lapping steadily, without any apparent effort, at something like one minute fifty-three.

Some bloke at the pits had spent a great deal of time dashing from shelter to hang out signals to me. My answer was to keep skimming his toes without seeing what was chalked on the board. In the end he threw down the board in disgust and walked off. I suppose he reckoned I wasn't taking too much notice; he was trying to warn me about the slippery conditions.

I gave up the idea of car racing there and then, and decided I was best fitted to motor-cycle racing. These were early days for me in bike racing and, up to then, I hadn't won a championship.

The bug to race cars didn't bite me again until 1962. Then, I thought, I was a little older, a little wiser and more ready to have another try. I was fairly well established on the motor-cycle race scene, but even so I was anxious to move over to cars. I thought about it, argued about it, and decided that the only way I could find out if I would be any good was to have a go.

I scratched my name on a cheque for £1,700 and bought a Formula Junior Brabham. Then I went shopping for a sky blue driver's suit, a pair of lightweight shoes and a large helmet . . . and went racing.

I drove my Dodge shooting-brake and trailer down to Weybridge to collect the car from Brabham's place. I'd entered myself at Brands Hatch for the following day. The car wasn't ready when I called for it, and I had to wait until 11 p.m. before I could pick it up. But, when I saw it being wheeled out, the waiting seemed worthwhile. The yellow paint gleamed and the Cosworth–Ford engine crackled crisply enough to make me tingle. The mechanics wished me luck and I set off for Brands – and my car-racing début.

I didn't get to Brands until the early hours of the morning. I slept in the back of the Dodge, but I was so nervous I don't think I got more than an hour's sleep all night. Everybody expected me to do well.

The car was brand, spanking new, and had never been run. When I took it out for training I was delighted to discover that it would top 108 m.p.h. I finished up with a good placing on the grid, and the world that morning seemed a much rosier place.

It was like coming home, racing at Brands. The circuit was as familiar to me as my own garden. The atmosphere, too, made me feel at home. All that was missing were the faces of motor-cycle riders. Instead I was surrounded by people I didn't know. This made it a new world to me. The flags, the crowds, the smell of high-octane fuel and the paddock were familiar, but that was where the similarity ended.

In this, my first race, I had to chase a man who later became famous outside motor racing. His name was Roy James, now in jail for his part in the Great Train Robbery. I certainly wouldn't envy anybody who had to catch him. I tried hard but all I ever saw was the disappearing tail-end of his car.

Roy James won and I managed fifth place. James was a fine driver, and, but for his other vocation, could probably have done extremely well in the car-racing business.

I was quite pleased with my first attempt – and I was delighted with the Brabham, it was a flyer. I painted its nose black and had a black line daubed up the centre of the yellow front. At least, I thought, I'd be noticed, however far back in the field I might finish; even if I couldn't win, the spectators would know I'd turned up for the meeting.

I took the Brabham to as many meetings as I could fit in between my commitments on motor bikes. At my second outing I managed to win, then followed it up with three more victories.

By this time I imagined I was ready for the big stuff, the Grand Prix scene. My confidence had increased, and I'd served a reasonable period of apprenticeship in the Junior ranks.

Reg Parnell, an old friend of Stan's [Hailwood's father] from pre-war racing days, had been trying for a long time to persuade me to make the break from bikes and change over to cars. He had been team manager for Bowmaker, and when they pulled out of racing he took over the cars, a Lotus 24 with a V8 Climax engine, and two V8-engined Lolas, both with Climaxes.

I'd been putting Reg off for months, but when he asked me once more I agreed. I was flushed with the success I'd had with the Formula Junior and felt ready to make my name in cars.

It took a great deal of heart-searching and critical self-investigation, but I concluded that there was little left for me on bikes. I'd achieved most of the things I wanted – the world one-hour championship was mine after a trip to Daytona, I had won world titles and scored TT wins.

I decided not to break completely, however, at least not until I was established and could make enough money to live on as I had done with motor bikes. I opted to mix both sports; I was making plenty of money with MV and I realized it would be foolish to throw it all over to enter for Grand Prix car racing as a private runner. I was hoping to do well enough in cars to be picked up by one of the works outfits; if that had happened, I would have stopped racing bikes altogether.

The Count had no objections to my racing cars, provided it didn't interfere with the world motor-cycle championship programme. One of the contracts he offered me every year was one to drive an MV car. He always said that one day he would build one and he would expect me to drive it for him. It never existed, not even on the drawing-board so far as I knew, but he still used to pay me £2,500 a year to drive it. I certainly wasn't going to turn down money for nothing; it's the easiest cash I ever earned.

After discussions with Reg Parnell I bought a half-share in his Formula One team and partnered Chris Amon. I thought this was the best way to go racing, the quickest way to be spotted by a works-team manager.

Reg, who knew motor racing inside out, was able to pass on a good many tips, and was able to give me more help than I could have got from anybody else. He taught me a few tricks of this very new trade, but it was clear to me that Formula One racing isn't the sort of sport that you can master overnight; you have to have years of experience to be fully versed in all its intricate arts.

The team went to Silverstone – again! – for tests. I'm convinced I saw the track staff belting for cover when they recognized me as the lunatic who had scattered them all two years before.

I was as much on trial as the Lotus we took there. Reg stared out from the pits watching my progress through his keen, critical eyes; he could see faults that I couldn't hope to notice. After a few practice laps he said he was pleased with my performance, and told me, 'Considering the car and your inexperience you did well, but there's a lot of room for improvement. You've a lot to learn.'

I don't think that even Reg realized quite how much there was for me to learn.

I tempered my tests with a fair amount of caution, in the light of the memory of the hairy outing I'd had on the same track two years earlier. There was, of course, the financial consideration, too. I owned a half-share and I wasn't too anxious to risk bending the equipment when I knew it was going to cost me money to put it right again.

The arrangement I entered with Reg was as much a business one as a plan to learn how to race among the big boys of Grand Prix events. I couldn't hope to make any big money out of it; I assumed that my principal value to the team was the publicity they would get from my joining them. For my own purposes and ambitions it meant that I had my own training ground, cars that were half mine. I wasn't responsible to anybody else for the machinery. Chris Amon was a salaried driver, but I was employed as a driver without wages; I was to take a part share of the profits. All I got were expenses and – this was a laugh – prize-money. The trouble was, there wasn't a lot of that knocking about.

After a while, when we found we weren't having any success worth talking about, we decided to invest in equipment that might give us the breakthrough. We bought a Lotus that Jim Clark had been using for two seasons, the car he'd been driving when he won the world championship. Originally it had been fitted with a Climax engine, but Reg thought it would be more economical to stick a BRM unit in. He argued that it would be much cheaper to maintain and would help cut down the running costs by a great margin.

When we collected the shell from Colin Chapman, he told us that if we did put a BRM engine in it the car would never go; he explained that the car had been designed for Climax torque and weight. He said a BRM engine couldn't possibly send it along as well as the car could go. However, Reg had his way, I bowed to his superior experience and knowledge, and we put the BRM unit into the Lotus.

As it turned out, Chapman's words of advice were painfully prophetic. The car never seemed to go right. The main trouble stemmed from the engine; then we had trouble with the five-speed gearbox, a new one, and, as if that wasn't enough to worry us, the car wouldn't handle properly.

We seemed to go through an engine a meeting, and it began to cost us a pile of money. One bill alone, from BRM, set us back £8,000 for a season's racing. It was a season of only a dozen races, too, with very little to show for it. I picked up a championship point for a sixth place at Monaco and Chris collected two or three points, including a fifth at the Dutch.

Clearly this was business lunacy, and something had to be done. My motor-cycle winnings were subsidizing my interest in the car team. I was like two different men – in the bike world I was having great success and loving every minute, in the car business I was getting nowhere and was as miserable as sin.

From *Hailwood* by Mike Hailwood and Ted Macauley (Cassell, 1968)

Principles of Competition Driving

Alain Prost

Installation in the car

Before turning a wheel, there is one thing which is very important and is worthy of mention: the adaptation of the driver to the car. Seat location and driving position aren't talked about very often, because they are usually taken for granted. But for me such things are of fundamental importance. I remember in 1988, with McLaren, I had five or six different seats made before I found one I was happy with. The mechanics had moved around the pedals, steering wheel and gear lever, but I never found a satisfactory driving position! Thus I could probably lap just as fast as usual, but as I wasn't comfortable I had to stop every three laps or so because of cramp. As I said, it is essential that you are perfectly comfortable in a car before you so much as turn a wheel.

And each driver has his own tastes: Niki Lauda and I employed totally different positions: he lay down a little more in his car; in the footwell, I preferred to have the brake pedal a little closer than the accelerator, while Lauda liked them both at the same distance. For my part, I have the steering wheel very close to the instrument panel because I sit quite close up, and I have the gear lever at a slight angle, while Lauda used to have it canted right over. Such preferences don't stop you driving a car if it's any other way, but you wouldn't be able to give it your best.

Sitting on the floor

There are many cars which don't have a rest for the left foot, and that is a big mistake! Of course you can drive without it, and that has happened to me. But to drive really quickly, particularly in fast corners, it's impossible. You lose too much of your feeling for the car. . . . In any case, if one isn't properly installed, one can't appreciate the reactions of the car or its settings.

For my part, I have another little trick which I have always used, which consists of sitting on the floor of the tub. Many drivers have a foam seat which reaches to the bottom of the car. I think that's stupid. I have much greater sensitivity for the car through sitting directly on the floor. You don't have to be held firmly in an all-enveloping seat. It's important that the shoulders and hips should be held firmly but I don't like to be wholly restrained, apart from by the safety harness.

Should you double-declutch?

Generally when changing down I go directly from the gear I'm in at the end of a straight to the one I need for the next corner: from sixth to second, for instance. I bypass all the gears in between. If it's sometimes possible to hear a couple of blips on the throttle, it's only during lengthy braking manoeuvres where for me it's a question of keeping the engine within the power band, rather than having to rev it at the moment where I would otherwise effectively need to double-declutch. I don't see the point in going right down through all the gears, but it's a question of whatever you yourself feel happiest doing, the main thing being to concentrate upon the braking when all's said and done. However, under hard braking or in the wet it's often worthwhile not to jump straight down the box in order to maintain the stability of the rear wheels.

As for double-declutching, it's something I do systematically, even if in a hurry it may seem brief, like a 'false' double-declutch. But I think it's essential you know how to do it. It won't matter over the course of a race; it will be more important over a whole season, and during the length of your career it will be invaluable. It's things like that that make you different from your team-mate and rivals: you miss fewer gears, do less damage to the gearbox, are a better driver for it and enjoy an enhanced reputation.

Racing lines in the wet

There is no firm rule about racing lines in the wet. On fast circuits, it's often advantageous to stick to the outside, running alongside the dry racing line. This is because that part of the track won't be covered in tiny rubber deposits, which are notoriously slippery in the wet.

But on a damp track, each driver has his own ideas about the best lines, and that can go from one extreme to another at the same corner: some stick to the inside, others to the outside, and there's barely any difference at the exit! Sometimes it's quite bizarre. There is, however, one thing that's certain. Be wary of trackside kerbs, which are terribly slippery in the wet, especially those that have been painted.

Attacking drivers

I did see both Keke Rosberg and Gilles Villeneuve driving almost sedately. But they were capable of doing things that I barely know how to do, or at least only in exceptional circumstances.

It is a brutal form of driving which, in a way, owes nothing to the car, its set-up or its fine tuning. For my part, I prefer to drive according to the settings I have chosen, then to change them depending upon what I've subsequently noticed. But for some drivers, their settings and the handling of the car were of little consequence: it had to be driven like that simply because they wanted to!

The pros and cons of different styles

For a driver who turns in early, as Jacques Laffite and I do, it's as much a means of defence as attack. It helps you avoid some of the specific problems at the entry to a corner, but if the circuit is greasy at the exit you tend to skate straight off. Drivers like Keke Rosberg or the late Gilles Villeneuve were always on the ragged edge at the entry to a corner, which meant that a change in the level of grip might take them unpleasantly by surprise on the exit. In reality, they were never taken by surprise, or at least a lot less than we were. A driver like Rosberg could never adapt to my driving style, whereas from time to time I adopted his. Perhaps not always, but certainly sometimes, and I think that was certainly an advantage for me. From the spectators' point of view, however, an attacking driving style is certainly preferable. It has never been proved that either of these two styles is appreciably faster than the other. I personally think that mine is 'quicker' over the course of a season, in that it limits the possibility of mistakes. I'm convinced of it! Note that cars lend themselves more or less to any style of driving.

The difference between Keke Rosberg's style and mine would be more striking in the wet. In difficult conditions of this kind, I always force myself to drive astutely, trying to exploit any available traction to its best effect, and I always look for the smoothest, neatest lines. As for Keke, he'd arrive with all wheels locked up – I'm not exaggerating! – sideways as he turned in, spinning the wheels, leaping over kerbs on the exit and winding up with two wheels on the grass! Certainly spectacular, and at one point during the corner doubtless a couple of tenths quicker than me. But on the other hand I don't think he'd be faster than me over a whole lap.

From *Competition Driving* by Alain Prost and Pierre-François Rousselot
(Hazleton Publishing, 1990)

CHAPTER FIVE

PORTRAIT GALLERY

The Devil from Mantua

Ken Purdy

Now that Nuvolari is dead, buried in his cloth helmet and his famous turtleneck sweater, a steering-wheel on his chest, lying beneath a marble tomb in Mantua, they will soon begin to say that there were others just as good — better, maybe. Mike Hawthorn at Rheims, Juan Fangio in Mexico, Froilan Gonzalez anywhere when he's running from behind — could Nuvolari have done it better? Certainly he could have. Any day, or night for that matter. And with one leg in a plaster cast or one arm strapped to his chest.

You can argue about it now, if you want to, although not for long and not successfully with anyone who ever saw the little man drive, but if you want to be sure you have only to wait. Let's see who else drives for thirty years, wins 72 races of the first rank in world importance, nearly 150 altogether, finishes second only seventeen times in his life, and then finally dies in bed, sixty-one years old and his last win only three years behind him.

It really isn't arguable at all. The men who knew the most about Nuvolari, the motoring journalists of Europe who watched him down the years, were all in essential agreement: the greatest driver of racing cars ever to hold a wheel in his hands.

The writer I can compare Ken Purdy to the closest is Hemingway. Ken took vast pleasure from writing about his heroes. He got a thrill from knowing them and describing the things they'd done. After the big shunt at Goodwood in 1962 which ended my career he said he wanted to do an article for *Playboy* and I said sure, come along. I'd met him before, but only as an American journalist and enthusiast who'd attend races and sometimes he'd write about them, sometimes he wouldn't. He had an enormous capacity for writing and I think he contributed to fifty-two magazines; but he was always amazingly worried about his next story, always had a feeling of great insecurity. I say amazingly because to people like me whatever he wrote was terrific, regardless of the subject. He had the gift of making it interesting. He committed suicide, a terrible tragedy. Whether that was the insecurity I don't know. [Moss and Purdy collaborated on one of the outstanding human racing studies, *All But My Life*, from which there is an extract later in this book. C.H.] I particularly wanted something on Nuvolari because to all the young men of my era he has to be the ultimate idea of a racing driver: a racer and a fighter. No anthology could be complete without looking at Nuvolari, Fangio, Clark and Senna. There are a lot of other drivers you put in, and no disrespect to them, but these are the four cornerstones.

S.M.

Not, as some romantics have suggested, that there was an element of black magic about Nuvolari. Much was made, in some obituaries, of talk in Italy that he had had a 'pact with the devil' like the virtuoso violinist Paganini – who had to compose much of his own music because existing works were not difficult enough to demonstrate his unearthly skill. Nuvolari had no pact with the devil. What he did have was much more useful: (1) the experience of a lifetime: racing was his whole life from his teens onwards; (2) absolute courage: he could probably conceive, with difficulty, of the possibility that he might be killed, but it was a small and insignificant thing compared with his lust to win. He knew he could be hurt, because at one time or another be broke practically every major bone in his body except his spinal column, but injuries he considered only nuisances; (3) a fabulous skill based on nothing more mysterious than abnormally, almost freakishly fast reaction. Said the English authority Gordon Wilkins: 'Nuvolari's reaction in emergency was so nearly instantaneous as to appear pure instinct, bringing him unscathed from a situation that wrecked other drivers. His truly amazing skill was demonstrated over and over again by his sensational performance with cars which lacked the speed of his rivals . . .' Nuvolari himself claimed another attribute: an incredibly fine sense of balance. He once remarked that he could tell to a kilo the amount of weight on any wheel of a car in any situation, cornering, accelerating, braking, drifting, whatever. No one who ever saw him sail through an S-bend, breaking every rule in the book, obviously anticipating the car's behaviour in tenth-seconds, his arms a blur as they flashed up and down, would doubt it.

And during most of his career, it should be remembered, the little man drove solid-axle cars, cart-sprung fore and aft: Bugattis, Alfas, Maseratis. He was nearing forty when racing cars began to use i.f.s., De Dion rear ends and the like.

Nuvolari had undertaken, not long before his death, to write his autobiography, and the portions of it that he finished may cast some light on whatever mighty force it was that drove him, for surely there was some great subconscious urge in him, an inborn addiction for speed and a carelessness of consequences. It certainly showed five years after his birth in the little village of Casteldaria, Mantua, in 1892. His father, Arturo, was a horse-breeder and Tazio used to sneak into the pasture, grab a horse's tail and goad it into running around the field while he bounced along behind, hitting the ground every ten feet or so. He picked up his first bone-fracture of record in that way: a horse kicked him in the shin, broke it, and put him to bed for three weeks.

He was a dark, solitary, moody boy, so undersized that his father had him marked as a jockey before he was a month old. Even fully grown he stood only five feet five inches tall and weighed 130 pounds. He had a short temper, accepted no dares and took no lip from the kids around him. He was a great tree-climber and a self-taught trapeze performer. He was a poor scholar and the schools saw no more of him than the law demanded.

When Tazio was fourteen his father bought a motor cycle and taught him to ride it. A year later he had his own bike, had seen his first motor-cycle race and had announced his intention to enter the first race he could get into. He raced bicycles first, and although he was good, he left them before he reached real distinction. In 1933, though, when he was forty-one, he bet Campari that he could beat him in a match race around the Monza circuit for a dinner, and did it easily.

He had a fling at flying, too, in his late teens. He patched up a Blériot monoplane that had crashed near his home, killing the pilot and being left where it hit, a total wash-out. He couldn't get it to take off under its own power after he had stuck it back together, so he disassembled it, took it to the roof, put it together and tied it to the chimney with a rope. Then he cranked up the engine, opened the throttle to maximum and cut the rope. The Blériot came in like a brick, fortunately hit a haystack and Nuvolari was able to walk away with only a broken shoulder to show for it. He did learn to fly, but not until he was fifty-six.

He was an ambulance driver in the First World War, but not the most esteemed in the Italian Army. When he was discharged his commanding officer urged him to find some other line of work. 'You'll never learn to drive a car,' he told him.

Nuvolari began riding racing motor cycles in 1920, didn't win a major race until 1923, when he won the Circuit of Parma, and quickly enough afterwards won Busto, Emilia and Piave. Forty cycles started the Emilia race and only fifteen finished. It was a mountain circuit, 637 kilometres long.

Nuvolari won 300-odd motor-cycle races, thirty of them of the first rank. A Monza Grand Prix is the one most people remember best. During practice he took a bad spill and broke both legs. The doctors put casts on his legs and told him to reconcile himself to a month in the hospital. The next day he was on the starting line, both legs in plaster, tied to the bike. Two mechanics held him upright until he got under way and stood by to catch him at the end. His doctor refused to have any part of the deal. 'If Nuvolari falls just once,' the surgeon said, 'he is a dead man. Don't call me. I won't even come. There would be no point in it.' Nuvolari ran 300 kilometres, won it all, and coasted in at three miles an hour to be picked up by the mechanics. This was in 1928.

Two years later, after an interim period in which he raced both cars and cycles, he began to devote himself altogether to cars. The greats of the day were Bordino, Antonio Ascari – the World Champion's father – Salamano, Campari, Brilli-Peri. Achille Varzi, Nuvolari's great rival from then until his death in 1947, began about the same time.

The Nuvolari-Varzi argument is still heard occasionally. Varzi was a great technician, a stylist. He drove in the classic manner, doing it all by the book, taking the mathematically correct line on the corners, always easy and unruffled. He never had an accident until he had the one that killed him. On the record, he was close to Nuvolari: of Laurence Pomeroy's list of the 200 most important races to 1939, Varzi won twenty-six to Nuvolari's thirty. But that isn't enough. Nuvolari still stands alone as the man who won more races than anybody else who ever tried, and in the intangibles that separate the great from the merely competent, comparison between the two is a milk-and-water thing. Varzi would win if he could, but Nuvolari would win when he couldn't. Nuvolari once beat Varzi in a Mille Miglia by hanging behind him for mile after mile in the dark, flat out, not a light showing. Varzi was pushing, not loafing, but he was secure in the belief that there was nobody behind him, since there were no headlights showing. Howling along in the pitch black, his foot in the firewall, his mechanic sitting beside him promising Almighty God never to sin again if only he were allowed to live through this one, Nuvolari gradually came up on Varzi, screeched level with him out of a bend, threw on the lights, passed him and ran away.

It was the bitter-end will to win, the lust for winning, the bone-deep need to win no matter what, that set Il Montavani Volante, the Flying Mantuan as the newspapers called him, apart from his fellows. It is this thing that has always set the champions apart, to use a word that has been cheapened in our own time. Nuvolari lived to win, he loathed losing and he didn't care who knew it. All really great competitors have this quality, and you cannot name one who did not. Tilden liked Johnston, but to beat him a set 6–2 instead of 6–0 racked the fibres of his soul. Dempsey had nothing against Willard the day he tried to cut him into bite-size pieces. Joe Louis respected Jimmy Braddock, perhaps admired him despite the price Braddock charged for a try at the title, but he hit him a shot that literally opened up one side of his face. Wilbur Shaw would give his friends – his *friends*, his drinking buddies – the choice of letting him through or going into the wall. All the really great ones are the same: they'll buy you a drink beforehand, and lend you money afterwards, but while you're in there with them they hate the air you breathe. These few are competitors. The rest are spear-carriers, nice fellows, sportsmen if you like, but in no danger of having immortality thrust upon them. They are contestants, and their function is to fill out the field. Nuvolari was a competitor, a killer.

Nuvolari broke up many a car, of course, while Varzi, like Rudi Caracciola, was a great conserver of cars. There used to be a cartoon on the walls of the Alfa-Romeo showroom in Rome which depicted Nuvolari finishing a race. He was shoving an Alfa across the line, wheeling it like a pedlar's cart, nothing left but front wheels, frame and engine.

From *The Omnibus of Speed*
Edited by Charles Beaumont and William F. Nolan (Stanley Paul, 1961)

The First Champion

Anthony Pritchard

By profession a solicitor, Pritchard has written motor-sports books since 1966 and contributed to a large number of magazines. The book from which this is taken recreates the lives of the World Champions from 1950 to 1972 and is particularly valuable for information on the first of them, Giuseppe Farina.

C.H.

Twenty-two years after he won the first World Championship, Nino Farina is both a legend and something of an enigma. When Farina was racing, drivers simply got on with the job of driving; only if they had journalistic leanings did they pen their own autobiography and it was rare indeed for a driver to collaborate with a journalist, rarer still for him to have a close enough friend to write his biography. Very little of what Farina felt about racing ever became known, there was no explanation for his harsh, forceful driving that sometimes bordered on ruthlessness or for his moods that on occasion resulted in him giving up the race in the middle of a chase and made life so difficult for his team manager.

Farina was born in Turin on 30 October 1906. He took his doctorate in political economy at Turin University and was related to Pinin Farina, the greatest of all Italian coachbuilders. In Turin, in the Corso Tortona, he ran with his brother his own coachbuilding company known as Stablimente Farina. The business flourished in postwar days and was responsible for a number of bodies fitted to early Ferraris, but as Ferrari turned to the Pininfarina concern more and more for new coachwork for his cars, the fortunes of Stablimente Farina gradually faded.

Giuseppe Farina is best remembered for his style of driving; the relaxed, inclined position and outstretched arms that was to influence a whole generation of drivers. Even in postwar days, when Farina was driving for the Alfa team, many of his contemporaries still sat crouched, fighting with the wheel. While the great stylist Farina applied art and intelligence to the driving of his car, the 'Pampas Bull', Argentinian Froilan Gonzalez, would hunch over the wheel of his Ferrari and urge it along with great heavings of his ponderous frame.

Farina's parents had comfortable financial means; there was

always a car in the family and before he was ten years old he was a rabid motoring enthusiast. Although his parents tried to steer him towards a more academic career, young 'Nino' was determined to become a racing driver. His first race, of a very unofficial nature, came in 1921 when he was only fifteen years old. He and his brother raced through roads near Turin with a brace of Temperino 1200 cc cycle-cars – there is, however, no record as to who won, but that this race did take place was substantiated by a photograph in Farina's family album.

While at university twenty-year-old Farina decided to buy a racing car without his family knowing. The only problem was money and Nino tried to raise this by speculating on the stock exchange. Soon he had accumulated almost all the money needed, but then disaster struck, his final speculation failed and he found himself hopelessly in debt. There was now only one thing that he could do – tell his father the full story. By this time Farina senior had become reconciled to his son's plans to become a racing driver. He paid off all the debts and agreed to buy Nino the Alfa-Romeo he wanted, but on the understanding that he, too, should have one so that they could compete together.

Their first event was the 1927 Aosta-Gran San Bernardo hill climb. Nino's run was first, but in a burst of over-exuberance he lost control at a corner, turned the car over and was taken off to hospital with a broken shoulder. At this point Farina senior put his foot down and decreed that Nino could forget cars and racing and concentrate on his studies. It was not until 1933 that Nino could afford another car for competition work, an 8C-2300 Alfa, which he drove into third place in the Naples Grand Prix. The following year he crashed again in a hill climb, hitting a wall at the first corner, less than two hundred yards from the start. This accident helped to tame his wild driving. He took his racing more seriously and later in the year switched to a Maserati 1500 cc Voiturette, with which he scored a number of successes including a win in the Circuit of Masaryk in Czechoslovakia and third place in the Circuit of Biella, a minor Italian 'round the houses' race. Both of these successes were gained at the wheel of cars entered by the Scuderia Sub-Alpina on behalf of the works and he continued to drive for this team the following year.

In the early part of the 1935 season he handled a 3.7-litre version of the new 6-cylinder Maserati that had made its debut in the hands of the great Tazio Nuvolari at Monza the previous year. This car proved hopelessly unreliable, as did the 4.4-litre V-8 Maserati which he handled later in 1935. Perhaps Nino's best drive of the year was in October in the Donington Grand Prix (the first international Grand Prix to be held on a true road circuit in England) which he led on a rain-soaked course for the first hundred miles until his V-8 Maserati expired with a broken half-shaft. Farina had become friendly with Tazio Nuvolari and the great Italian helped and encouraged the young Maserati driver.

Farina's driving greatly impressed Enzo Ferrari who later wrote of him: 'He was a great driver, but I could never help feeling apprehensive about him, especially at the start of a race and one or two laps from the end. At the start, he was not unlike a highstrung thoroughbred, liable to break through the starting tape in its eagerness. When nearing the finish, he was capable of committing the most astonishing follies, although it must be admitted in all justice that he risked only his own safety and never jeopardized that of others. As a consequence he was a regular inmate of the hospital wards.'

Ferrari's remarks are of considerable interest, but it is impossible not to question whether one can trust what he wrote of Farina, any more than one can trust his undoubtedly prejudiced descriptions of Fangio or Fangio's equally prejudiced comments on Ferrari! Certainly Farina was involved in many accidents, so many that he could not remember them all, but his moments of folly came mainly in later years when both he and Ascari were driving for Ferrari (to be beaten by the younger man was more than his pride could stomach). In pre-war days Farina appeared to be gripped by a ruthless determination to succeed, a man who had made a scientific study of motor racing and drove with forethought and precision. If he took a risk, it was a calculated risk and not a chance.

Enzo Ferrari invited the slim, austere Farina to join the Scuderia for 1936. At this time Italian motor racing was in a very sick state. Since the introduction of the 750 kg Grand Prix Formula at the beginning of 1934, a Formula imposing a maximum weight but no maximum engine size, the German teams, Mercedes-Benz and Auto Union, had been racing cars of considerable technical complexity. Their annual racing budget was many times greater than that of Alfa-Romeo, the leading Italian contender that had dominated racing in the early thirties. The outcome of so much effort applied was inevitable; there was a Teutonic stranglehold on Grand Prix racing that the Italians could rarely break and Farina's chances of success in Grand Prix racing with Alfa-Romeo were slim.

Farina's first drive for Scuderia Ferrari was in the Mille Miglia road race in April and at the wheel of one of the new 2.9-litre supercharged Alfa sports cars, closely based on the design of the team's Grand Prix machinery. He finished a bare half-minute behind team-mate Brivio whose car had covered the last twenty-five miles of this 992-mile race, the latter stages run in the dark, with smashed headlamps. In Grand Prix racing he achieved a fourth in the Eifelrennen at the Nürburgring and thirds at Milan, Modena and Barcelona, but his year was marred by a horrible accident in which he was not blameless. In the Deauville Grand Prix, in the absence of opposition from the German teams, Farina was leading the race with his 8-cylinder Alfa-Romeo when he collided with the ERA of Marcel Lehoux which he was lapping. The accident cost the life of Lehoux whose car caught fire.

For 1937 Farina remained with Scuderia Ferrari, finishing second in the Mille Miglia with a 2.3-litre unsupercharged Alfa-Romeo, taking other second places in the Circuit of Turin and Milan and winning at Naples. Alfa-Romeo decided to resume racing cars on their own behalf in 1938 and Farina now drove for this works team proper which was given the name of Alfa Corse. 1938 started badly for Farina; he crashed in the Mille Miglia and at the Tripoli race he was involved in yet another fatal accident when he collided with the Maserati of Laszlo Hartmann who was killed. In this first year of a new Grand Prix Formula the latest German cars were not entirely *au point*, and it was for this reason rather than any other that Farina achieved more Grand Prix successes than in the past. In the Coppa Ciano at Leghorn he took second place to Hermann Lang's Mercedes, a fortnight later he finished second to Caracciola's Mercedes in the Coppa Acerbo at Pescara, he was fifth in the Swiss Grand Prix and second again in the Italian race. For the second year running he was the winner of the Italian Championship.

From an Italian point of view the most significant event of 1938 had been the introduction of the new Alfa-Romeo Tipo 158 1500 cc Voiturette which, after teething troubles in its early days, was to enjoy a run of racing success that persisted until the end of the 1951 season. In 1938 these cars had appeared in four races and won two of them, but Farina did not drive a 158 until 1939 when all major Italian races were held for 1500 cc racing cars and the Tipo 158 spearheaded the Alfa attack. At Tripoli the 158s were trounced by two new Voiturettes from the Mercedes factory, cars that no one knew existed until shortly before the race. After an early effort in which he held second place ahead of Caracciola's Mercedes, Farina retired with engine trouble.

The new Mercedes only appeared the once and in the remainder of the year's Voiturette races Alfa-Romeo had a comparatively easy time. The Dottore won the Coppa Ciano, after leading the race for the whole distance, took third place in the Coppa Acerbo and won the Voiturette class of the Swiss Grand Prix. Farina drove a fantastic race at Bremgarten, for in the final in which the Voiturettes and Grand Prix cars ran together, he was in second place to Lang's Mercedes at the end of the first lap and it took seven laps before Caracciola could force his Mercedes past into second place. At the finish he was still leading a works Mercedes and a works Auto-Union. In the whole of his career this was the race that gave Farina the greatest satisfaction. One final victory in 1940 before Italy entered the war and Farina joined the army, came in the Tripoli Grand Prix in which he again drove a Tipo 158.

Alfa-Romeo – and Giuseppe Farina – returned to racing in June 1946 in the St Cloud Grand Prix run through the streets of a Paris suburb and incorporating a half-mile-long tunnel – much longer than the tunnel at Monaco. The Alfas were driven by Farina and Jean-Pierre Wimille, but both retired with clutch trouble; a direct result of the cars' long hibernation during the war years. What was remarkable about this failure was that it was the only postwar defeat of the 158s until Gonzalez pushed Fangio back into second place at the 1951 British Grand Prix.

The Alfas' second outing was at the Grand Prix des Nations, on a street circuit at Geneva the following month, and here Farina's team-mates were Wimille and Achille Varzi, two of the greatest drivers of all time, and Count Felice Trossi. The race was run in two heats and a final, and at the end of the first lap Nino came round in second place behind Nuvolari's Maserati, gesticulating wildly, and it was apparent to everyone that Tazio had been baulking him every inch of the way! Farina pushed his way past on the next lap and won the heat from team-mate Trossi. In the final, Nuvolari succeeded in ramming Wimille's leading Alfa, which spun off, and rejoined the race in third place. Farina was the winner, again leading Trossi home.

Farina retired with transmission trouble on the very first lap of the Turin Grand Prix and the race was won by another Alfa driven by Varzi. At this time there was a great deal of dissension in the Alfa team because the company insisted on picking the winner, and quite often signalled the leading Alfa driver to ease off and let another Alfa driver overtake him. The usual practice when teams were running three or four cars for fairly evenly matched drivers would be to let them sort out their placings for themselves in the opening laps and then signal them to hold position, a much fairer arrangement. At Turin, Wimille was forced to ease off to let Varzi win and as result of the altercation after the race he was dropped from the team at the Milan Grand Prix. In this race Farina finished first on the road in his heat, but was penalized a minute for jumping the start and classified third. It seems that Trossi was supposed to win the final and after a few laps Achille Varzi let him through to the front. A furious duel between Varzi and Farina developed in which Varzi appeared more concerned in stopping Farina from going after Trossi than holding on to second place. Farina's brakes began to play up and when he spun at one of the corners, instead of carrying on in a safe third place he retired in a huff because he was not being allowed to win. 'During the evening after the race, in the café in the Galleria della Duomo,' wrote John Eason Gibson, 'Farina put on a terrific act: aloof and sulky.'

The net outcome of these nursery antics was that Farina was told by Alfa-Romeo that they no longer required his services, thank you very much, and when Farina failed to appear on the circuits in 1947 everyone concluded that he had retired. Nino bounced back again in the South American Formule Libre races early in 1948 and won the Mar del Plata Grand Prix with a 3-litre Maserati. In European races he drove Maserati 4 CLT/48 cars for two seasons and soon revealed that he had lost none of his old sparkle. In 1948 he won the Grand Prix des Nations at Geneva and the Monaco Grand Prix, but despite driving really hard in 1949 his only success was second place in the *Daily Express* Trophy race at Silverstone. He appeared at the 1949 Italian Grand Prix at Monza at the wheel of a new version of the

Maserati known as the 'Milano', one of two cars built by the Scuderia of that name to win the special starting money prize of six million lire (£3000) offered to any entrant of two new cars. The Milano, with an engine much more powerful than that fitted to standard Maseratis, proved really fast, but it still lacked the speed to catch the latest Ferraris which were also making their debut in this race. Yet again Farina's difficult and disagreeable temperament let him down. He was in third place when he retired in a huff, merely because he could not catch the two leading Ferraris – one of these retired and if only he had had the sense to keep going, he would have finished second!

After a year's absence Alfa-Romeo returned to racing for 1950 and there is no doubt that they were desperately short of drivers. Of their old team, both Varzi and Wimille had been killed in motor-racing accidents and Count Trossi had died of cancer. At the time Alfa-Romeo must have felt that they were scratching about rather when they signed up promising Argentinian Juan Fangio, who had but one season of European racing behind him; veteran Luigi Fagioli who was another driver thought to have retired; and, as team leader, Nino Farina who was given another chance.

As events turned out, this trio proved to be one of the most successful that had ever raced together, and more than a match for the Ferrari opposition driven by Ascari and Villoresi. Just as in 1947 and 1948 the Alfa team won every Grand Prix entered and Farina took the Drivers' Championship, newly inaugurated for that year, with victories in the British, Swiss and Italian races. Nino also scored victories in non-Championship races at Bari and Silverstone. At Monaco he spun on water that had broken over the sea wall, hit the wall and rebounded broadside across the road where his Alfa was rammed by Gonzalez's Maserati. This triggered off the multi-car accident that eliminated half the entry. He fell back with gearbox trouble to finish fourth at Spa and after fuel pump trouble was classified seventh in the French race. At the Grand Prix des Nations he crashed his car into the straw bales to avoid Villoresi who had lost control, hit a kerb and was thrown out.

In 1950 Farina was at the peak of a career which now went into a gradual decline. The following year he won his heat of the *Daily Express* Trophy race at Silverstone, but the final was abandoned because torrential rain flooded the track. At the Swiss Grand Prix, another race run in heavy rain, he drove a car which bulged with supplementary tanks to get him through the race without refuelling. All the extra tankage affected its handling and he fell back to finish third behind team-mate Fangio and Taruffi with one of the new 4.5-litre Ferraris. A minor victory in the Ulster Trophy race in Northern Ireland followed, and setting the pace right from the start, he won the Belgian Grand Prix at Spa.

His Alfa was delayed by tyre trouble in the French Grand Prix and with his car crippled in the closing stages of the race by a faulty magneto he finished fifth, banging his fists in frustration on the sides of the car as he tried to snatch fourth place on the last lap from Parnell's 'Thin Wall' Ferrari which had been slowed by transmission problems. His car expired with an under-bonnet fire in the British race, the gearbox failed at the Nürburging and at Monza his Alfa retired after only five laps. Farina took over team-mate Bonetto's car and started a frantic chase after the leading Ferraris. When he stopped to refuel, the Alfa was stationary for two minutes, an inordinately long time, all the ground he had gained was lost, but once more he began to fling his Alfa round Monza in vain pursuit of Gonzalez's Ferrari. His car had developed a fuel leak, he stopped again for the tanks to be topped up and as he accelerated away from the pits, fuel could be seen spewing from the tail of the Alfa. Despite the fire risk, the Alfa was not black-flagged, and after one of the most gallant and hard-fought races of his career Farina took third place. In the last round of the Championship at Barcelona he again finished third.

When Alfa-Romeo withdrew from racing at the end of the 1951 season, Giuseppe Farina signed up with the Ferrari team. For the next two seasons he fought a personal battle to beat Ascari, a battle that he was bound to lose, for Ascari was by far the better driver; more controlled, faster and more precise. At forty-five Farina found that his ability was waning, he could not match Ascari's lap times, and time and time again he threw away good placings by overdriving his car. At Marseilles in 1952 he took the lead when Ascari stopped for new tyres and carried on at undiminished pace until he shot into the straw bales and wrecked his front suspension; at Montlhéry in the Paris Grand Prix he was overtaken by team-mate Taruffi and while trying to regain the lead, he ended up in a ditch and was disqualified for receiving help in getting the car back on the track; at les Sables d'Olonne he was eliminated in a multi-car crash that was no more his fault than anybody else's; and he crashed again at La Baule in August. His best performances during the year were wins in the Naples and Autodrome Grands Prix, and in Championship races he finished second at Spa, Rouen, the Nürburgring and Zandvoort.

Farina's last full racing season was to be 1953. At the beginning of the year he was involved in a horrible accident in the Argentine Grand Prix when his Ferrari mowed down a crowd of spectators who had strayed over the safety barriers to watch the race from the edge of the track. Ten onlookers lost their lives. After such a terrible accident, however little he was to blame personally (the real fault was lack of crowd control) many a driver would have felt unable to carry on driving. But only a fortnight later Farina reappeared at the same circuit with a Ferrari and won the Buenos Aires City Grand Prix.

For 1954 Farina remained with the Ferrari team, finishing second in the Argentine Grand Prix, co-driving the winning car with Maglioli in the Buenos Aires 1000 kilometres sports car race and winning at Siracusa in the first European Formula One race of the season. In the Mille Miglia he drove one of the new and monstrous 4.9-litre Ferrari sports cars, but crashed into a tree not long after the start while trying to avoid a spectator who had run on to the road. Farina's injuries included a broken arm and although he reappeared two months later at the Belgian Grand Prix he was not really fit. He had another bad crash during testing at Monza and did not race again until 1955. After running without conspicuous success during the first few months of 1955, Farina was still badly troubled by leg burns and once again withdrew from racing. He was entered with one of the Lancia V-8s, which Ferrari had just acquired at that year's Italian Grand Prix, but non-started after tyre trouble in practice.

Farina was now approaching his forty-ninth birthday, older even than Fangio when he retired, but, admittedly, not as old as that motor racing wonder Tazio Nuvolari who drove in his last Grand Prix at the age of fifty-six. He decided that the time had come to hang up his crash helmet for good and he never raced again. He had hoped to round off his career by running at Indianapolis, a life-long ambition, but failed to qualify in 1956 or 1957 when he appeared with cars entered by American Ferrari concessionaire Luigi Chinetti.

Giuseppe Farina was not a great driver by the standards set by Nuvolari, Fangio, Moss and Clark, but he was a very fast driver of great courage and determination. He was too audacious and too temperamental perhaps for his own good, sometimes too obstinate when the odds were weighted heavily against him, sometimes throwing in the towel before the race was lost. Farina died on 30 June 1966 when he lost control of his Lotus–Cortina on a slippery road near Chambéry in France while driving to the French Grand Prix. His car went off the road and demolished two telegraph poles and Nino was killed outright.

From *The World Champions* by Anthony Pritchard (Leslie Frewin, 1972)

A Gentle Guiding Hand

Walter Hayes

The story of Walter is a story of success. He worked as a journalist, joined Ford and persuaded them to go into racing. In time he had as much say at Ford as Ford himself — Henry would turn and ask, 'What do you think, Walter?' and Walter would reply, 'We should do this' or, 'We should do that' and it would happen. I'm sure he saw in Jimmy Clark someone whose enormous skill helped Ford with what they set out to do. Ford entered Grand Prix racing with the Cosworth engine. Once Lotus and Clark had it they were extremely difficult to beat, not to mention Jimmy's exploits in Ford Cortinas. Walter never forgot that a lot of the success which Ford enjoyed came because Jimmy was so good.

S.M.

I made the point in a short obituary I wrote for *Ford Times* that other people drove motor cars but Jim Clark was able to show what a motor car was capable of. And there is quite a phenomenal difference between the two types. In all his conversation he would never say what he could do or what he thought, he would always talk about the car and what the car could do. Some drivers drive as though they have to dominate the machinery but I think Jimmy drove like a ballet dancer, he had the lightest feet and hands on earth. He had immensely strong shoulders and arms but this was the only part of him that was strong physically.

He was a great dancer in motor cars, gentle with them, kind with them and I feel that the reason he was a great driver was that there was always the feeling of participation with the motor car, so the driving almost became sixth sense with him in many cases. At Nürburgring I once dumped my eleven-year-old son into the back seat of a Cortina–Lotus when Jimmy was going off round the Ring. Now, I wouldn't let this little boy be passenger with racing drivers because he is precious to me, but you would let anybody drive with Jimmy.

I never knew anyone to say anything nasty about Jimmy. I know this is the kind of thing you get after someone has been killed, an obituary insincerity, but people didn't say horrid things about him because he never did anything horrid.

I think there is an image of Clark that one must try and bury and that is this thing about Jimmy and the sheep. The reason Jimmy would go back to the farm was because his family was there – and it isn't a sheep farm anyway, it is an arable farm. I think he liked going back to it in the earlier days, but I think later he went only to see the family for I don't think he cared very much about the sheep. All this stuff about Jimmy the shepherd with his little flat cap was nonsense. He wasn't a great shepherd. He liked to go back to the family every so often to rediscover who he was.

I am not suggesting that Jimmy wasn't interested in farming, but the public version of Jimmy going back to tend the sheep was a long way from being true. The background to the family had also got more than a little twisted for they were not the Highland shepherds some people have suggested they were. One of the most invigorating things to my mind in the weeks following Jimmy's death was the unbelievable strength of his father, a fabulous character by any standards.

It was probably late in 1962 that I first came into contact with Jim Clark when the Cortina was coming along and we were about to think intelligently about going further into the competition business. I had known Colin Chapman for a good many years and indeed when I used to edit the *Sunday Dispatch* and he had his small garage up in Hornsey, I had hired him as motoring correspondent. He was an unknown sort of boy at that time, but obviously a bright up-and-comer.

When we decided to come into closer touch with the sport we decided that one of the things we would do would be to go into motor racing with Lotus, and so I had a part to play in bringing Lotus and Ford together with things like the Lotus Cortina. When we decided to do a proper racing programme it seemed natural we should talk about drivers and then of course came the first meeting I had with Jim Clark. Even then I had the feeling there were a number of people who didn't know too much about him. He had a comparatively brief time at the absolute top and from then on we had a friendly-cum-business-cum-advisory sort of relationship which lasted right up to the very last minute.

The arrangement we always had was that we had a contract with Colin Chapman and a separate contract with Jim Clark because there were a number of things we wanted him to do for us which had nothing really to do with Lotus. He did a lot of testing and the occasionally rally. He was very interested in helping the motor industry and he used to do a tremendous amount of ambassadorial work for us overseas. The number of places where the Cortina was introduced to the public by Jim Clark was quite exceptional. On one occasion he agreed we would do a Scandinavian tour which required travelling to Sweden, Norway and Denmark and it was all laid on. His father's back had been bothering him so Jimmy insisted that he go home to see his father and I sent a private Dove aircraft to Edinburgh to pick him up and fly him to Stockholm, which is a terrible journey in a Dove. I met him in the early morning and we then did all the various trips, finally arriving in Denmark. The Danish press were so enthusiastic that when we flew out to go to Holland the airline held up the plane while he gave a press conference. Then for the first time I saw Jim Clark's magic at work.

When we were in Holland and went into a night club things were getting tedious and boring until I noticed this beautiful hostess at the bar. I went over to talk to her and she asked me if I would do something for her. I said anything, and she asked if I would get her Jim Clark's autograph. I decided that night that when a little hostess in a Dutch night club could recognize on sight this little man and crave for his autograph he must be a great man and he gave her the autograph with a certain amount of pleasure.

When I first met Jimmy he found it extremely difficult to speak in public and he was exceptionally shy about it. In the last years of his life he was really very good, not as good as Graham Hill but good all the same. The great and extraordinary thing about him was this sincerity which seemed to come over. He could say things and people knew he was telling the truth, because he was so patently sincere in what he was saying. You could never get him to say anything he didn't really believe. There was no question of this, and one would have been insane to try to dictate what he said, so although he used to ask us what he should say about the car we used to tell him to say what he liked about it. He was endlessly willing to drive people around circuits, talk about cars and discuss cars and he was always very interested. He really was a tremendous ambassador for us overseas.

In the early days you could look at him and he wasn't so well dressed as he became when he was an international personality, nor was he as suave or worldly as he became. Later his suits improved and so many things about him changed. In those early days he was a tremendously simple young man and this was the awe-inspiring thing about him. I used to stand and look at him endlessly and ask myself, 'What is it, how is it possible?'

My wife has a theory that there are only two racing drivers who look like racing drivers – Jo Bonnier and Graham Hill. She doesn't think that any of the others look like racing drivers. She thought Jimmy was very handsome but somehow he didn't look as a racing driver should look, and I must say in the early days I would have agreed about that.

He was terribly unbusinesslike. To my knowledge September had arrived one year not so long ago and there were still no signed contracts with anyone. Where we were concerned we would tell him what we would like him to do and he would tell us what he wouldn't do, and we would then agree how much we thought we ought to pay him. Then we would say 'fine' and it was never referred to again, never mentioned. I used to have in the early days a slight suspicion that he wouldn't really argue for money and he never ever asked us for more than we offered. One became very protective and felt one had to take care of this young man because he didn't know how to ask for more. There was one occasion when he rang me up and asked me if I could meet him in London and he said that he had never really thought about money – and this I swear was after he was World Champion – but now he was in a difficult situation for he was getting into the bigger time and could I advise him as to how much he should ask people? He emphasized it had to be on a reasonable basis because he didn't want to be greedy and yet at the same time he didn't want to let the other drivers down.

I don't believe he ever had the first idea of his market value until the last two years of his life. Now I know this isn't the popular belief, and it isn't what people say, but the first year Clark drove for us we paid him £1500. We paid him this because I didn't know any better and he didn't know any better. When I said to him halfway through the season, 'I don't think it's enough', he replied, 'Why not?'

This certainly isn't the popular impression of Clark, who is supposed to have made a great deal of money. I think he did know what it was all about fairly recently because along came Jackie Stewart. Jackie was the great catalyst in money and he has been more instrumental in jacking up racing drivers' fees than any other man in the business. The so-called fabulous sums of money Jimmy was supposed to be getting he never really did get until the last two or three years. The point I am trying to make is how unworldly-wise he was even when you would have expected it not to be so. Take the other top racing drivers of the day – I don't think any of them have this sort of unbusinesslike approach.

A man is influenced by his surroundings and you find you can afford things you never thought possible. At Watkins Glen last year we had dinner in a tent in the garden of Cameron Artensinger (who runs the American Grand Prix). The table consisted of Colin Chapman, Graham Hill, Jim Clark and Denny Hulme and I was the only man at that table who didn't have his own aeroplane. A considerable amount of the conversation was concerned with landing in here and what radio aids you need there and lurid descriptions of Graham Hill landing at Stranraer. So there we were sitting at the party on the evening of the United States Grand Prix and I had to ask if they minded changing the conversation as I felt out of it all. And they said 'Oh you've got to have your own aeroplane' and they were talking about it not like *nouveaux riches*, but like people to whom a private aeroplane had become indispensable.

You may not care about international restaurants and the finest menus in the world but after a while you stop thinking 'here I am in a famous restaurant'; it comes quite naturally to you. Your tailoring becomes better not because you have consciously thought that your tailoring should become better but because it becomes quite natural to go and buy your clothes from a famous tailor. What had happened to Clark was that familiarity with this kind of world in which he lived rubbed off on him in a way that I think just changed his outward appearance but not himself, not at all.

From *Jim Clark: Portrait of a Great Driver* Edited by Graham Gauld
(Paul Hamlyn, 1968)

Racing is Also This

David Tremayne

There was much of Jim Clark about Thomas Maldwyn Pryce's character, and perhaps that was why I identified so instantly with him. He was quiet, humble, utterly devoid of any side or pretention. I remember watching him at the International Trophy race meeting at Silverstone in 1972, standing by his Royale, deep in thought. Just as I was about to walk over his attention was called elsewhere. It would probably have been a toss-up which of us would then have been more shy on first meeting.

The Executive Editor of *Motoring News* and *Motor Sport*, Tremayne corresponds to Danny Blanchflower's dictum that 'a sportswriter is a fan with a notebook'. However, Tremayne tempers that with a steady, knowing eye. His reports of races miss no detail despite their scope and length, but you always feel, like Purdy, he's happiest pursuing his great love – his heroes. The book from which this is taken, *Racers Apart*, is an outstanding example of this, showing Tremayne at his best.

C.H.

The record books reveal only one victory for him in a Formula One race – the 1975 Race of Champions at his beloved Brands Hatch – but oh, could Tom Pryce ever drive! In the Formula Three race supporting the 1972 Race of Champions he had simply pulverized the Hunts and Williamsons to take a tremendous victory. He won by fifteen seconds, and his rivals were so incensed they protested that his Royale RP11 must be under weight. It wasn't.

That day at Brands Hatch in 1975, the same raw ability had simply been geared up another notch as he took pole position for the Race of Champions and then savagely cut the lead he had allowed Jody Scheckter to establish after making a poor start. He had that sinister black UOP Shadow slithering beautifully round the greasy circuit as he ate up the Tyrrell's lead. Just as he was preparing to pounce, the South African's engine scattered, and Tom romped home to victory and a standing ovation. He set fastest lap, too, and matched it again in a race in which he had trounced luminaries such as Ronnie Peterson, Emerson Fittipaldi and John Watson.

Brands Hatch was *his* circuit. He lodged just down the road at West Kingsdown when his childhood love of cars and motor racing had taken him to England to compete in the racing drivers' school

Motor Racing Stables' Formula Ford races that counted towards the *Daily Express* Crusader series. The prize was a new Lola T200, the deciding race the support to the 1970 International Trophy race at Silverstone. Tom walked it. With the Lola went fuel, oil and tyres, and he moved permanently to the south to work as a mechanic on the MRS cars.

The short-wheelbase T200 wasn't the easiest car to drive, as Tom found when he shunted it heavily coming out of Clearways in his first race with it. 'There was this pile of junk sitting on top of the bank, and I just didn't have a clue what to do with it. I didn't know a thing about the business, where to get it fixed, or who to approach.' It sat in a Brands lock-up for days as he wondered what to do, but a trip to Arch Motors and £50 later he was back in the right direction. The incident was typical of the man who didn't open a bank account for years after moving from an agricultural engineering background in Ruthin, and who usually spoke only Welsh to his highly supportive parents.

The Lola taught him the car control he later displayed for Bob King's Royale company in SuperVee and the short-lived F100 sportscar series in 1971. It was a poor formula, but a good way of getting experience at someone else's expense. In the Royale RP11 in 1972 he was also running away with the Oulton Park Good Friday Formula Three race until he had an unaccountable spin, and at Monaco he broke a leg when, having stopped at Casino Square with engine trouble, he was run into by Peter Lamplough. 'I just couldn't believe it. I just froze on the spot,' he admitted. Nevertheless, five weeks later he was back on pole at Brands Hatch and the momentum continued. By 1973 a menu of Formula Three, Formula Atlantic and Formula Two won him the top Grovewood Award for aspiring drivers, and Formula Two drives with Bob Harper for 1974.

In 1973 he had been invited to test one of Ron Dennis' Formula Two Motuls and had got a drive in one courtesy of property developer Chris Meek. Characteristically, Pryce was modest about his selection. 'He had drawn up a list of names and I seemed to be the first one who was home when he rang!' At Norisring he had led until brake failure dropped him behind Tim Schenken. By chance, he then became involved in the unusual Token Formula One project when Meek put up the money for a Cosworth DFV for a car which had been created by Rondel's Motul designer, Ray Jessop, and Rondel backer Tony Vlassopoulo made up the rest of the budget.

They raced the car in Silverstone's International Trophy race, four years after he had won his Crusader Lola, and then he made his Grand Prix debut at Nivelles in the Belgian GP, where he qualified an excellent twentieth, but retired after Jody Scheckter struck the car as he limped it to the pits with engine trouble. Then came Monaco and the turning point. The organizers refused to allow the Token to start, and instead Vlassopoulo offered him one of his Ippokampos Marches in the Formula Three race. 'I wondered if it was the right thing,' Tom admitted, but he thought of the potential Token sponsors who would be present and went ahead. He won the race going away, dominating in a style rarely seen in the highly competitive formula. 'When I'd won, all I thought was that we had some money to go towards the Token. I never dreamt there would be so much fuss.'

Suddenly, everyone wanted Tom Pryce's signature on a Formula One contract. His press-on style had been evident for a long time, and frequently drew comparisons with that of Rindt and Peterson, so perhaps it was fitting that it was Shadow team manager Alan Rees, who knew both stars well, who won the day on behalf of the team's owner, Don Nichols.

'Tom was my choice when Brian Redman quit after Monaco. I was very keen on him. I thought what he did at Monaco at that race was almost unique because he wasn't in Formula Three any more. It is a terribly difficult race to win, for a number of reasons, and he came back on a one-off deal and won it in a very impressive way. That was one of the most impressive things I remember about any driver. It's very difficult just to win it, let alone do what he did and come out of a different formula. We needed a driver then, and he was the obvious guy.'

First time out in a Shadow DN3 at Zandvoort he qualified eleventh, but collided with Hunt at Tarzan just after the start. Next time out at Dijon he was sensational.

'Suddenly Tom went out on the normal Goodyears we were getting at Shadow in those days,' recalled former Shadow mechanic, now Jordan Grand Prix team manager, Trevor Foster, 'and he was *very* quick. He qualified third, right behind Lauda and Peterson and ahead of Regazzoni, and people just couldn't believe it. The garages at Dijon are literally the same now as they were then, and he just came in and sat quietly in the corner. He had this plain white racing suit, the one he'd always had, with just "Tom Pryce" written on it and his blood group, and that was it. He just couldn't understand what all the fuss was about, that's the thing. It didn't overawe him at all. Everyone wanted to interview him, wanting this and wanting that, and he said, "All I'm doing is just driving a Formula One car."'

He scored his first World Championship point at the Nürburgring, and blended unobtrusively into the milieu of Formula One. Alan Henry, journalist and close friend: 'He and Nella were very quiet. You've got to remember she was a child almost. She married him at nineteen and was a widow at twenty-two. Talk about growing up in one compressed space of three years. They were very private people. They were both good company with a good sense of humour, but they kept themselves away from the main company at the races. Very much the way that Martin Donnelly and his fiancée did in 1990 ... I remember them sitting there at Monza, dining alone. That would have been Tom and Nella. Nella didn't like motor racing, she was scared of it.' Like Clark, Tom was utterly unassuming out of the cockpit, but a tiger within it. Funnily enough, he ate his finger ends as well.

From *Racers Apart* by David Tremayne (MRP, 1991)

Master James

Maurice Hamilton

The *Daily Express* called him 'Britain's Golden Boy'. The *Sunday Times* purred in patronizing fashion that he was 'Master James'. In every publication, James Hunt was simply good news.

This was around the time of a roller-coaster ride to victory in the 1976 world championship. Hunt's progress thus far had been nothing short of sensational, a never-ending series of sometimes ridiculous protests, brilliant drives and disappointing results — all of them crammed into nine months between the first race in Brazil and the final, hugely theatrical, shoot-out in the teeming rain in Japan.

When it was all over and the novelty value had worn off, Hunt became the *enfant terrible* of the press. *Vogue* called him *l'anti seducteur*, a typically striking cover using his fulsome blond locks to frame a bored and slightly arrogant look.

The winter of 1976/77 and the spring which followed became open season on James Simon Wallis Hunt, son of a stockbroker, ex-public schoolboy and dashing sportsman who frequently shouted off his mouth with flowing use of a plummy accent. He was, allegedly, ill-kempt and ill-mannered. And he seemed to love it. The more indifferent he became to the views of the media, the more hostile the world at large seemed to become.

The impression was that he was intolerant. That bit was true. Ever a pragmatist, James Hunt wanted to win by the most direct method available. If he did not succeed then, yes, he became angry with those around him. More than anything, though, he became

Truth to tell, James Hunt wasn't in the Fangio-Senna-Clark class. Of course he was a good driver — he became World Champion — but there are a lot of other World Champions at the level James reached. As a man he was a trifle odd, but in racing you always get odd men, men who are different. I think there were more like that then than now, because these days there is pressure to conform and so much more money involved. I also think that today technology has increased to such an extent that the guys at the back of the grid are not that far from the guys at the front. When James did become World Champion and he'd attend official functions wearing jeans, I was disappointed. James would turn up with plimsolls when he should have had a tuxedo. That was bad, and he did himself no justice. He'd been well brought up, well educated, he was well spoken, he came from a good family and he had so much to give the sport. If he hadn't known any better that would have been different. You could forgive him because he was such a great bloke but I always felt you shouldn't have needed to.

S.M.

Hunt, a public schoolboy, drove in ninety-two Grands Prix between 1973 and 1979 and won ten times. Subsequently he commentated on the BBC, where his uncompromising views enraged or delighted viewers. He died of a heart attack in 1993.

C.H.

extremely annoyed with himself. And it was that absence of self-pity which would carry him through impossible odds simply to make it into Formula One in the first place and eventually to become world champion.

Hunt's gangling, hunched appearance militated against him from an early age. He was rejected as a bus conductor because he was too tall, this potential line of business being one of the many he explored as a means of raising enough cash to purchase and prepare a Mini and take up racing.

To the dismay of his parents, James's future ambitions were diverted by a visit to Silverstone in 1965 and he subsequently abandoned plans to go to medical school. The aim of the trip had been to celebrate his eighteenth birthday; the outcome was an immediate attraction to a branch of sport in which, hitherto, he had taken no interest whatsoever. But, typically and without bragging, James felt it was something he could do rather well.

With an Alexis bought on hire-purchase, he began hesitantly, learning enough to confirm the feeling that he could make a name for himself, and then moved into Formula Three during 1969. Racing a two-year-old Brabham powered by an engine which was more elderly still, Hunt did enough to permit the purchase of a Lotus and lay claim to some sponsorship for the following season.

As ever the money was nowhere near sufficient, particularly as James had now embarked on a hand-to-mouth tour of Europe. He scored two wins and several reasonable placings, the shortage of cash imposing worthwhile restraint on his driving. Hunt hardly ever crashed (that would soon change) and he reckoned his repair bill for the season came to no more than £600. A large slice of that had been accounted for by a well-publicized incident at the Crystal Palace circuit in south London.

Hunt became locked in combat with Dave Morgan, another young charger with more than reasonable talent even if his wild brake-locking moments did not suggest it on this October afternoon. The battle was for third place and, at the exit of the last corner, Morgan tried an impossible move. The result was two wrecked cars, Hunt's Lotus beached in the middle of the track with both right-hand wheels missing. James sprang from the wreck, marched over to Morgan and, in full view of the nation's viewers, promptly thumped his startled adversary.

It was the first public hint of Hunt's short fuse and a clear indication of his high adrenalin level when in a racing car. Hunt later claimed he drove better that way, his nervous system reaching such a peak that he would vomit into a bucket moments before a Grand Prix and sometimes explode in an uncontrolled release of pent-up emotion when the race was over. And if his race ended prematurely and not in Hunt's favour, then it was best to give him a wide berth, as Dave Morgan learned that Saturday afternoon in 1970.

For the following season, James had a works-supported March at his disposal. It was an average car and his results appeared to reflect it. The truth was that the degree of uniformity of these under-powered Formula Three cars allowed those without talent to mix disastrously with those who were more generously blessed. Invariably, if Hunt could get clear of the field, he would race into the distance. There were wins at Montlhéry and the Nürburgring. But there were also impressive accidents, particularly at Zandvoort where a collision with another competitor sent James motoring on his head for several hundred feet. The title 'Hunt the Shunt' grew ever more popular.

In 1972 he slithered further downhill, a ride with the works March team ending with an argument at Monaco early in the season. Having progressed no further than Formula Three, his future seemed seriously limited. It appeared to take a turn for the worse when he subsequently joined forces with an unlikely band of racers. In fact, this was to be the beginning of one of the most colourful and romantic episodes in motor racing.

James Hunt was to drive a Dastle Formula Three car for Lord Alexander Hesketh. His team-mate would be Anthony 'Bubbles' Horsley. It hardly seemed a combination likely to set the Formula Three world on fire, never mind gaining recognition in the lofty peaks of Formula One.

'Bubbles' was running the operation for his lordship and he speedily approached Hunt when the rift with March became final. The smirking and the sniggering became widespread when Horsley crashed more often than not and James then had a massive shunt during practice for the support race for the British Grand Prix at Brands Hatch. As was frequently the case, the accident was not Hunt's fault. On this occasion, a car ahead lost control and Hunt, in attempting to avoid a collision, merely succeeded in having an even bigger accident as he turned the Dastle upside-down. For good measure, 'Bubbles' crashed elsewhere on the circuit and James was hospitalized briefly after becoming involved in a road accident on his way home.

It was enough to make anyone give up. But, as Horsley was to note, it was precisely this sort of situation which made James more determined than ever. Presented with a seemingly hopeless cause, Hunt would simply refuse to be defeated. Besides, Lord Hesketh and James got along famously, each sparked the other's passion for racing and matters British.

The original scheme was to enter the Formula Two championship, but a brief venture into Formula One at the Race of Champions prompted Hesketh to raise his game. The team had hired a Surtees and James used it to finish a very creditable third in the race at Brands Hatch. Having tasted life in this upper echelon, the thought of returning to the more basic world of Formula Two did not appeal to his lordship.

With typical quirky logic, Hesketh reasoned that if he was to spend a fair sum to get moderate results in Formula Two, he might as well invest the same amount and struggle along in the infinitely more acceptable world of Formula One. Hesketh and Grand Prix racing would unite at Monaco. All three seemed made for each other.

The Hesketh 308 was ready in time for the 1974 season and the entourage duly returned to Silverstone for the non-championship International Trophy. When James won, it seemed this fairy-tale enterprise knew no bounds. Despite the heady euphoria, Hunt none the less had his feet firmly on the ground. The feeling was that the car was workmanlike, but he would be hard-pressed to challenge the likes of McLaren. So it proved.

During the long haul round Europe, Hunt had but a couple of third places to show for his endeavours. Then, improvements to the car at the end of the season brought a fourth in Canada and third place at Watkins Glen. There was the thought that 1975 could be much better.

He led the opening Grand Prix in Argentina for nine laps before the excitement of the moment caused him to spin. A strong recovery brought him into second place, but when he led in Spain and then crashed, paddock opinion had it that James could not deal with motor racing's ultimate pressure. He was to blow that theory apart in the most convincing manner at Zandvoort in June.

In a race run in wet/dry conditions, Hunt not only made a wise tactical move by being the first to change to slick tyres, he also held off a relentless attack by Niki Lauda. Hunt did not make a single mistake and his first Grand Prix win was earned in circumstances which he relished. Now that he had established his credentials, all James needed was a car capable of matching his ability.

Then, in an extraordinary sequence of events, a vacancy arose within a top team. At the eleventh hour, Emerson Fittipaldi told McLaren he would be leaving. Within seconds of receiving the news, Teddy Mayer, the McLaren director, was on the telephone to Hunt. A deal was completed within thirty-six hours.

The opening Grand Prix of the 1976 season was at Interlagos, a sinuous and difficult circuit on the outskirts of São Paolo. The date was 25 January, which meant there had been very little time for James to settle in with the team, let alone drive the car. It showed in many ways, not least in the fact that he did not fit the McLaren properly when he climbed on board for the first official practice session. By the time that had been sorted out, there was little opportunity to work on the car.

The following day, the Ford–Cosworth engine blew up in the first session. Engine changes were a more haphazard affair than they are today and James watched his mechanics at work, not really knowing the full extent of their competence. The feeling was mutual. James knew that in an hour or so he was going to have to get into that car – a car he didn't really know – and wring its neck. After all this frantic effort, the mechanics would expect him to come up with the goods.

James went out and put the McLaren on pole. He immediately had everyone's respect. The year of Hunt the super-star was under way.

James retired from the race with engine trouble, but not before he had run competitively with Niki Lauda. When he finished second to Lauda's Ferrari in South Africa, it became clear that these two were likely to set the pace although no one in their right mind would have contemplated such a dramatic turn of events as the season unfolded. Hunt *versus* Lauda would become the sporting catch-line of the year.

James tangled with Patrick Depailler's Tyrrell on the streets of Long Beach, Hunt doing himself no favours by standing on the track and shaking his fist each time the Frenchman came by during the next few laps. The next round in Spain was to prove a critical one.

James claimed pole but Lauda led to thirty-two laps before the pain from broken ribs sustained in a tractor accident forced him to ease off and let the waiting Hunt through. When James won, it could not have been more satisfactory from his point of view.

Then the scrutineers moved in with their rulers and the McLaren was found to be 1.8 cm too wide across the rear wheels. Hunt was excluded. The arguments began.

A mistake had been made by the team and the penalty had been harsh. But no one dreamed that any performance advantage could be had from such an infinitesimal amount. And yet, during the races which followed, Hunt was nowhere.

The Spanish Grand Prix had coincided with the introduction of new regulations calling for, among other things, the mounting of the rear wing further forward. The McLaren, in its new guise, had obviously gone well in Spain and now it was handling badly. The only change since then appeared to have been the reduction in width by 1.8 cm.

Not quite. The team had also moved the oil coolers to the side pods for the Spanish race and then, fearing they might be breaking other regulations, they had returned them to the original position beneath the rear wing. That seemed harmless enough but it took the team three races to discover that the new location for the oil coolers, about an inch further forward than before, was seriously affecting the airflow around the rear wing in its new position. The oil coolers went back to the sidepod – and James Hunt simply flew to victory in France. The British Grand Prix was next.

By now, James Hunt was in the front pages as well as on the back of every tabloid newspaper in Britain. His unconventional manner and casual style of dress either infuriated or delighted the nation. He added grist to the media mill by appearing to behave in a petulant manner on the Tour of Britain, a mixture of racing and rallying which he had won a few years before.

There was a full house on 18 July to see James start from pole. Regazzoni barged through from the second row to challenge Lauda for the lead. To Hunt's amazement and initial delight, he watched the Ferraris tangle at Paddock Hill Bend. Then he realized he was to be a part of the accident as well. The McLaren briefly became airborne, bending the front suspension as it crashed back on to the track. Cars went in all directions. The race was stopped.

The next thirty minutes were totally chaotic as the stewards experienced great difficulty in deciding what interpretation to place on the vague regulations covering these matters. It was announced that any driver who had failed to complete the first lap would be ineligible for the restart. It was also suggested that the use of spare cars would not be permitted.

Either way Hunt was in trouble – but not half as much as the organizers. They became aware of mounting agitation within the spectator enclosures on this hot summer's day; beer cans flew higher and the chanting grew louder. The organizers, showing commendable flexibility to match the mounting need for self-preservation, suddenly found a rule which said Hunt could start because his car had been moving, albeit slowly, at the time the race was stopped. Everyone, except Ferrari, was happy.

Lauda led for forty-five laps but, when Hunt forced his way through, the place erupted. Lauda did not respond and James was left to cruise to one of the most emotional victories of his career. As he motored slowly through Paddock Hill Bend, and up the rise towards Druids, James raised both arms aloft. Arthur Partridge, a spectator perched high in the grandstand, caught the moment on film and that evocative photograph is the only racing picture on display in James's home.

A court of appeal had since returned Hunt's victory in Spain but, even so, Lauda's second place at Brands Hatch meant the gap was still twenty-three points in the Austrian's favour. There was nothing for it but to battle on, James arriving at the Nürburgring with a desire to win which went beyond the simple accumulation of points. Success at this demanding track would provide immense personal satisfaction and he started off in the best possible way by putting the McLaren on pole. Lauda would share the front row.

The game plan changed on race day when rain hung in the air and everyone, with the exception of Jochen Mass, started on wet rubber. At the end of the first lap, it was clear Mass had made the correct decision, Hunt leading a number of cars, including Lauda's Ferrari, into the pits for slicks. By the time they rejoined, Mass was into a comfortable lead. But what should have been the driver's day of days was to be interrupted in the most terrible manner.

For some unaccountable reason, Lauda crashed on the far side of the circuit, his Ferrari bursting into flames. The Austrian driver was eventually pulled free by four drivers, but when he reached hospital his burns were considered to be too great to offer hopes for survival. A priest gave Lauda the last rites.

James suddenly realized how much he had depended on Lauda's presence. Feeling helpless but fervently hoping the Austrian would survive, James sent a provocative telegram in the hope that it would both enrage and encourage. Against all predictions, Niki was back in action six weeks later.

In the intervening period, James had finished fourth in Austria and won at Zandvoort. By the time Lauda had returned at Monza, the gap between them was down to two points. The Italian authorities were determined to have their say and Hunt's McLaren was forced to start from the back of the grid as a penalty for an alleged fuel infringement. The resulting battle through the field ended ignominiously when he had an unnecessary collision with another car. Lauda, meanwhile, had finished fourth.

On to Canada now and any hope of a decent confrontation seemed to be demolished when Ferrari's appeal over Brands Hatch was upheld. Nine points were taken away from James; three more were given to Niki.

Hunt responded brilliantly by taking nine points at Mosport while Lauda scored none. James repeated the performance a week later at Watkins Glen. That made it Lauda sixty-eight points and Hunt sixty-five. Only the Japanese Grand Prix remained.

A place on the front row at Mount Fuji would be more important than ever. Hunt, technically minded only when he needed to be, adopted a typically pragmatic approach when it came to sorting his car to suit the 2.7-mile track.

During the first day of practice, he made very little progress. Vain attempts to balance the M23 between oversteer on the fast corners and understeer on the slow ones only succeeded in mystifying James. At the end of the day, he examined the lap times and concluded that the fastest drivers had probably decided to abandon a technical approach. They had either said 'to hell with it' or they didn't care about such complicated matters in the first place. James followed this line of thinking and used sheer willpower and reflexes to hurl the McLaren on to the front row. Lauda was third-fastest. So far, so good.

On race day it rained, as only it can in this part of Japan. There were doubts that the race would be held at all but, after much indecision, suddenly it was on, Hunt powering off the line to take full benefit of his grid position. He pulled away in inverse proportion to Lauda's progress towards the back of the field. Unhappy with the appalling conditions and possessing a sharper realization of the dangers involved and the meaning of life – *his* life – Lauda decided to stop even though it meant throwing away the championship. Lauda did not care about that any more than he cared about making his views public. James Hunt had it made.

Then the rain eased, the breeze finally blowing the swollen clouds away and drying the track. With two-thirds of the race completed, Hunt pressed on, Depailler closed in with his Tyrrell and took the lead, and still Hunt pressed on, the team choosing not to give him instructions either way concerning a tyre change. Not even when they could see that he had a punctured rear tyre. With so much at stake, this was a matter for the driver, they reasoned. Lauda may have retired, but if Hunt finished lower than fourth, the title would go to Austria. Better to let James make the decisions.

In the end, the choice was made for him. The left-front tyre suddenly failed, the result of running the wet-weather rubber on the drying track. Luckily for James, the pit entrance was close at hand and he dived in, had all four tyres changed and returned, convinced he was out of the championship. In a state of blind fury, he drove like a man possessed. Along the way, he passed two cars and moved into third place without realizing it. At the flag, he was still third and therefore the 1976 World Champion. Everyone knew it except James.

From *Grand Prix British Winners* by Maurice Hamilton
(Guinness Publishing, 1991)

There's a Way

Derick Allsop

Like many national newspaper journalists, Allsop came to motor racing by chance. There's a vacancy and you're filling it! His arrival coincided with that of Nigel Mansell, with whom he formed a close working relationship, leading to their collaboration on Mansell's autobiography *Driven to Win*. Allsop, formerly of the *Daily Mail*, now covers motorsport for the *Independent*.

C.H.

Nigel Mansell's stature at the end of the 1980s served to remind everyone that a drivers' World Championship title is not the only badge of greatness. In the minds of the vast majority, he ranked alongside Senna and Prost – even in the minds of those who had dismissed him out of hand during the first half of the decade.

There were some who always gave him a chance, Pat Mennem [of the *Daily Mirror*] for example: 'From the outset he had fantastic guts and determination. I was struck by that from the time he came into Formula One. I admired him enormously. He has deserved everything he's achieved since then.'

Peter Collins, who worked at Lotus when the young Mansell was striving to make an impression in Formula Three, was another. Collins was sufficiently impressed to recommend Mansell to Colin Chapman. He, too, recognized the raw qualities that gave Mansell the will to succeed, but he also saw the driving potential that would blossom in the late 1980s.

In 1987, when Collins was team boss at Benetton, he watched from the back of the paddock in Hungary as Mansell set fastest time in qualifying. He said: 'People go on about Nigel's courage and determination but that lap was also about skill and precision driving. It was brilliant.'

Relieved of the pressure and anxiety to prove himself, Mansell had, by then, begun to give fuller expression to his talent. Confidence lifted his driving to a new plane. Not only self-confidence but the confidence he generated around him. People were believing in him and he responded. The move to Williams came just when he needed it. They gave him the car and the opportunity to win races, and he repaid them. When the team lost Honda engines he felt betrayed and neglected.

Enter Ferrari, again just at the right time. Apart from an association with the greatest name in motor racing and all the public attention that entailed, they offered him a warm embrace. They were willing to cosset him, even to spoil him a little. Mansell, still basically a down-to-earth family man, was made to feel at home, wanted, and he liked that. He was content and relaxed. It showed in his driving and it showed in his manner out of the car.

Ferrari is no charity refuge for waifs and strays. Mansell gave them – and indeed all Italy – what they demanded in return. They had a man at the peak of his powers: fast, aggressive and bold, but also controlled, cunning and mature. All these qualities were evident at that unforgettable 1989 Hungarian Grand Prix. On a circuit where overtaking is difficult, he forfeited a reasonable grid position to fashion a winning car. In the race he was forceful when he had to be and cautious when he had to be. Then came the final, showman's flourish to take Senna for the lead.

The style and spectacle were in keeping with the Ferrari tradition. The *tifosi* loved it and the team loved it. Ferrari chief Cesare Fiorio was moved to say: 'It was one of the greatest drives I have ever seen and Nigel is one of the greatest drivers Ferrari have ever had.'

The thoughts of one of the greatest team bosses in the history of Formula One, Ken Tyrrell, are typical: 'I couldn't understand what Frank Williams was up to when he took on Nigel. He used to go off and make mistakes. Then he won the Grand Prix of Europe at Brands and it was like turning a switch. All of a sudden he became a racing driver. I can't explain it but now he's a fantastic driver. That win in Hungary proved the point.'

Innes Ireland is another who has revised his opinion: 'I didn't rate him very highly in his earlier years but he's certainly got himself together and now he can be as quick as anybody. And I mean as quick as Senna on a hot lap – though I wouldn't care to be sitting next to him on that lap. He has to have very good reflexes and very good car control.'

Rob Walker was at least served notice of Mansell's emergence: 'I was told way back that he was a good driver to watch for, so I kept an eye on him and he has, indeed, become an extremely fast, extremely good driver. I think what impresses me most of all about him is his passing. He passes the way Surtees used to when he first came into car racing. He still defeats me, though. Family man, wife pushing a pram while he's winning an important race. Not the way you usually think of a racing driver. But there's no doubt about it, he's extremely good.'

At the climax of the 1986 season James Hunt stirred up a hornets' nest with the assertion that Mansell would not be a suitable champion. He now sees a different Mansell: 'It's unfortunate that Nigel's two chances of winning the Championship came when he wasn't ready. I don't think he had the right persona then. But things have changed. He's a better driver now and a different person. He came of age in 1989. I noticed a new maturity in him. It was there in the car and it was perhaps even more noticeable out of the car, when talking to him. Anyone who has known him over that period of time will agree. Now he's ready and capable of winning the Championship – if he has the car with which to do it.'

Mansell's domestic 'rival' Derek Warwick could be forgiven a touch of envy. After all he, too, had talks with Williams about a drive in 1985, but chose to stay at Renault. Warwick says: 'It was the right decision at the time and even now I can justify that decision, but as Nigel went on to win thirteen races with Williams you obviously have to say it was the wrong decision. But all credit to Nigel. He deserves it.

'People ask me if I get hacked off because Nigel, another British driver, has won all these races. I get hacked off when *anybody* beats me. It doesn't matter who he is or what his nationality is. Yes, I'd rather it had been me winning those races, but there are no grievances on a personal level at all.

'Nigel has probably done more for British motor racing than anybody. I hope he doesn't go through his career without becoming World Champion because he deserves to be Champion. The way he is driving he can still do it. He has time.'

Mansell's driving has provided inspiration for a younger generation of British hopefuls. Johnny Herbert, planning a more successful second attempt at Formula One, says: 'There have been certain drivers I've looked up to, heroes really. Lauda was one, Villeneuve was one, and Nigel is one.'

Julian Bailey's ill-starred venture into Formula One in 1988 left him with mixed feelings about the sport's upper classes, but it gave him a sharper appreciation of the leading drivers: 'Nigel has made himself special. He and Senna are the best and fastest drivers in the

One of those occasions you never forget. I present Ayrton Senna with the *Autosport* International Driver award at the Grosvenor House Hotel, London, in December 1991. Murray Walker, Master of Ceremonies, seems happy, too. (*Autosport*)

Top: A boyhood hero, the great Tazio Nuvolari, seen here in the pits at Reims. Look at the tyres! (LAT)

Above: Nuvolari during the 1935 French Grand Prix in circumstances I knew well: straw bales to one side, a verge and an unprotected crowd to the other. (LAT)

Top: Jackie Stewart, the fastest calculator, in the Tyrrell Ford at Montjuich Park, Spain, in 1973. (LAT)

Above: Yes, these are Ferraris, never mind the numbers 11 and 12! It's 1979 and Jody Scheckter leads Gilles Villeneuve. Ferrari assumed their now famous numbers of 27 and 28 in 1981 – and Villeneuve made 27 immortal. (LAT)

Nigel Mansell as he became – a
winner and World Champion.

Above: **A rare picture of Mansell in the famous Red 5 Williams. Rare? He's stationary!** (Canon Williams-Honda)

Top: Nigel Mansell as he was – with the Williams Honda team in 1985. (Honda)

Top: **Prost and Senna, the uneasy partnership at McLaren.** (Marlboro)

Above: **The unfulfilled partnership. Williams designer Patrick Head and Senna, 1994.** (ICN UK Bureau)

A compression of the action, and a
brace of Marlboro McLarens. Alain
Prost leads Ayrton Senna at Monaco,
a circuit both mastered absolutely.
(Marlboro)

Top: Virginia Williams, smiling as she copes with a different kind of life. (Transworld)

Above: Frank Williams, the man who overcame terrible adversity and still ran one of the strongest teams in the world. (Mike Hewitt/Allsport)

world. I like drivers who drive hard and fast and that's the way these two guys drive all the time.'

Mansell himself acknowledges the benefits of maturity and a more relaxed manner. He talks of his 'new perspective' and his 'sense of values'. But don't run away with the idea that the beast has become a pussycat. He remains a ferocious, hungry competitor. He has made more than enough from the sport, and from his business interests outside, to retire and keep his wife and three children in luxury for the rest of their lives. But into the 1990s, the familiar ambition and willpower still lure him to the track: 'I go on because I feel I am driving as well as, if not better than, at any time of my career. I still enjoy racing, I still enjoy competing. And I would still like to win the Championship. It is not an obsession, but it is my remaining ambition in racing.'

Mansell went into the 1990 season with a new partner, reigning champion Alain Prost, and an old travelling companion, determination. 'When I joined Ferrari in 1989 I had a definite two-year plan. The first year went fairly well. I won a couple of races and with better reliability might have been able to challenge for the Championship. The plan was to be ready for the onslaught in the second year.'

He had had to carry the burden of not only his own Championship expectations but those of an entire nation. He arrived at the fortieth anniversary of the World Championship with little prospect of being able to share the load. Seven years had passed since another Briton – John Watson – had won a race.

From *The British Racing Hero* by Derick Allsop (Stanley Paul, 1990)

When the World was Young

Alan Henry

I said to Jenks [Denis Jenkinson, navigator when Moss won the Mille Miglia in 1955], 'You know what we should do? We should reproduce the pace notes. A lot of Americans would pay a lot of money to have them as a memento – and there's no other use for them after all this time.' Jenks wouldn't hear of it. What he said was, 'It would lessen the importance of the original.' I replied that to have cribs, so to speak, around would make the original far more important. 'Well,' Jenks said, 'you're going to have to wait until I kick the bucket and get it from Alan Henry, because I'm leaving it to him.' That demonstrates the esteem in which Jenks holds Alan as a man as well as a prolific writer.

This extract is about Frank Williams, who reminds me of Enzo Ferrari in a specific way: he got to where he was by using other people in their correct context. Frank gets great people around him and will then delegate – something I admire because I have great difficulty doing it. Frank is one of those who delegates and gets a better job done. He was not a particularly good racing driver but that doesn't matter. Compare it with someone who can't paint masterpieces. What they can do is organize an art gallery, organize studios, create an atmosphere that allows others to paint masterpieces.

S.M.

Cars – especially racing cars – have been the inspirational force in the life of Francis Owen Garbett Williams ever since his schooldays. Born on 16 April 1942 in South Shields, on Tyneside, the young lad grew up imbued with a resilience and fighting spirit indigenous to that hard, unyielding, often deprived outpost of England's industrial heartland.

His father, an RAF officer, split up from Frank's mother who brought up her child alone in Jarrow, the bleak township that spawned the hunger march to London by a vast army of unemployed labourers during the great economic depression of the early 1930s.

He talks of his mother in respectful tones, yet with a sense of distant formality. He has met his father only about four times in his life. There was not much to be said between the two of them. Frank's mother made a career out of teaching sub-normal and backward children, but found it difficult to relate to her own son. 'It was as if she didn't allow him too close,' recalls his friend Jonathan Williams, 'almost as if because he was normal he therefore did not need her affection and support.' Jonathan also recalls that when he and other friends visited the Williams home near Nottingham, Frank's mother steadfastly wanted nothing to do with them. Nevertheless, Frank stands up for her stoically: 'She skimped and saved to give me a decent education and I'll always be very grateful for that. In the end, I was the one who left home to follow my own life.'

From an early age Frank was mad about cars. 'If there was

nothing else, a ride on the bus provided my excitement. I read *Autocar*, *Motor*, knew all the prices, the cubic capacities, the horse-power and so on. I could quote you everything. Then, gradually, when I was in my early teens, a competitive element began to surface.'

He was educated at St Joseph's College, Dumfries. 'Ecurie Ecosse country,' he recalls. In the mid-1950s, the great Edinburgh-based Scottish team was at its zenith, fielding private Jaguar C- and D-types at Le Mans, which they won in 1956 and 1957. The parents of a friend were acquainted with David Murray, the Ecurie Ecosse patron. Frank confesses to being 'virtually speechless with excitement' when he was offered a ride in a Jaguar XK150S, one of the most covetable of sports cars in the late 1950s. 'After that, I was in. There was nothing else but motor racing.'

Of course, the prospect of realizing his lofty ambitions brought Frank face to face with one crucial tangential consideration. Lack of cash. Breaking into motor racing was no easy task in the early 1960s. Although the costs involved were minuscule by comparison with the outlay involved in the most junior category of racing today, even adjusting figures for inflation, it was far beyond the resources of the average enthusiast.

Sponsorship as we know it today simply did not exist. Club racers might occasionally receive the odd free set of tyres or can of oil, at best some fleeting assistance with the preparation of their car from a friendly local garage. But beyond that you just had to dig deep into your personal resources, a luxury which Frank Williams was ill-equipped to indulge.

Jonathan Williams remembers first meeting Frank at a Mallory Park club meeting in 1962. Sitting atop the bank at Gerards Corner, against which he had firmly parked his own Austin A40, Jonathan was hypnotized by the sight of this 'complete idiot in a grey A40 getting progressively more and more out of shape each time he came through the corner. He looked the part all right . . . straight-armed driving style, Herbert Johnson crash helmet perched on the back of his head a bit like Stirling Moss . . .'

Inevitably, Williams F. joined Williams J. sitting on the bank, surveying their bent motor cars. Frank had a lot of style behind the wheel, Jonathan concedes, 'but he was prone to the odd memory lapse'.

After a couple of seasons' saloon car racing, during which he was attempting to hold down a succession of jobs ranging from Campbells soup salesman to filling station attendant, in 1963 he tossed aside all his inhibitions and moved to London. He was going to be a racer. More precisely, he was going to be Jonathan Williams's mechanic, working on his newly acquired Formula Junior car.

Jonathan was to become a member of a now-legendary *demi-monde* of Formula Three drivers and hangers-on who helped to make the mid-1960s so rich in variety and fascination. While racing an Austin A40 in 1962, Frank had frequently scrounged space on a sofa in a house in Lower Sloane Street shared by Sheridan Thynne, scion of the Marquess of Bath's family, and brewery heir Piers Courage, known to his pals as 'Porge' or 'Porridge'.

'I also used to go in during the day and kip in one of their beds,' recalls Frank with some pleasure, 'and even borrow one of Porridge's striped shirts . . . that sort of thing.' The glee with which he recounts these minor tactical triumphs almost thirty years later is enhanced by the fact that he often does so in front of Sheridan who is now Commercial Director of Williams Grand Prix Engineering.

In assessing Frank's expertise as a mechanic, Jonathan concedes 'he sometimes stood at the right end of the car'. But he acknowledges a genuine debt to his namesake for looking after him throughout the rest of the European season after he had crashed his Merlyn at Monaco practising for the Formula Junior classic which traditionally supported the Grand Prix.

More specifically, Jonathan recalls that it was quite clear that Frank took life a bit more seriously than his more privileged contemporaries. 'For the rest of us, the main priority was to ensure that the fun times kept happening, but Frank was different,' he says firmly. 'Frank was always going to be somebody. He had ambitions. He was going to make something of his life.'

'I replaced the Merlyn with a Lotus 22,' remembers Jonathan, 'but I drove for the rest of the year suffering with delayed concussion. Frank was more than my mechanic. He was my minder. I kept asking where we were, what race we were supposed to be at the following weekend. It drove him mad, I think.'

On the basis that whom you know is more important than what you know, Frank made a crucial breakthrough in late 1963 when he began sleeping on another sofa, this time in what was to become a notorious motor-racing flat in Pinner Road, Harrow. Here he expanded his social circle and met such diverse characters as Charlie Crichton-Stuart, grandson of the fifth Marquess of Bute, whose family owned much of Cardiff city centre; Charles Lucas, the son of a wealthy Yorkshire land owner; and wheeler-dealer Anthony Horsley – 'Bubbles' to all and sundry. He also got to know Piers Courage much more closely.

They were lighthearted days dedicated to keeping the good times rolling, where the nicknames – Charlie Stu, Sherry, Luke, Bubbles, Porridge – rolled off the tongue like something from the pages of P. G. Wodehouse. Frank was delighted to gain acceptance within this exclusive and good-humoured motor-racing enclave, but was conscious of being the poor kid on the block. He had to live on his wits.

Frank would do anything – anything – for a bet. Charlie Crichton-Stuart wagered him ten shillings (50p) that he wouldn't run, stark naked, across the road outside the flat on a Sunday morning when the church next door was just decanting its congregation.

'We locked the door by the time he returned,' Charlie recalls with glee. 'But, being Frank, he called our bluff. He went back into the middle of the road and started leaping around like a dervish, banging his fists on his chest, with us hanging out of the window pleading for him to come in again.'

Charlie tends to endorse Jonathan Williams's view about Frank's mechanical aptitude: 'He had none at all, absolutely zero. He also claims the first time he did anything for me was when I asked him to do an oil change on my Cooper. I can't remember whether that's right, but I'm sure it is. I wouldn't have had the faintest idea what an oil union was, anyway. Frank had obviously advanced to the level where he could take a sump plug out, well ahead of my capability!'

The flat quickly developed into a clearing house for motor-racing talent, with the likes of Innes Ireland and Jochen Rindt passing through from time to time.

For 1964, Frank teamed up with Bubbles and they embarked on a programme of European Formula Three races. Horsley was a wheeler-dealer *par excellence*. Charles Lucas recalls with delight how 'Bubbles was working in a hamburger joint somewhere in Fulham when he overheard a couple of Americans apparently talking about a

Formula One team. Somehow he managed to strike up a conversation with them and offered his services as their team manager.'

Thus the amiable Bubbles became van driver cum general dogsbody for the Scirocco-Powell Formula One team, a short-lived private venture funded by Americans Tony Settember and Hugh Powell. It was based in a small motor racing *demi-monde* in Goldhawk Road, Shepherds Bush, behind a car dealership owned by moustachioed extrovert amateur racer Cliff Davis. It was here, in this nest of fledgeling racing drivers and motor cyclists, that Bubbles first met Frank Williams in the summer of 1962. He was attempting to sell a winter overcoat.

The domestic British motor-racing scene of the 1960s is an essential element of the Frank Williams story. It was a time when enthusiasts could scrimp, save, barter and deal, live on a diet of egg and chips, prepare their own cars and go motor racing on a shoestring. Moreover, within the confines of this particular story, the early racing careers of several key players were as firmly intertwined as the aristocracy's blood lines.

There were dozens of Formula Junior (Formula Three from 1964) races dotted all over Europe in those days in out-of-the-way places, enabling the impecunious enthusiast to earn a living and avoid racing against the better financed young rising stars. It was not necessary to race against the leading lights if you trailed your Volkswagen pick-up truck, containing its old Cooper or Lotus, to Roskilde in Denmark, to Vallelunga in Italy, to Brno in Czechoslovakia or Schleizer-Dreiack in East Germany.

Seldom has the mood, atmosphere and camaraderie of the moment been better captured than by Jonathan Williams. Contributing to a beautiful little private circulation biography of the late Piers Courage in 1971, he explained it thus:

'A meal in Dover, the midnight boat, bacon and eggs in Aachen with the lorry drivers, gaining skill at passing frontiers quickly with race cars and trailers. East Germany on Thursday, laughing at the Communists, but a bit in awe of the guards in their tall towers.

'Another race, another result, getting better, learning how to do it . . . moving to Monza, revelling in the unaccustomed heat, the excitable people, different food and new sounds. Refusing to stop when blackflagged in the race, so strong was the desire to do well, to "show them".

'Constantly moving about Europe, Italy, France, Germany and Holland, always laughing with Picko, Bubbles, Charlie Stu and Frank in a great mob after the race, making fun of each other's incidents. Feeling rich with starting money on Monday morning, having splendid breakfasts and then splitting up until the next week-end.' Small wonder that Frank Williams was drawn hypnotically into this Aladdin's cave of enthusiasm and excitement.

From *Williams: The Business of Grand Prix Racing* by Alan Henry (PSL, 1991)

CHAPTER SIX

THE WIVES' TALE

A Different Kind of Life

Virginia Williams

Professor Vincintelli cleared his throat. In an impersonal manner he started to describe the details of the operation he had conducted on Frank during the night. There had been various minor injuries to be attended to, he said, and he outlined what they were while I struggled to comprehend the French medical jargon.

On Saturday 8 March 1986, Frank Williams left the Paul Ricard circuit in the south of France in a hire car after supervising a test session by his team. He crashed. His wife Virginia flew to the hospital in Marseille where he'd been taken and met the head of neurosurgery who'd operated on him.

C.H.

Then his voice seemed to take on a different intonation. It had, he informed me, been a very long operation. There was a reason for that, which I ought to know. It had been necessary to remove part of Frank's hip-bone in order to fuse broken vertebrae in his neck. Professor Vincintelli gestured with a little chopping motion to his neck in case I had misunderstood and looked me straight in the eye.

'*Vous avez compris?*'

I stared at him in disbelief, certain that my schoolgirl French, previously put to the test only on shopping expeditions with girl-friends, had let me down. I must have got it wrong. Not his neck! Not in my worst imaginings during the last few hours had I considered a broken neck.

I looked around the room for reassurance and my eyes met those of Nelson [Piquet] seated on the filing cabinet. And I saw that Nelson, twice the World Champion driver, always in command of the situation, always bubbly and cheerful and ready with a joke, had tears streaming unheeded down his cheeks. Nobody spoke.

I heard a terrible strangled noise and realized with surprise that it must have come from me. The professors looked uncomfortable. Professor Watkins [Formula One's resident doctor] had his eyes fixed on my face and I felt he was challenging me to be controlled. Eventually when no one else moved, Peter [Windsor, team-member] came over and put his arm around me. I was immensely grateful. But there was no escaping the question I had to ask. I took a deep breath.

'Is he paralysed?'

Professor Vincintelli nodded silently. I wanted to cry loudly and violently but the presence of those five men in the room prevented me. A couple of tears did escape and ran down my face and Professor Vincintelli looked disapproving. Sternly he said that I had to show courage in order not to distress Frank. My husband was going to need a lot of support, not more stress than he already had. When my silent tears continued to flow he learned forward and said in an exasperated voice that unless I was able to pull myself together he would not allow me to see Frank. The shock of his words and the lack of sympathy behind them jolted me back into control. Perhaps that was his intention.

I was conscious of a sudden raging headache. Apart from that I felt numb. I was only vaguely aware of being led out of the office, back down to the ground floor and towards the intensive care unit. Patrick [Head, the Williams designer] followed me. A nurse took me into a small side room and gowned me up. I stood unprotestingly as my hair was tucked into a plastic hat, my feet were encased in rubber boots, my hands were gloved and my whole body covered from head to toe in a sort of white shroud. Only then was I permitted to walk through two sets of doors into Frank's ward.

It was stiflingly hot. The side ward I was directed to had three beds. Each contained a still silent body surrounded by batteries of hi-tech equipment. I felt sick with fear. I had no idea which patient was Frank and I turned to the nurse at the central station for help and recoiled. The nurse's face was terribly burnt — so badly scarred and mutilated that it was impossible to tell if it was a man or a woman. I felt as though I was living through a nightmare. Following the direction of the nurse's gesture I walked towards the bed in the corner. I was unprepared for what I saw.

Frank lay motionless on the bed, covered from the waist down by a thin white sheet, a human clearing in a forest of machinery.

Behind him monitor screens bleeped and flashed, recording every conceivable bodily function. Four or five drips and bottles of blood on stands were attached by tubes to his limbs. More tubes drained from his body into ominous looking bags filled with dark fluids slung under the bed. His hair was matted with dried blood, the inside of his ears and nostrils encrusted with it. Even his fingernails were black with blood. Overriding all my other reactions I felt an irrelevant sense of outrage that no one had even bothered to wash him.

Frank, the man I had lived with for fourteen years, was almost unrecognizable. His face was bruised, cut, and horribly swollen, his forehead covered in stitches. His body, which only yesterday had been so fit and lean, was distended to horrendous proportions. At every rasping breath his lower abdomen heaved up and down with effort. A long livid freshly stitched incision ran across the front of his neck. His eyes were closed. I wanted to speak to him but found that I was unable to open my mouth. It was as though I was paralysed myself. Behind me I was aware of Patrick staring down in shocked silence.

I don't know how long I stood there. It could have been a few minutes or as long as half an hour. Then gradually I became aware of a slight pressure against my stomach and when I glanced up I saw that Frank was looking at me – his eyes bloodshot and unfamiliar but the gaze as piercing as ever. Somehow he had forced his arm towards me. He was trying to say something but his voice was little more than a whisper and I bent over him to catch his words.

'Did my arm move?' he asked slowly.

I nodded, speechless.

'What have they told you Ginny?'

I was unable to answer him. Patiently he rephrased the question, struggling to articulate each word.

'Have they told you that I'm paralysed from the neck down?'

Haltingly, I told him that I thought they had said it was a possibility. There was a long silence. Hot tears streamed down my face.

Frank watched me, dry-eyed. He was so much braver than I was. As I fought to control my sobs he spoke to me again very clearly.

'Ginny, as I see it, I have had forty fantastic years of one sort of life.' He paused and stared at me unblinking. Then he said very slowly and deliberately. 'Now I shall have another forty years of a different kind of life . . .'

From *A Different Kind of Life* by Virginia Williams with Pamela Cockerill (Doubleday, 1991)

The Other Side of the Hill

Bette Hill

When Graham was racing many thousands of miles away, I used to write my daily thoughts and emotions down. One early entry says: 'Separations are bad and uncertainty dangerous. One has to be assured of a person's love. Without this the mind can run wild.' Another note reads: 'Ten days now – and still no word. Guess I literally sink out of sight and mind as he turns the corner.' If one is honest every marriage goes through a bad patch – and that must have been a down moment. Then, a few days later, there is an entry which says: 'Miss Graham terribly. It's impossible to believe he has one iota of affection for me otherwise he would be phoning or writing.'

When he did write he imparted such vitally useless bits of information as . . . 'I watched two of the boys playing cards last night. One of them owns a little monkey which kept grabbing their cards and dealing himself a hand. They got pretty fed up, especially when he jumped on to their shoulders and stuffed his tool in their ears! He really is a randy little sod – very embarrassing for Marianne who was in the room at the time.'

Graham was a shocker at keeping in touch and yet later on, in the last five years or so, he sent us postcards wherever he went and even phoned. In Australia, towards the end of his driving career, he rang after every single race . . . and what did I do? I began to get suspicious because I thought what the hell is he ringing for, doesn't he trust me – or do I trust him?'

Obviously he couldn't take me everywhere – but I hated the separations. I wanted to go racing with him, it was a lovely life, and if the children could be there too he was delighted because he liked having us around. He said we were a great joy to him – and I know we were.

Sometimes I am asked why I enjoy racing, whether it was the

You can state that Graham Hill's success was totally due to Bette. She really did help him and they worked together as a team. He'd been a mechanic who'd come up the hard way, and if she hadn't given what she did, Graham wouldn't have had the opportunities to achieve what he did. It wasn't just moral support. She went to the circuits as an active helper, taking lap charts and so on – and don't forget that racing wasn't well paid in the sixties.

S.M.

noise of the engines that did something to me perhaps? The only thing the noise does is make me deaf! It's the general atmosphere and excitement of the race that I like. As Graham became increasingly successful we got to know more and more people, it grew more glamorous and we just got swept along.

I enjoyed it from the word go, brushing shoulders with both drivers and spectators in the early days. It was like a horse-race meeting with everyone out to enjoy themselves. One saw people, met people and got to know still more people. At Goodwood, for instance, there were the beer tents – and the drivers would stand around having a glass of orange or whatever, as the mechanics trotted across to have a beer. Everyone mixed and when the Dog-house Club was formed it became even more friendly. We had a little caravan, and roped enclosure to serve as a crèche, so that wives could leave their children there to play in safety with someone looking after them. It meant that many of the girls could be at the circuits where, without it, they would have had to stay at home.

Our three children were born into motor racing. Brigitte went to Silverstone when she was seventeen days old in a carry-cot and in those days there were no facilities at all. I had to feed and change her in the car. When that was done there still wasn't anywhere to go even when it was cold and raining. We had to put up with these things.

The caravan grew into bigger and better things until the Dog-house eventually ended up with a clubhouse at Silverstone, another at Brands Hatch, and one at Oulton Park in Cheshire. They are used regularly by the wives and their families, not only during the Grands Prix but for all the races held at these circuits throughout the year from saloon and sports car races to Formula One and Two. One girl wrote to me recently and said how much she had appreciated it. Her husband, who was a racing car designer, and the team had been testing at Silverstone on a freezing day in mid-winter. She had cooked them all bangers and mash in the clubhouse.

It was good for the wives to be at the circuits in other ways. When Graham said you can't motor race unless your wife is all for it he wasn't just talking about me. I can't think of any wife, certainly during the last ten years, who hasn't supported her husband. They couldn't afford not to . . . imagine if they didn't support them and something happened. They're an exceptional bunch of girls, as are the drivers, team managers, designers and mechanics – because of their dedication, sportsmanship and competitiveness – apart from being super people.

The excitement of racing gets into the blood. I've seen people like Nora Tyrrell absolutely drained after a race when the dicing hasn't only been for first place, but second or third places so vitally important to the Championship points. If the wife is with the winning team – well, the sheer joy makes all the anxiety and exhaustion just fade away. The excitement of winning isn't followed by an anti-climax . . . it carries on to the next race. It's infectious because everyone feels involved.

When Graham won at Monaco, as he did for the fifth time in 1969, after the victory celebrations around the pits I always walked back to the hotel. He still had things to do so he'd say: 'Here, take this . . .,' and he'd give me the bag containing his helmet and other gear and I'd climb the hill with this damned heavy load and his trophy. By the time I got to the hotel everyone there would be celebrating, someone would grab me and I'd just fall into the bar and the drinks would flow. Graham would be whipped away in a car to get away from the crowds – but not before he's spent a good hour with them signing any bit of paper or programme. When he walked into the bar to join me everyone would cheer and they'd pat him on the back and me too. This usually went on for some time and meant that we'd be late for the Ball. After a quick bath and change they would still be there to applaud him as he walked through the Hôtel de Paris to the ballroom.

The next morning as we drove to the airport there would be congratulations from another sea of smiling faces. At the airport more bows and smiles, 'Ah – Monsieur Grahame Heel, Grahame Heel.' Then we'd get on the plane and the air hostesses would give him devastating smiles, enough to turn any man's head, shower attention on him and make sure we were comfortable. Then, in no time at all, we'd be at London airport with the press there all around – then reach home, where there would be still more photographers and pressmen.

It's wonderful how the reflected glory flows through to the milkman, the butcher and the people down at the shops who all know you. The excitement continues for days before it gradually peters out. Then, before you know what has happened, you're at the next race where you hope people will be congratulating your husband again. Then that race is over and you're up there again . . . or down!

If it was a down, a good race but something broke, Graham didn't look back except for experience – only forward to the future. If some part failed and lost him the race – that was that and nothing could alter it now. But in looking forward he made sure that any mechanical part that had broken wouldn't do so again.

He took his disappointments well – whereas I used to be an *if* and *but* person in the very early days of Graham's racing. Many times I said, 'If only . . .', but I came round to his way of looking at things in the end. There was one occasion, in 1960, when he came pretty close to winning the British Grand Prix at Silverstone. He was in the lead with only a few laps to go with Jack Brabham chasing him when he came upon a couple of back-markers at the approach to one of the corners. His brakes had been giving trouble and he had to make a quick decision to follow the two cars through and risk Jack catching him . . . or to go through ahead of them, and this is what he did. The decision turned out to be the wrong one, his brakes failed just when he needed them, he spun off the track and lost the race – even though he had put in the fastest lap.

As he got out of the car and walked back to us in the pits the crowd gave him a terrific ovation, shouting and waving their hands and programmes. Tony Rudd, BRM's Team Manager and Chief Engineer, was marvellous and just the right man. He patted Graham on the shoulder and said: 'Well, bad bloody luck,' or something like that – but I was in tears.

Graham saw me and said: 'What are you crying for?'

'I wanted you to win.'

'I made the wrong decision.' That was the only comment he made to me after the race that Saturday. I walked into his study at Parkside on Monday, he was just sitting there. I asked him what was the matter and he said: 'I'm kicking myself for having made a nonsense of it at Silverstone.'

It was the only time he ever looked back and regretted some-thing. From then on he always looked to the next race. Any previous race was over and done with – only the next race mattered.

He would dearly have loved to have won the British Grand Prix but never managed to – even though he won fourteen other ones. People often wondered why this was and one interesting theory was put to me by someone after they had been watching a BBC2 television programme over Christmas, in 1976, on golf. Peter Alliss and Harry Carpenter were guests of Henry Longhurst at his lovely home on the Sussex Downs. They were discussing the past golfing year and re-living some of the great moments and personalities with play-back film clips.

Severiano Ballesteros, the brilliant Spanish player, had an impossible task to hole a putt or something – but he did. As they watched the play-back someone said it must be very difficult for that man because he couldn't speak a word of English – and there he was performing that miracle in front of the British crowd. Peter Alliss chipped in immediately and said: 'No – when I go abroad I always play better because I can't talk the language, and I get no distractions.'

The person who was telling me this wondered if this was why Graham never won the British Grand Prix and why he managed to do so well abroad. I don't personally think that was the reason because Graham could divorce himself from situations – that is one of the reasons why he never had a favourite circuit. But there's no shadow of doubt that he always had far greater pressure on him at the British Grand Prix. Not only because he wanted to win it, and so did I, but also because the crowd were rooting for him. Their enthusiasm and willing him to win affected *me* time-keeping and their excitement infected me. But I don't think it distracted Graham – though it certainly made him more tense.

I enjoyed all race meetings whether they were at home or abroad. Each one had its own atmosphere. At some places we stayed in terrible hotels – at others in glamorous ones. Sometimes we stayed where there was no one else from motor racing – but more usually in hotels where there were lots of others involved in the sport. The general sportsmanship in motor racing is terrific – but now with big business, the parties with everyone tend to stop. It didn't cost so much to run cars and teams then, naturally, so sponsorship is important today as it helps motor racing to keep going.

Drivers are killed, friends are lost. When it first happened my feeling was one of disbelief. I just couldn't believe that I wasn't going to see someone again. Then as another of our friends was killed I was not only sad, I became horrified by it as well and I began to wonder what it was all about.

Jimmy Clark was killed in a Formula Two race, having taken·part in all those Grands Prix. I really did wonder what they were doing. But through all the years I tried to remind myself that nobody put them in the cars, switched them on, and sent them off. They knew the risks and so long as the public were safe – then they were in there to motor race because they wanted to. They loved to race and they gave a great deal to the public.

From *The Other Side of the Hill* by Bette Hill (Hutchinson Stanley Paul, 1978)

CHAPTER SEVEN

GILLES

Bad Blood at Maranello

Nigel Roebuck

Imola provided a salutary lesson for Gilles Villeneuve: never trust anyone. Not even someone you think you know.

Everyone was staggered when Didier Pironi appeared in the lead on the last lap – and none more so than Gilles. As they completed their slowing down lap Villeneuve rocketed his Ferrari into the inspection area, flung his belts off, stepped out and strode away. There was never a glance at Pironi, nor any question of joining him for the lap of honour. Briefly they stood together on the rostrum but there was no handshake, no eye contact, nothing.

There is no more correct or honourable man in motor racing than Gilles and I was puzzled by the display of apparent petulance. It seemed wholly out of character. 'Yes,' beamed Pironi. 'I am very happy to win for Ferrari in Italy. Every Ferrari driver dreams of it ...' Villeneuve in the meantime was away, walking quickly to his new Agusta helicopter parked on the infield.

A couple of days later I rang him. 'I left because otherwise I would have said some bad things,' he said. 'He was there, looking like the hero who won the race, and I looked like the spoiled bastard who sulked. I knew it would look like that, but still I thought it was better to get away ...'

I judge that Nigel is a great writer but also a top-class investigative journalist, in the sense that you will have an appreciation of how things really are in Formula One by reading him. I'm thinking particularly of his Fifth Column in *Autosport*. This extract from a specially poignant Fifth Column is important because it shows the seedy side – or the unattractive side, or whatever you want to call it – of what can happen between drivers. Gilles had enormous flair, was very talented, one of those who could make a car do extraordinary things: wring a car's neck. That's why his appeal is so enduring.

S.M.

On 25 April 1982 Didier Pironi won the San Marino Grand Prix at Imola from his team-mate – the legendary Gilles Villeneuve – by 0.366 of a second. It was not, however, quite so straightforward.   C.H.

The explosive anger of Sunday was gone now. Villeneuve spoke in a calm, detached manner, but still there was no doubting the resolve in his voice. Had he discussed the race with Pironi? 'No,' came the answer. 'I haven't said a word to him and I'm not going to again – ever . . .' Was he serious? 'Absolutely. I have declared war. I'll do my own thing in future. It's war. Absolutely war . . .'

So how had everything gone wrong?

'I'll tell you the facts,' he replied, 'and leave you to decide. First of all – before the race even started – we knew we were extremely marginal on fuel. [Mauro] Forghieri [in technical control of Ferrari] told us to save fuel as much as we could. In fact, the cars were topped up on the grid.

'So for three-quarters of the race we were fighting with [René] Arnoux [Renault], lapping at around 1m 35s. When René blew up I took the lead, and we got a "slow" sign from the pits. It is just not true that there are no team orders at Ferrari. You get a "slow" sign, and that means "hold position." That has been the case ever since I have been there.

'Let me remind you of a bit of history. At Kyalami in '79, I stopped to change from wets to slicks and lost the lead to [Jody] Scheckter, who had started on slicks. I caught him again, and he was holding me up because his tyres were shot but I never tried to pass him. Finally, he had to go in for new tyres and then I took the lead. And do you remember Monza the same year? I sat behind Jody the whole way, knowing that this was my last chance to beat him for the World Championship. I 'oped like 'ell he would break! But I never thought of breaking my word. I know all about team orders at Ferrari.

'Imola was going to be my race, because I was in front of Pironi when Arnoux dropped out. If it had been the other way round, tough luck for me. I can tell you and I know it to be true that I would not have tried to take it away from him, and I expect the same from him. Jesus, we've been living together at Ferrari for the last year and a half. I thought I knew the guy . . .

'As soon as the Renault was out I relaxed, slowed the pace. The only thing in my head was making the fuel last. Pironi had dropped back, and that let him catch up. I made a mistake coming out of a corner, and he passed me. I wasn't worried: I figured he would lead for a couple of laps, then give it back. Maybe he wanted to put on a show for the public, impress the fans. OK, fine. But what did worry me a little was that he was going so quickly, which meant that I had to go quickly, too. How can you obey a "slow" sign if your team-mate doesn't? So I got back in front on lap 49 and slowed things down again.

'Can you imagine a scene where two Ferraris, leading a race in Italy, run out of fuel on the last lap? That was the only thought in my head. So I lapped in one minute 37, one minute 38 for three laps, and then he passes me again, and now we're back in the one minute 35s. I thought it was bloody stupid.

'Then, on lap 59, I passed him again on the approach to Tosa. I thought he lifted a little, but he says he had a small engine problem. Whatever it was, I got by, and even at that stage I thought he was being honest. He was obeying the original pit signal. He'd left it late, but never mind. I led that lap, having slowed the pace yet again.

'I went into the last lap so easily you can't believe it, still very worried about the fuel. I changed up a thousand revs early. I was almost *cruising* down the straight before Tosa, because I was not expecting him to pass me again at *all!* And all of a sudden I saw him coming up to me. I didn't block him – if you look at the TV you will see that I *never* defended myself against him. And he comes up inside me with wheels almost locked, passes, and wins the race. He let me by on lap 59 because he wanted to draft me at the same place on lap 60. And I was stupid enough to believe he was just being honourable.

'After the race I thought that everyone would realize what had happened, but no. Pironi says that we both had engine problems, and that there were no team orders, but what really p—— me off was that [Marco] Piccinini [team manager] confirmed that to the press. My engine was perfect and there *were* team orders.

'People seemed to think we had had the battle of our lives! Jesus Christ! I'd been ahead of him most of the race, qualified a second and a half quicker than him. Where was my problem? I was coasting those last fifteen laps. *He* was racing. I think I've proved that, in equal cars, if I want someone to stay behind me . . . well, I think he stays behind . . .

'I guess it looked like I was mad at finishing second. OK, I'd have been mad at myself for not going quick enough if I'd been plain beaten. Second is one thing, but second because he steals it, that's something else.'

As I left the Press Office on Sunday evening, I picked up a list of the drivers' lap times. Does close scrutiny of these bear out Villeneuve's story? Yes, it does. Here are the last fifteen laps together with their leaders.

Lap 45 – 1m 36.578s (Villeneuve); lap 46 – 1m 36.451s (Pironi); lap 47 – 1m 35.828s (Pironi); lap 48 – 1m 35.406s (Pironi); lap 49 – 1m 35.967s (Villeneuve); Lap 50 – 1m 37.372s (Villeneuve); lap 51 – 1m 37.321s (Villeneuve); lap 52 – 1m 38.123s (Villeneuve); lap 53 – 1m 35.409s (Pironi); lap 54 – 1m 35.571s (Pironi); lap 55 – 1m 35.555s (Pironi); lap 56 – 1m 35.307s (Pironi); lap 57 – 1m 35.213s (Pironi); lap 58 – 1m 35.906s (Pironi); lap 59 – 1m 37.020s (Villeneuve); lap 60 – 1m 36.271s (Pironi).

Villeneuve is now into his fifth season with Ferrari, and most of the time he's been working with loaves and fishes. As we talked, I formed the distinct impression that Imola may finally drive him away from Maranello.

'Of course I was disappointed with Pironi, because our relation-ship has always been good, and I trusted him. But I was furious that Piccinini backed up his story to the press. I didn't like the way things were done at Imola at all.'

Will he stay at Ferrari next year?

'I don't know. If Pironi is there then the answer is no, for sure. Even without him, I'm thinking about it. But we cannot both stay because any team needs co-operation between the drivers, and there will be no more of that with us. If we go testing, I'll tell the engineers all the information, and they can tell Pironi if they want to. It's up to them.

'You know,' he went on, 'I guess people will say I'm overreacting, but I don't see it that way. I trust people until they give me reason not to, but if they let me down, that's it. I would have to be very weak to shake hands with him and say, "Let's forget it." I can't do that. We were not fighting for fourth place. This was a matter of a Grand Prix victory.

'Pironi has been on French TV, and they say to him that Villeneuve is not very happy. He says again that there were no team orders, and comes out with sweet sugar talk about he understands because it's always hard to be second, blah blah blah . . .'

Supposing, I said, that the same situation were to arise again. He responded vigorously.

'If we get a repeat of Imola, running 1–2, short of fuel, then I guess we're both going to run out of fuel, right? If it's a matter of trying to pass him at the end of the straight in Belgium, I'll take the same chance as if it was a Williams or a Brabham. I'll do what I should have done at Imola – go balls out on the last lap, and forget about the fuel. D'you know how much gas I had at the end? Enough for another half lap . . .'

On the Tuesday after the race, Enzo Ferrari took the unprecedented step of issuing a press release about the controversy, in which he expressed a certain sympathy for Pironi, but came down solidly on the side of Villeneuve.

'I guess it's nice to know that you have the boss's support,' said Gilles wryly, 'but it doesn't alter what happened on Sunday, does it?'

From *Autosport*, 6 May 1982

Time Runs Out

Gerald Donaldson

The Grote Prijs van Belgie, which would have been Gilles Villeneuve's 68th Grand Prix, began with practice and qualifying on Friday, May 7 1982, at the Omloop Terlamen Zolder. Much of the attention was concentrated on the Ferraris, for the Villeneuve/Pironi controversy was now the talking point of Formula One. The tension in the team's pit was obvious, with Gilles briskly going about his business looking more preoccupied than usual and studiously avoiding any contact with Didier. He was also reluctant to discuss the matter with journalists. 'Nothing has changed since Imola,' said Gilles. 'I still don't talk to him and I'd rather not say anything more.'

There was one exception, when Gilles took Nigel Roebuck aside. 'I was standing near the Ferrari pit and he beckoned me over. We started talking about the car and I gave him a copy of the story I'd written. Then Pironi came into the pits and got out of his car. Gilles saw him coming and said, "Let's get out of here." He wasn't going to stay in the pit as long as Pironi was there. He wouldn't look at him, let alone talk to him. It was as serious as that.

'The next day he came over to me and told me about the article. "That's exactly what I wanted to say. I'm glad that it's in print. That's my side of it and I think the facts bear it out. And thank you for doing it so fairly." That was the last time I ever spoke to him.'

On Friday Gilles set a best time of 1 minute, 17.507 seconds, which was fifth fastest of the day (behind the 1.15.903 set by Arnoux's Renault), while Didier was slower than his team-mate at 1.18.796. Gilles complained that his car was quite undrivable on the harder-compound Goodyear tyres. 'In fact', he said, 'I scared myself several times. We just don't have enough grip, but it was better on softer tyres.'

Gilles also mentioned that the steering seemed to lock momentarily in the straight-ahead position as he was going through the left-right curves over the hill toward Terlamenbocht, and because of that it was not easy to go flat through that section – where the accident was to take place. He was also irritated by the traffic problems, with up to thirty cars on the 4.262-kilometre circuit at one time. There were tremendous speed differentials between faster and slower cars as drivers were cruising to warm up their qualifiers, slowing down after their quick laps, waiting for gaps in traffic to go for a quick time, and so on.

'It's no worse than usual, I guess,' said Gilles, 'which means it's very bad. Every time I was on a quick lap I came across someone going slowly. Like I've said a million times before, it's crazy having only two sets of tyres to get your time with. You're forced to take fantastic risks.'

The incident report for Friday quoted Gilles talking about the difficulties. 'The French Canadian expressed himself absolutely amazed at the early braking habits of some of the slower drivers, and confessed to having a couple of nasty moments when he nearly collected a Renault and a March.' The March was the number 17 car driven by Jochen Mass; Gilles had had to brake hard to avoid running into the back of it.

On Friday, too, the Grand Prix Drivers Association held a meeting to work on the safety problems in Formula One. President Didier Pironi and vice-president Niki Lauda formed a committee of drivers to investigate ways of lessening the hazards in the sport, particularly those encountered in qualifying. One of those nominated to the working committee was Jochen Mass.

Also on that first day in Belgium, Gilles was interviewed in the newspaper *Le Soir*. He was asked about the danger of racing. 'It's normal to have one or two accidents in a season. I know I risk finding myself in hospital. This does not frighten me, because I am aware of the risks. But there are times when one cannot do anything. If at Zolder my car skids, all I can do is call mama and cross myself.'

Gilles was alone at Zolder and the motorhome was not at the circuit. Joann only missed half a dozen of her husband's Formula One races and this time she had remained with the children in Monaco to make preparations for Melanie's first Communion, on Sunday. Gilles was staying at a hotel near Zolder and on Friday evening he had dinner with a Belgian acquaintance who lived in Canada and had helped him secure some sponsorship back in Formula Atlantic. His dinner companion noted that Gilles still sensed there was a conspiracy against him and he was distracted and preoccupied to a very noticeable degree.

*

On Saturday the final hour of qualifying began at one o'clock. The Renaults of Prost and Arnoux were fighting over the front row while the Ferraris seemed set to be close behind them on the grid. With a little over a quarter of an hour remaining Pironi's was the faster Ferrari with a time of 1.16.501, while his team-mate was slightly slower at 1.16.616. Gilles's time worked out to an average speed of just over 200 k.p.h. As the minutes ticked away more and more cars took to the circuit in attempts to improve their positions, among them Jochen Mass, whose best time of 1.19.777 had him on the last row of the grid.

With less than fifteen minutes to go Gilles was still out on the circuit using his last set of qualifying tyres. He had already established his fastest time but continued to circulate on the used tyres, trying to improve. As Gilles came by the start-finish line Mauro Forghieri showed him the 'IN' signal on the pit board.

'I called him into the pits because his tyres were finished. He had already done three fast laps on them before and was close to the best time of Pironi and there was nothing more he could do. He knew he couldn't do any better and was coming in. Gilles was coming in to the pits on the lap on which he had his crash. But even when the car was coming into the pits it was travelling at over 200 kilometres per hour. That was Gilles.'

Gilles came over the brow of the hill and into the left-hand kink before the Terlamenbocht corner at a speed estimated later to be 225 k.p.h., just about 140 m.p.h., and saw the March in front of him. Competing in his 100th Grand Prix, Jochen Mass was a careful and considerate driver and was watching for following cars. He was in fifth gear but cooling his tyres and moving much slower than the oncoming Ferrari. 'I saw Gilles in my mirrors and expected him to pass on the left. I moved right and couldn't believe it when I saw him virtually on top of me. He clipped my right tyre, bounced off the front tyre and was launched into the air.'

The accident was of aircraft proportions and, unlike when a car skids and then hits a solid object, there was no loss of speed, no deceleration before impact. The Ferrari just kept flying and was airborne for over a hundred metres before it slammed down nose first into the earth, buckling the front of the car in on the driver. But the energy was scarcely dissipated and the accident went on and on.

The car catapulted high into the air again and began a series of horrific cartwheels, at one point touching down on an earth bank some distance behind the guard rails on the right side of the entry to Terlamenbocht. On its return to the circuit the uncontrolled red projectile very nearly landed on the following March. Mass was just able to swerve on to the grass to avoid being crushed.

The Ferrari chassis began to disintegrate, with pieces flying in all directions. The driver, the seat and the steering wheel became detached and were hurled nearly fifty metres through the air to the left side of Terlamenbocht and ploughed through two layers of catch-fencing. Gilles's helmet flew off and rolled to rest some distance away from his body.

A doctor was on the scene in seconds and began to try to revive Gilles with mouth-to-mouth resuscitation. He banged his chest and gave him heart massage. More doctors arrived and were surrounded by marshals as the frantic lifesaving attempts continued. Jochen Mass stopped and rushed over to the gathering crowd. As the black flag was shown around the circuit Didier Pironi halted at the accident scene and ran toward Mass, who turned him around and led him away. René Arnoux and Derek Warwick joined them and the shaken drivers walked back toward the pits.

Among the medical personnel attending to Gilles was the president of the FISA Medical Commission, Professor E. S. Watkins, who is on hand for emergencies at each Grand Prix. Also head of neuro-surgery at the London Hospital, Sid Watkins 'was very upset . . . not because it was in any way avoidable once the circumstances which produced the accident had fallen into place – but because I knew him very well. He was always rational and reasonable, a thoroughly nice person to deal with. When I first met Gilles he was extremely polite, a gentleman. I remember he said, "I hope I never need you." When I identified his car as we arrived on the scene of the accident . . . well, I just thought of those words.'

Gradually everyone filtered back into the pits and many drivers hid their feelings behind their helmets as they walked into the paddock behind pit lane. But some didn't and wept openly, among them Alain Prost, who said: 'I've lost my motivation for the race. He was my friend.'

The last portion of the accident was seen on television monitors and its enormity was immediately apparent. The disaster was shown in endless replays and many people burst into tears on viewing it. Gloom and grief spread along pit row and throughout the paddock. The deeply shocked Ferrari team packed away the equipment and left for Maranello. Marco Piccinini stayed on, saying, 'a miracle is still possible.'

The crash occurred at 1:52 p.m. and just eleven minutes later a helicopter took Gilles to the University of St Raphael Hospital in nearby Louvain. At 5:40 p.m. the doctors at the hospital announced that he was unconscious and suffering from severe injuries to his neck and brainstem, officially a fracture of the cervical vertebrae and the severing of the spinal cord. His vital functions were being maintained by a life-support system.

Then came a final official bulletin from the hospital: 'Gilles Villeneuve died at 21:12 (9:12 p.m.).'

From *Gilles Villeneuve: The Life Of The Legendary Racing Driver* by Gerald Donaldson (MRP, 1989)

One cannot help being aware of the tremendous potential which exists at Ferrari; all that is lacking is a sense of direction. Somehow they have never really grasped the fundamental principle that you should all aim for the same objective. And if you are going racing, that is to win. There is no room for personal battles

John Surtees

Ferrari starts bellowing again. We go at it for another hour or so until he finally asks again, 'How much do you want?' And I drop another 4 per cent. My final offer. 'OK, ebreo,' says Ferrari. OK, Jewboy. He's entitled to say that – he's paying. The next moment he is pleasant and friendly again. A charming old man, the most delightful company anyone could imagine.

Niki Lauda

How did I get on with Enzo Ferrari? Good, very good. I didn't speak the language, but you know he liked to speak about girls, I liked to speak about girls, so it went well. I know Niki had problems with him, but I didn't. I never had any problems with him, not one.

Gerhard Berger

He took me out in a small two-seater GT car. Out of the factory, we turned left and soon were winding our way up into the mountains, through little villages with cobbled streets. It was here I come to know how Enzo Ferrari retained his great flair as a racing driver, his braking points and his gear-changes, precise and crisp, the little car on the limits of engine revs in every gear, the limits of adhesion on every corner. On our return, the village streets were lined with locals, all clapping their hands and cheering, our first pass alerting them to the fact that the great man was out in his little car.

Innes Ireland

On my visits to him during the past five years the routine was always the same. I would be ushered into a waiting room and would hear the slow, shuffling footsteps of an old man go past in the corridor outside. Then I would be shown into his big, always darkened, office with the picture of his mourned-for son Dino on one wall and a black glass replica of the prancing horse behind the powerful figure sitting behind the big desk, with his fine head and big beak of a nose.

Philip Turner

Ferrari was so successful at making cars that he could pick his customers.

Anon

I was never a works Ferrari driver, although I did drive Ferrari cars on thirteen occasions. I had a row with Enzo when I was young. He asked me to drive and I went all the way down to Bari in southern Italy and I found he'd given the car to somebody else — Piero Taruffi. He was fully entitled to do that but he shouldn't have commissioned me. I vowed I would never drive for him. Just before my crash in 1962 I went to Italy and we kissed and made up. He said, 'Tell me what you need to drive for me and I'll have it designed and built for you.' I said, 'A Formula One car and if you paint it in Rob Walker blue I'll drive it.' We had that agreement, but of course it never came to anything because of my crash. Enzo was dictatorial, absolutely dictatorial, and tough. He never went to the races but he had people feeding him information right after practice so he knew exactly what was going on. Like Frank Williams, he could use his powers of controlling people to put things right. I remember him as a dynamic man of considerable character.

S.M.

CHAPTER EIGHT

BEYOND FORMULA ONE

The World Land Speed Record

Sir Malcolm Campbell

We left England early in February, arriving at Daytona at about one o'clock on the morning of Sunday, 12 February 1928. I had arranged to stay with friends, and at the first opportunity I went down to look at the beach. My first impression was one of disappointment; the weather was cold, the sea was rough, and the sand was very uneven.

My father knew Malcolm and I knew his son Donald. I don't think either of them was a particularly nice person, but, no two ways about it, Donald was a courageous man and that must be true of his father. I have always considered that bravery and stupidity are closely related. Whatever, to do what they did you had to have courage, as this shows.

S.M.

The beach is formed in a very odd way, and is not part of the true coastline. It lies along a narrow spit, which is divided from the mainland by the Halifax River, and stretches for twenty-three miles. Four long bridges link it with the city of Daytona.

Its entire length is not available for record attempts, because a pier cuts the beach in two. The course is set south of this and only a stretch of about ten miles is available. At the north end the pier limits the course, and at the south the Halifax River bends round to the sea.

When the tide is out, it leaves a broad stretch of firm sand, with one side bounded by the Atlantic rollers and the other by soft sand which runs up to the dunes. The beach is very sensitive to weather conditions, demanding a wind from the north-east before it can be left really smooth. If the wind is in the wrong quarter, the sand becomes rough and lumpy, and sometimes strewn with shells. When we arrived, the wind was blowing from the south. We could only make the car ready for its tests, and hope that conditions would improve.

We had brought out three cases of spare parts, and two special gas engines for starting up the power unit. There was a big case containing a spare engine, and ten others held spare wheels and tyres. Two more cases were filled with spare parts for the engine and the gearbox. This made eighteen cases in all, apart from the huge crate which contained the car itself.

I was impatient to test 'Blue Bird', because the machine had never run under its own power; it was not possible to discover how the machine would behave, or what adjustments might be necessary, until it had been tried out. The sooner we could do this, the more time would be available in preparing for official attempts.

The car was ready by Tuesday afternoon, but it was then too late to run, because the state of the tide would not permit it. We hoped to have a chance on Wednesday, but a strong wind was blowing and the sand was very rough. Next day, Thursday, conditions were still bad, and the wind was high, but I could wait no longer. I did not ask to have the course marked out, because I had no intention of trying for the record; I simply wanted to test the car.

The police cleared the beach and, like everyone else at Daytona, they were most friendly, willing to do anything they could to assist us. Visitors to the town left the sands readily; Daytona was crowded with people attracted by the idea of three cars competing in an effort to travel faster than machines had ever run over land before. So far, neither [Ray] Keech nor [Frank] Lockhart [due to make attempts in American cars] had brought his machine out, regarding the conditions as unfavourable.

'Blue Bird' was towed down while the beach was still being cleared, but it was not long before everything was ready for the first run. Spectators lined up along the dunes, protected by a broad patch of soft sand which lay between themselves and the course; if a car chanced to get out of hand, the sand would check it before it could dash into the crowd.

While we were waiting, and while the engine was being warmed up, some of the police came over to us, and I soon gathered that the sympathy of the entire force was with myself and my mechanics. Many of the officers had some sort of connection with England, and mentioned towns from which their relatives had come – Birmingham, Lincoln, London, and there were many men from Ireland.

I slipped into the cockpit when word came that all was ready, the engine was restarted and, almost at once, I sent the machine away, driving towards the south end of the course. The car gathered speed, but I made no attempt to use full throttle. I hit one or two bumps before I changed into top gear and then, moving at about 180 m.p.h., the car hit a bad ridge which was immediately followed by another.

The machine jumped, travelling fully thirty feet with all four wheels clear of the sand. It landed with a crash, and I was jerked right out of my seat, while the car started to skid, a great cloud of sand spraying up at one side. As I straightened, slowing down, I heard a clattering from beneath the machine, and knew that some damage had been done, although I had no means of telling what it might be.

I ran on to the far end of the course, knowing that Villa and other mechanics were following. When their car reached the spot where the machine had jumped, they discovered part of the under-shield, which had been torn away. We examined the car, and found that half the underpan had been ripped off and was doubled right back under the tail. Shock absorbers were broken and the rear springs were so much damaged that the rear of the car – which should have had a clearance of some five inches – was all but touching the ground.

We could only tow 'Blue Bird' back to the garage and begin repair work, having learned very little from that first test. The mechanics worked all night, changing the rear springs and making new parts for the shock absorbers, while we engaged panel beaters to hammer out a new undershield and repair a damaged section of the body. The work occupied two or three days, with a cold wind blowing all the time, and even when the machine was ready again, the sands were too rough for further attempts.

The machine was ready for another test on Saturday, but there was heavy rain and a high wind; nothing could be done, except hope that Sunday would bring an improvement. The rain stopped on Sunday morning, and we decided to try the car again; this time, I asked for the beach to be marked out and official times taken. There was no suggestion of making an attempt upon the record, but before we brought the car from its garage I told the mechanics that I would put my foot hard down if there was the least chance of reaching record speed. From a survey made earlier, there was not much promise of a really smooth beach, but it was in better condition than when we had last taken the car out.

More and more visitors had poured into the town. The knowledge that thousands of people were on the scene made it very hard to wait quietly for ideal conditions, because I now felt that everything was right with the car.

When we set out for the beach there were heavy clouds, and a strong cross-wind was blowing from the north; this would be behind me during the first run and would help the car, but it would be against 'Blue Bird' on the return journey. By the time we had made all ready, the course had been set out with true American efficiency, and I received word that I could start as soon as I liked. Villa and the other mechanics looked around the car for the last time, when I sent the machine away. When I left the men behind I had no idea that I was about to face the worst experience of my life.

One of the difficulties with 'Blue Bird', and which I had discovered during the first test run, was in changing gear, because it was impossible completely to free the clutch. When I shifted into top gear, at about 150 m.p.h., it was as much as I could do to ram the gear home; the top-gear dogs kept kicking against one another, and the gear lever had to be forced in by sheer strength.

The car went away well, and I changed into top safely, then devoted myself to handling the machine, and that was not easy. As the speed mounted, 'Blue Bird' seemed to become alive, and terribly strong. I had actually to wrestle with the car to maintain a straight course, fighting against a tendency to snake from side to side, clinging to the steering wheel with all my strength.

Struggling to control the enormous power of the car, I had to concentrate everything upon physical effort. There was no chance to consider that what was happening was dangerous. There was no time, no thought for anything, except to use all the strength that I had in fighting the machine. As I neared the start of the mile, I glanced at the revolution counter. It was showing 210 m.p.h. and, with my foot hard down on the throttle pedal, I went into the measured distance.

All visibility now became an impression of the beach rushing to meet me, everything else forming a blurred kaleidoscope which raced past me on either side of the car. I could not distinguish anything that I passed, except as merged and hazy shapes of different shades. I kept my eyes focused directly ahead, and the objects which I was able to pick up – seen from the corners of my eyes – became vague as they rushed towards me, merging into the shapeless blur which constantly streamed by.

'Blue Bird's' speed rose all the way through the mile, and when I neared the end I looked at the revolution counter again. It now showed 220 m.p.h., and hardly had I seen this when, just clear of the timing tape, the car hit a bump. The impact shot me upwards out of my seat and into the truly tremendous air-stream which rushed past the cockpit.

The air felt solid. It tore my goggles from my eyes and forced them down on my face. I was exposed only for the fraction of a second, but the wind seemed as if it would lift me from the car; I believe I should have gone, but for the tenacious grip that I had on the rim of the steering wheel.

I dropped to my seat again, but my foot had lost pressure on the throttle pedal. The engine, which had been pulling at the moment we hit the bump, now exerted a braking effect – because the throttle had been partially closed – and the machine pitched into a skid, shooting into a great stretch of soft sand. 'Blue Bird' was now all but out of control – caught by the side wind, and skidding in a huge cloud of sand at over 200 m.p.h., while I was half-blinded because my goggles were jammed aslant across my face.

If ever I imagined that my end had come, I believed it in the moments which followed, and it was instinctive action which saved my life. I did not attempt to correct the skid, as I would have done had the surface been hard; instead, I helped the car to work itself out of the soft sand. Had I tried to straighten out deliberately, the chances would have been all in favour of the machine turning over. As it was, it required nearly a mile before I had 'Blue Bird' back on a safe course.

The car was still travelling very fast when I adjusted my goggles and looked for the mechanics who had been sent to the far end of the course. I saw them as the car slowed right down, and in the back of my mind I was working out that my speed through the mile must have been something very close to 215 m.p.h. I had crossed the first tape at 210 m.p.h., and the second at 220 m.p.h., and the average of these two speeds gave me the car's approximate rate of travel through the distance. The record I had to beat stood at 203 m.p.h., so on this run I had surpassed it, but to gain the record I had to return over the course.

The realization that I had to cover the same ground again, that I had to fight 'Blue Bird' once more, was not in the least pleasant. Sitting in the cockpit, using the brakes carefully, I felt exhausted. The muscles of my arms were wrenched, and my whole body felt strained. And I was tired. According to programme, I should have halted to change wheels as a safety measure, but I decided not to do this. I knew that if I stopped and got out of the car, I should never step into the machine again. Near the waiting mechanics, I began to turn, then waved to them and started straight back again.

I put my foot down and 'Blue Bird' gathered speed once more. It was only when I came to change into top gear that I discovered just how much that first run had sapped my strength. I could not get the gear in, and, travelling at 150 m.p.h., I had to take both hands from the wheel, using the last of my remaining strength to force the gear-lever home. It went in, and I snatched at the wheel, my foot going down on the throttle pedal.

The wind was against the car now, and this, as the pace rose, tended to make the machine even less tractable than it had been before. I had to fight over every yard, and it was when I sighted the entrance to the measured mile that I remembered the bump and the soft sand that lay near. This was just in front of what was now the start of the measured distance. If I hit the bump, and if there was another skid, I knew that I should not have enough strength to hold 'Blue Bird', while the skid would send the car towards the sand dunes, the spectators, and the machines which were packed in front of them.

The start of the mile flashed nearer, and I held my breath as the car pitched towards it. There was an instant of suspense, then the machine was over the tape, clear of the bump, and racing on with everything rushing past me. I now seemed detached, no part of the blurred world that came to meet the car and vanished behind. I could hear only the rush of the wind, and saw nothing clearly except the far end of the mile.

There were long-drawn moments of suspense before I reached it and cleared the tape, then I began to ease my foot on the throttle pedal, doing this very carefully, while the car travelled more than another two miles before I attempted to use the brakes. 'Blue Bird' slowed, ran to the end of the course, and stopped. I remained in the cockpit while the mechanics hurried over. I felt weak and they helped me out, then came news which was like a tonic.

On my first run, 'Blue Bird' had covered the measured mile at 214.79 m.p.h., and the return had been at a fraction below 200 m.p.h. The mean speed for the two runs was 206.956 m.p.h., which meant that we had broken the world's land-speed record by a clear margin. Leaning against the side of the car, finding it hard to stand, I realized that we had accomplished all that we had hoped.

From *My Thirty Years of Speed* by Sir Malcolm Campbell
(Hutchinson and Co, 1935)

RAC Rally: The Early Years

Maurice Hamilton

At the beginning of December 1931, a motorist lost a sack of almonds somewhere between London and Ipswich. The incident was reported to the weekly magazine, *The Autocar*, for inclusion in the 'Lost and Found' column. A typical week would include the discovery of a wallet containing £2 on the roadside near Brighton, and the finding of 'three lady's hats in a cardboard box: Southampton to Salisbury'.

Those were honest times when motoring was still a novelty and nothing was spared to return wayward items to their rightful owners. Judging by the action of the motorist bound for Ipswich, this was also a period of financial constraint. A lost sack of almonds, apart from the obvious hazard to other motorists, was not to be dismissed lightly.

Unemployment was high and, with Britain in the grip of a vicious recession, the government called for a temporary halt to the spending of sterling abroad. That may have been only a severe handicap for the enterprising businessman; for the sporting motorist it was a disaster. It meant the end of British participation in the Monte Carlo Rally for instance – assuming the average motorist had a conscience. But, since vehicle ownership was usually the privilege of the few, it seems the majority of motorists felt duty-bound to heed the government's suggestion.

Picking up the cudgels on behalf of their readers, *The Autocar* published a strong editorial on November 20 1931. Under the heading 'A Rally at Home? Combining Sport with the National Economy' it said:

For many years past one of the most popular of the annual international motoring fixtures has been the Monte Carlo Rally. Quite a number of British competitors have taken part, with no little credit to themselves and to their cars, and the whole affair has provided good British propaganda on the Continent. In the present economic emergency, however, we have to consider whether or not the results, from the point of view of increasing the demand for our products abroad, justify the very considerable sums of money that the British participants spend in France and Monaco.

Frankly, we think that, however sporting a trip the great rally may have been, it was only worthy of support so long as the pound sterling was valued in France at about 124 francs. Recent events have put a very different complexion on the subject. A request not to spend money abroad has been issued to the nation, and the appeal applies to motorists just as much as to other travellers. Is there, then, no way in which the fun of the Monte Carlo Rally can be enjoyed without doing anything which is deprecated by the Government?

The answer, we think, is in the affirmative. A rally is good for trade, and a rally should be held and widely supported; but why not keep the course within the boundaries of our own country? This subject was discussed at the Scottish Motor Show last week, and it was considered that a very attractive rally at home could be organized. Several of our South Coast resorts would be suitable rallying points – Torquay was one which was favoured – and the starting points could be any towns in England, Scotland, Wales or Northern Ireland, marks being given for distance covered, just as is the case in the Monte Carlo Rally.

If, in addition to the rally proper, there were to be a *concours d'élégance*, the appeal of the event would be widened, and it might be decided that the cars should be sent over a supplementary reliability course on Dartmoor.

The idea is well worthy of serious debate.

That is a revealing insight into the purpose and format of rallying at the time, but the plea for a major event within Britain should not create the impression that the sport – if it could be called that – was unheard of in the United Kingdom.

Indeed, thirty-one years earlier, a wonderful collection of snorting, clattering vehicles had gathered in the Agricultural Hall in London before setting off on a 1,000-mile trial. This eighteen-day run through England and Scotland required a great deal of courage on the part of the sixty-five entrants. Not only were they asking much of their machinery, some of them were setting out for such far-flung places as Sheffield and Edinburgh in vehicles running on solid tyres and steered by a device resembling a boat's tiller. It was a pioneering event which, to put it in perspective, preceded Louis Blériot's flight across the Channel by several years.

The fact that they actually managed to reach their destination did much to increase the popularity of the motor car. With confidence in the horseless carriage knowing no bounds, motoring outings – generally known as trials – because a popular pastime. It was the shrewd Monegasques, however, who first introduced the word 'Rally' to the world of the automobile.

A Stroll South

With trade in Monaco being somewhat slack in the winter months, it was decided that an international rally, starting from various points in Europe and finishing in the Principality, would do much for the balance of payments. Thus, in 1911, the *Rallye Automobile vers Monte Carlo* was born.

Described at the time as a 'comfort race through Europe', the event attracted visitors with the desired credentials. They had not been under the slightest pressure during the runs from Paris, Geneva, Boulogne, Vienna, Brussels and Berlin since the generous time allowance called for an average speed of around seven miles per hour. Barring mechanical misfortune they were able to eat and sleep in a civilized manner on the adventure.

Having arrived safely – although not always in comfort since one or two of the vehicles were open-topped – a prize was awarded for the best decorated motor car, the winner triumphantly posing by a machine festooned with flowers and garlands.

The latter-day image of Roger Clark grinning from a Ford Escort decked in freesias is difficult to imagine, as is also a driver of Clark's calibre tackling a section of a rally as *slowly* as possible. But that is exactly what was required when *The Autocar* editorial was heeded and Britain's first RAC Rally got under way.

According to Graham Robson, the eminent rallying historian and a long-time contributor to *The Autocar*, the magazine was, in a manner of speaking, a front for the Royal Automobile Club. It was not surprising, therefore, that Commander F. P. Armstrong RN, the Secretary of the RAC, gave his full approval in a letter to the magazine. He wrote:

The RAC would gladly give its support to the scheme and undertake the organization of the competition. I am confident that any proposals which have for their objects the retention in this country of money which would ordinarily be spent abroad, and the drawing of the public attention to the attractions of British coastal resorts, would greatly appeal to the governing body of motoring sport in this country.

Sounding a note of caution, however, the 'Disconnected Jottings' column in a subsequent issue of the same magazine said:

> Participants in the Monte Carlo Rally keep the flag flying abroad. . . . It must not be forgotten that there are many people to whom the warmth of the Riviera is a real necessity rather than a luxury. Townsend Brothers' Ferries have succeeded in making arrangements with certain hotels on the Riviera to agree for all payments for hotel accommodation to remain in this country and to be invested in British funds.

The columnist then argued that rather than being seen as a substitute for the Monte Carlo Rally, the British event should be considered separately and could not aspire, for the first year at least, to being more than a 'jolly all-British affair'.

Winning as Slowly as Possible

Once the nod of approval had been given, the prime motivating force turned out to be Captain A. W. Phillips MC, a mercurial man with a sharp eye for detail.

With the date set for 1–5 March 1932, Torquay was selected as the finishing point since the boost to the resort's trade would be welcomed. (In fact, the event was officially known as the Torquay Rally.) Edinburgh, Newcastle-on-Tyne, Liverpool, Harrogate, Buxton, Leamington, Norwich, Bath and London were chosen as the starting points.

Each route covered 1,000 miles – but that was not as severe as it may seem since the RAC's main objective was to make sure *everyone* reached Torquay, where a series of tests would decide the winner. At the end of the rally there would be also a *concours d'élégance*, an essential part of any motoring event and for many entrants the sole purpose of taking part.

The routes, then, were something of an ambitious venture without overtaxing the competitors unduly – at least, not by modern standards, although at the time a forty-five-mile trip to Brighton was considered to be the limit of reasonable endurance.

The slogan 'Enter the Rally and see Britain' said it all. Three hundred and sixty-seven motorists responded. There were lords and earls, dukes and countesses, racing drivers and record-breakers. Three hundred and forty-one cars took the start – and only forty-seven were penalized en route to Torquay, an indication of the straightforward nature of the road sections, where an average speed of 22 m.p.h. for 1,100cc cars and 25 m.p.h. for those with a larger engine was required.

None the less it was not all plain sailing. There were no overnight halts and opportunities for rest were limited. One competitor fell asleep at the wheel and rammed a telegraph pole near Exeter. Another skidded on ice – of which there was thankfully very little – and overturned, while a similar fate befell Miss R. H. Grimsley when her car collided with a horse. She had travelled a mere eight miles from the Leamington starting point. *The Autocar*, in its twelve-page report, noted:

During the night, near Cambridge, a rabbit committed suicide beneath A. G. D. Clease's Jaguar SS1, and in the early morning a partridge did likewise near Chester while a few minutes later a pheasant just cleared the windscreen. R. M. V. Sutton killed a pheasant with his Lea-Francis and sent it home to his wife.

Realizing that the rally could not possibly be decided on the road, the RAC laid on a series of three tests along the Torquay promenade. For the first, cars had to be driven for 100 yards in top gear – as *slowly* as possible. Then followed an acceleration test, at the end of which the distance taken to bring the car to a standstill was measured.

The last two results were clear-cut, Donald Healey accelerating his Invicta along the 100-yards straight in 7.6 seconds. However, a complex formula had been dreamed up in an effort to equate the enormous variety of cars taking part and, in the event, it soon became clear that a very slow performance on the first section would count favourably. And one or two cars could move at a pace barely perceptible to the eye.

This was achieved thanks to a fluid flywheel which allowed the cathedral-like limousines to transport their occupants with the minimum of fuss and vibration. The winner, by a considerable margin, turned out to be Col. A. H. Loughborough, his lofty Lanchester ticking over gently to inch serenely along the prom at an average of 0.66 m.p.h.! Indeed, once the good Colonel and his passengers were under way, there was almost time for the judges to take tea before the finish.

As it turned out, the judges were kept on their toes by the devious thinking of some competitors as means fair and foul were employed to keep their cars at a crawl. The feathering of the clutch was strictly forbidden and observers were forced to watch the back seat passengers as well as the driver since at least one entrant was found to be receiving assistance by means of trap doors in the rear footwell area!

The inevitable *concours*, or coachwork, competition on the final day did not affect the result. In theory, there was not an outright winner of the event but Colonel Loughborough enjoyed the best individual performance to become, with the mellowing effect of time on statistics, the winner of the first RAC Rally.

From *RAC Rally 1932–1988* by Maurice Hamilton (Partridge Press, 1989)

Thereby Hangs a Tale

John Davenport

If Formula One holds a fierce attraction to some, rallying holds the same for others. Davenport has written about rallying, organized, co-driven and team managed for more than thirty years. He navigated some of the great names – Timo Makinen and Hannu Mikkola among them. He ran British Leyland's motor-racing department for ten years.

C.H.

Rallying is a motorized adventure pursued by somewhat reckless people who would probably be in one kind of scrape or another even if they had stayed at home. With the expansion of their horizons achieved by the simple act of entering a rally, the possibilities for laughter, disaster and eccentricity multiply quicker than a Cray computing the odds on the Grand National. Thus rallying is rich in anecdote, and the only unhappy thing is that large amounts of it are unprintable.

What follows in this chapter is an attempt to show the variety of things that may occur to test the resourcefulness of the rallyman and how perfectly normal rally situations can easily turn into legend.

Perhaps the best example with which to begin is the occasion in 1967 when Timo Makinen was trying extremely hard to complete his hat trick of 1000 Lakes victories in a BMC Cooper S. Equally keen to deny him were Simo Lampinen in a Saab V4 and a young Hannu Mikkola in a Volvo 122S. Less than four seconds separated Saab and Cooper when they came to the longest stage on the rally, Ouninpohja, full of the classic jumps for which the 1000 Lakes is rightly infamous. Makinen's engine was running hotter than it should have been, so he removed the bonnet-mounted lights and left the bonnet slightly open, restrained only by a leather strap. With only ten of the twenty-seven kilometres gone, the strap failed when the Cooper S landed heavily after a jump. The bonnet flew up and blocked all but a tiny strip of the driver's forward vision through the windscreen. A prudent person would have stopped and closed the bonnet, but not a Finn in full flight. Makinen was not going to cede one second more than he could help to his rivals and kept going. By slackening his seat belts, he could crane his neck to see a little further round the obstacle and somehow managed to keep the little red missile on the track all the way to the end of the stage. His time was only ten seconds slower than Lampinen and represented an average speed of some 104 k.p.h./ 65 m.p.h. He went on to win the rally by eight seconds from the Saab driver, which means that had he stopped, it must have cost him the victory.

The ability to figure the odds in situations like that is what gives experienced rally drivers the edge when it comes to winning. Their most difficult choices come every Monte Carlo Rally when they arrive at the service point before the start of each special stage to be greeted by an enormous pile of tyres and the members of the ice note crew that have looked at the stage just before the police closed the road. In five minutes or less, they have to digest what the tyre specialists have to say, the information from the ice note crew, the evidence of their own senses and come up with a choice of tyre for the special stage so that the mechanics can fit them to the car. Very often the ice note crew, experienced rallymen themselves, will come up with a recommendation, though this can sometimes be less than helpful. One works driver was told by his ice note crew: 'I know exactly which studded tyres you want for this test, but they don't have them here.'

The possibility for error is enormous simply because the choice of tyres is large and the conditions on the stage can be very mixed. The only time the choice is easy is when the conditions are the same throughout. A most significant tyre choice, which in fact decided the result of the 1985 Monte Carlo Rally, was one made by Walter Röhrl. With four wins in that event already to his credit, he came to the start of the twenty-seventh stage with his Audi Sport Quattro comfortably in the lead from a charging Ari Vatanen driving a Peugeot 205 T16. His lead was largely due to an error on the part of Vatanen's co-driver, who two days previously had checked in at a time control four minutes early, thus bringing Vatanen eight minutes of penalization. This deficit Vatanen was determined to catch back, and he was doing quite well with just eight tests remaining.

Whether he would have done it unaided will never be known since Röhrl effectively shot himself in the foot. The information on the stage was that there were eight kilometres up to the summit of the Col St Raphael which were one hundred per cent snow and ice, after which there were twenty-two kilometres of dry road descending in the valley on the other side. It is the worst possible choice to have to make and Röhrl plumped for racing tyres with a tread pattern but no studs. His gamble was that, with four-wheel drive, what time he might lose on the snow he would gain back, and more, on the tarmac which followed. Unfortunately, the 500-plus b.h.p. of the Sport Quattro was not helpful when it came to controlling the grip going up the hill on the snow and Vatanen, who had chosen a winter tyre with studs, started two minutes behind Röhrl and overtook him long before the first eight kilometres were done. His advantage over Röhrl on the whole stage was in excess of two minutes, which meant that the estimate of the gain of the racing tyres on tarmac was not correct. Though there are those who say that, in sitting beside Ari for those twenty-two kilometres on tarmac with most unsuitable tyres, Terry Harryman paid in full for his previous error. Vatanen went on to win the rally from Röhrl and set Peugeot on the road to their first World Championship.

Röhrl's choice was made in full knowledge of the conditions, but when the drivers arrived at their service points prir to the Moulinon–Antraigues stage on the 1972 rally, the situation was none too clear. In the manner of many classic Monte Carlo stages, this one climbs for some seventeen kilometres to the Col de la Fayolle and then descends for another twenty to the village of Antraigues. The col is not particularly high and for years the stage had always been clear tarmac where racing tyres could be used. Indeed, this was the recommendation of every ice note crew who had been over the stage not more than an hour or so before. The dilemma came because it was raining in Le Moulinon.

It was not ordinary rain; it had a slightly solid quality to it and the drop in temperature made some drivers think that a little further up the hill there could be something much more interesting than cold rain falling. As it was, the tyre choices were immensely varied, with some competitors going on slick racers, others opting for racers with treads, and then there were those who chose winter tyres, again some with studs and some without. The plain fact was that this stage was one where racers had always been used and few service crews had many studded tyres available, so those who wanted them had to search in the back of trucks to see what they could find. That search proved immensely valuable since, within six kilometres or so of leaving the start of the stage, the cars were on pure, fresh snow. Those who had chosen racing tyres, like the Porsches of Bjorn

Waldegaard and Gerard Larrousse and the Alpine A110 of Jean-Luc Thérier, had a terrible struggle to get through at all and were rewarded with penalties on both the stage and the subsequent road section. Timo Makinen, who chose winter tyres with 300 studs for his Ford Escort RS, said afterwards that he regretted not having ones with 600 studs.

The choice of tyres is not the only thing that can ruin a rally crew's performance, and the catalogue of mechanical mishaps is greater in rallying than almost any other branch of motor sport. One particular failure has led to a variety of ingenious solutions and that is throttle cable failure. It is typical of rallymen that, faced with an otherwise perfectly functioning car, they are prepared to adopt the most physically dangerous methods to be able to drive the car. One example was on a Geneva Rally in the 1960s when this problem came to Gunther Klass in a factory Porsche 911. Undaunted, his co-driver Rolf Wutherlich, the same man who had been in James Deans's Porsche at the time of his fatal crash, climbed on to the rear bumper, held open the bonnet with one hand and operated the throttle with the other. In that fashion, they were able to get out of the section and to the Porsche service. A more recent example was on the 1000 Lakes Rally of 1990 where Juha Kankkunen had to get out and sit on the windscreen of his Lancia Delta Integrale with his legs and arm under the bonnet while Juha Piironen steered the car out of the stage. In a twenty-kilometre stage, they somehow only lost five minutes, which says a great deal for their speed of diagnosis, resolution and co-ordination.

Inevitably, someone raised the question as to whether Kankkunen had been breaking the rules in completing the stage with no seat belts. On close scrutiny, it turned out that the specific requirement was for seat belts to be worn by the crew while travelling inside the car on the special stage. Just as well for Arne Hertz in the 1983 Lombard RAC Rally, as he had to travel sitting on the right rear of Hannu Mikkola's Audi Quattro in order to keep the car level after the left front wheel had been torn off in an accident. Mikkola went from leading the rally to twenty-sixth, but pulled back to finish second overall. A similar problem assailed Ari Vatanen with his Peugeot 205 T16 Grand Raid when he folded a front wheel underneath the car on the spectator stage outside Paris during the 1987 Paris-Dakar. To provide the necessary counterbalance to lift the collapsed corner off the ground and get the car out of the stage, he persuaded several hefty spectators, who were presumably Peugeot fans, to hang on to the rear using the roof rack to support themselves. The ploy was successful, though coming as it did at such an early stage, he did drop to 276th overall. But with such a long distance still to come in the desert, he was able to recover the lost time and went on to win the rally outright.

Redistribution of weight was behind the rearward location of Christian Geistdorfer's seat in the Fiat Abarth 131 of Walter Röhrl during the 1978 Lombard RAC Rally. Team engineer Giorgio Pianta had tested the car on several occasions with weights in the back and he was certain that moving the co-driver, while not increasing the all-up weight of the car, would give a significant increase in traction. The sight of the co-driver residing in the rear caused quite a stir, and for a while Röhrl was convinced that it worked. At least he finished sixth on the RAC, but when they tried the system again in practice for the 1979 Monte Carlo Rally, it didn't seem to work so well. Then on the stage from Pont des Miolans to St Auban, which ends with a series of uphill hairpins, Geistdorfer tried the car with two seats fitted in it. He started in the front and got in the back to go up the last part of the stage, but neither would say if they thought it was better or not. In any case, FISA quickly ruled that the co-driver had to sit in the front and that was the end of such experiments.

Of course there are events where having three people in the car is normal. The early marathons indulged in this form of crewing for the very simple reason that it was judged that, while a man might be permitted a few cat-naps while navigating, this was not desirable for the driver. Thus two drivers were taken who could share the work of two or more days non-stop driving. A three-man crew was also quite a normal sight on rallies like the Monte-Carlo in the 1950s when private owners would often take a full complement in the car and share the duties between them. It could have some drawbacks, as Raymond Joss discovered on the 1963 Monte Carlo when he briefly put his Rover 3-litre off the road on the Chartreuse special stage. When he went off, he had a crew of three, two of whom got out to push, but when the car was freed, he set off with such dispatch that only one of them was able to regain the interior of the car. The other spent a pleasant night with the locals drinking mulled wine in the local bakery and watching the rally. Although the Rover reached

Monte Carlo, it was promptly disqualified for not having the full crew abroad.

From *The Guinness Book of Rallying* by John Davenport
(Guinness Publishing, 1991)

Rallying is the most complete branch of motor sport. It has the problems of continuous relocation in addition to those of time, speed and skill which it shares with other motor sports.
John Davenport

An Initiation Test

Jean Todt with Jean-Louis Moncet

Everything he has done so far has been a success and he's been a major contributor to motor sport with Peugeot. Now, in 1994, he's taken on the most difficult job of the lot in trying to turn Ferrari round after so many years of failure. I'll be watching fascinated to see what he makes of it – and how.

S.M.

In order to make their debut at the Corsican Rally, in May 1984, Jean Todt had to find two drivers for the 205 before the end of 1983. He had already hired one, Jean-Pierre Nicolas; he was still looking for a second who had to be exceptional. 'Who's going to drive the car? It's the question I was most often asked, especially by the press. I made two lists, trying to be as precise as possible. The first one contained the names of those I felt to be the best rally drivers in the world. The second list, a little longer, included the drivers I considered to be just behind the ones who were "first-class".

'On the first list were four names: the German, Walter Röhrl, and the three Finns, Markku Alen, Henri Toivonen, and Ari Vatanen. Among these four, I made no distinction in talent. One of them, however, was in a difficult situation at the time, and might feel more pressure than the others to win, and more inspired to join a new team with an unknown car: this was Ari Vatanen. I first contacted him in April 1983, at the Intercontinental Hotel in Nairobi, to explain briefly our programme. He was driving an Opel at the time, for the Rothmans stable, and ended up winning the rally. In May, before leaving for Greece, he visited me in Paris, and I took him, at night, in secret, to see the car.

'At the beginning of September, I talked to Alen, Toivonen and Röhrl. The first was committed to Lancia for a long time to come, the second hesitated, and the third was leaning towards Audi.

'A few weeks later, we were all at the San Remo Rally. One morning, at the Hotel Royal, rally headquarters, the breakfast waiter thought he was going crazy: I ordered three breakfasts in a row, one for each meeting, the first with Ari, then Markku, and finally Henri. We decided to take some time to reflect, and by evening Ari had decided to accept. From that moment on, I knew I had made a good choice. He had been World Champion, suffered a lean spell, and was making a fresh start. Later, he admitted, "I had decided to accept right after breakfast, but I waited till evening to tell you. I didn't want the whole thing to seem too easy." Ari was worried, however, about their timing schedule.'

A year after the launch of the normal production 205 model, Peugeot revealed a new, sportier model in the GTI. Before launching her to the public, Vic Dial gathered his troops, 'the European sales force', at the Empire Theatre. He had invited Corrado Provera and Jean Todt to speak about the motives behind their work at Peugeot.

The key to the meeting was the arrival of Ari Vatanen in a running 205 Turbo 16. Provera recalled: 'Jean Todt was a wreck. He could only imagine the worst: that the car wouldn't start, that they would have to push it, that the whole thing would turn out to be ridiculous . . . when suddenly, Vatanen rolled on to the stage in a car that roared and kicked. This was in February 1984, three months before the 205's first event, the Corsican Rally.'

Before the start of the Corsican, something truly incredible happened. One evening, Jean-Pierre Nicolas went out on a recon-naissance drive with his navigator, Charley Pasquier. For the first time, the 205 went on the road alone, without following the usual testing procedure, whereby a group of engineers and mechanics watched her every move. In fact, no one could believe it; surely Jean-Pierre would come back in a minute. In the car, Jean-Pierre told himself the same thing. In a minute, some minor incident would send him back. Instead, he drove on for a staggering eighty kilo-metres driving hard to take useful notes. Jumbo looked at Charley with a forced smile; Charley responded with a doubtful glance. And they drove on for another 200 kilometres. This time, Jean-Pierre smiled widely. At the end of the night, after covering 500 kilometres without a problem, he and Charlie burst into laughter, like two children playing.

Finally, they were in hysterics a few hours later, when they saw Bernard Darniche, Markku Alen and others out on a recce. Jean-Pierre's characteristic optimism surfaced, 'incorrigible', according to his colleagues, when he boasted 'You'll see, suckers, with this baby we've got you licked.' The others piped in, 'Sure, fats, but even if you drove a three-wheeled taxi cab, you'd tell us the same thing! Sure fats, we know you . . .'

At his office in Paris, Jean Todt was not laughing. Not in the least! 'Before boarding the boat for Ajaccio, I had to work at a furious pace to finish the 200 retail cars and the twenty Evolution Group B models in time to register the 205 Turbo 16. Without this approval we would not be able to take part in the Corsican Rally. (Federal officials came to count the cars.)

'With this step out of the way, I then had to set the Peugeot-Talbot Sport operation in motion. This meant verifying the support vehicles and checking their contents: parts, tyres, supplies, maps, road-books. We had to devise a support plan, and form teams of mechanics, some of whom were new to rallying. I had refused, for this first rally, the use of helicopter assistance, preferring to be modest.

'Moreover, I had to arrange the travel for the members of our executive board, who would be attending the car's debut. It was a crucial day. From the start, I kept asking myself the same questions. How far would the car go? (It didn't occur to me that it could go all the way to the finish.) How would the car behave, especially on relatively unfavourable ground?

'This time I had really stuck my neck out, and with me, the team technicians. The Company had invested a great deal in the 205 Turbo 16 project. It had, moreover, opted for an original competitions policy that went against traditions and, in some instances, our convictions. The Company was waiting for a response, the response that would emerge during the first kilometres of the race, where anything could happen; for the essence of the rally car is risk and uncertainty itself.

'Then Vatanen arrived as if he were heading for any old race. And the engine of the 205 whirred gently. We made it. Ari clocked in fifth, which was more than honourable. In the second stage, he made a record time, which was the best time ever achieved for that stage: Röhrl made it in 26'36, Fréquelin in 27'15 and Ari in 26'16. Instinctively, I put my hands to my heart for fear it would burst.

'If I didn't maintain and demand a strong sense of decorum with my team, I would have stopped people in the street to tell them how important these results were: Vatanen had broken the record in Corsica!

'For us, the Rally could have ended right there, with the results of this second stage.

'But it was in the cards that we would reach even greater heights in Corsica. Seven more stages went beautifully, and we were becoming accustomed to the car's stunning performance. Succeeding is all too easy to get used to. Ari held the lead in the Rally and Jean-Pierre Nicolas was in second place. With Peugeot ahead of Lancia and Audi, the world had turned upside down. Jean-Pierre finally ran into some trouble, with among other problems, a flat tyre, and fell behind. At the end of the second part of the event, however, Ari was still in first place.

'The next day, in Calvi, the last stage began at six in the morning, under a black sky and pouring rain. André and I had left in our 205 Turbo 16 road car, paying close attention to the time limit for assistance. We had no radio contact. Near Venaco, we met a group of spectators who told us Ari had dropped out of the Rally.

'Our hopes had run wild, and suddenly the reality of rallying struck us. I was crushed. André cried. He was convinced that a mechanical breakdown was the cause of what we had learned: Vatanen's violent spin off the road. In fact, Vatanen had been surprised by a stream of water, invisible in the dark, stormy morning. There was only one thing left to do. We had to carry Jean-Pierre to the finish, on our backs if necessary. Nicolas ended up fighting like a lion against Blomqvist and came in fourth at Ajaccio. For our first World Championship rally, the results were superb.

'That evening, part of the team came with Vatanen to the auberge of a friend, Paul, in Bastelicaccia. All of the other teams were there and gave Ari a standing ovation, paying homage, moreover, to the efforts of Peugeot-Talbot Sport.

'The results of the rally had a tremendous impact on the public. There were fans waiting at the airport in Paris to greet the Peugeot team. We were just beginning to realize how our presence had shaken up and altered the rally world.

'The press unanimously saluted our programme. Their support was due not only to the team's merits but to the efforts of the media and Public Relations Department. The Department, consisting of Jean-Claude Lefebvre, Jean-François Bouzanquet and Jacqueline Klein, had worked hard to bring the best out of our operation. Corrado Provera, the Public Relations Director, developed an innovative system of press cars and radio hook-ups that allowed journalists to keep up with the rally at close range. He was a firm believer in an open press. He wanted to give the media a chance to get out on the road and follow the thread of a spectacular sport. He achieved his goal, and this has since proved to be a wise move. Thanks to him, numerous journalists have discovered a new dimension in rallying.'

From *Peugeot 205: The Story of a Challenge* by Jean Todt
with Jean-Louis Moncet (Flammarion, 1985)

CHAPTER NINE

UNINVITED GUESTS

You might think that birds and animals (and people) would not pose a hazard for two obvious reasons: instinct and the noise of the cars would propel them in the other direction – and fast. You'd be wrong. A hare once tried to overtake Ronnie Peterson at Silverstone, snakes wriggled onto Enna, the circuit in the middle of Sicily and . . .

C.H.

Dog Run in Mexico

Bill Gavin

The temperature was down to 10 degrees F for Saturday's practice, another four-hour session lasting from 1 to 5 p.m. A dog on the track caused a perilous diversion for a while shortly after the training commenced.

[Before the race] the drivers seemed unusually disciplined as they lined up to shake hands with the President. At 12.15 thousands of balloons were released and a private plane amused the crowd by carving through them and sending many bits of deflated rubber hurtling to the ground. The warm-up lap provided its own drama – a dog was loose on the circuit once again, and Mike Spence managed to spin his Lotus.

From *Autosport* 1964

Mexican Stand-off

Jeff Hutchinson

It had been sixteen years since the last Mexican Grand Prix. Back in 1970 it was, in the words of Jackie Stewart who took part in the race, 'a farce. We should never have raced, but everyone was frightened not to race because it would have resulted in a riot. People were lining the track and even sitting on it and despite repeated appeals from Pedro Rodriguez it did little to help. The race was delayed and I remember very well the organizers finally coming to us and saying, "Everything is OK now, we have taken insurance and it doesn't matter if you kill anyone."

The race went on and Pedro Rodriguez came close to killing a young child who ran across the road, while Jackie Stewart's race was equally scary when 'I hit a great big Alsatian dog at around 140 m.p.h. which destroyed the car and came close to putting me off the road and into the crowd.'

From Autosport, 1985

Tragedy at Spa

Jim Clark

The Belgian Grand Prix in July 1960 was only the second of Jim Clark's career. The story begins with the Lotus of Innes Ireland spinning off on lap 14.
C.H.

He managed to keep some semblance of control of the car and kept it on the road as it spun round and round about five times. He was so furious with himself that he dropped it into bottom gear and let the clutch in. The wheels were spinning round and round like mad for he had let the clutch in far too quickly, but he thought he had clutch slip again. So he started fiddling round in the cockpit. Suddenly the wheels gripped when the car was pointing sharp right and he shot off the road and down the bank.

The funny thing was that you could see all this from the marks on the tracks. As you came to the corner there were these black marks criss-crossing in figures of eight all the way up the road where his car had gone round and round and then about twenty yards further on there were two black marks and then a sharp zigzag off the track and nothing else to be seen. The next lap round an irate and very steamy looking Innes had reappeared and was standing by the side of the road cursing his luck.

But if I laughed at poor Innes' plight, a few laps later I was almost put off racing completely, for I was the first to arrive on the scene at Burneville when Chris Bristow was killed in his Cooper. Chris was a very keen young driver who was one of Stirling's protégés, and he tried very hard indeed in every race in which he competed. In this race, he was driving one of the Yeoman Credit team Cooper Climaxes and was in the midst of a tremendous battle with Willie Mairesse, who was having his first Grand Prix drive in a Ferrari. Mairesse has a similar temperament to Bristow in that he went into racing hell for leather. Coming down the hill, I heard Bristow got himself over on the outside of the bend and in the wrong line. He tried to get the car across to the other side but lost control completely. The car rolled over and over, killing him instantly before throwing his body out on the circuit. Mairesse just missed being involved in this ghastly crash.

I came bustling down behind them and no one had any flags out to warn me of what was round the corner. I saw a marshal suddenly dash out on to the road, waving his arms and trying to stop me, and the next thing I saw was another marshal run from the far side of the road. I remember thinking, 'Where is he going?', and then he bent down and grabbed this thing by the side of the road. It looked just like a rag doll. It was horrible and I'll never forget the sight of his mangled body being dragged to the side. I was almost sick on the spot. I remember at the end of the race finding that my car was spattered with blood, and this put me off completely.

When a thing like this happens you vow that you will never drive in a motor race again. You honestly lose all interest in racing, and just want to get as far away from a car as possible. Then your mind begins to function again and slowly everyday things start to crowd their way back. I don't think I am callous but I have somewhat been blessed with a bad memory for such things. A day later you feel a little better, three days later and you are packing your bags for another race. You keep telling yourself that you must overcome emotion, but at their height your emotions can wield great power over your body and your mind. You can make rash decisions and you have to live with them until you regain your self control. You assume the burden in your own mind even though it was not your fault. It is a kind of guilt by association and you don't initially realize what everyone in such a predicament should realize – no matter how you feel you still have to come back to reality and the living world.

Towards the end of that tragic race, my team mate Alan Stacey was also killed by a freak accident. A bird flew into his face when he was travelling at high speed and his car went off the road. Alan was killed instantly and the car disappeared into a field, catching fire, and was completely burnt out. Thankfully I didn't see the accident or the car and I was only told about it at the end of the race. Had I seen his accident right after Bristow's I am convinced that I would have stopped there and then and retired from motor racing for good.

I had only known Alan for a year, for I met him at Le Mans in 1959. He was a terrific personality and very good company. He thought a lot about the techniques of racing and could explain things. He had tremendous guts, for very few people knew that Alan had only one leg. His right leg had been amputated below the knee in a childhood motor-bike accident, and he had an artificial leg. He always used to have a machine with a motor-cycle twist-grip throttle on the gear lever because he couldn't heel and toe. He had developed a technique of blipping the throttle with his twist grip and changing gear while using his feet on the clutch and brake.

Despite his disability, Alan was determined that nothing and nobody should stop him racing. Not only did he develop his own racing technique, but also one for hood-winking the doctors at the compulsory check-ups which were insisted on before races by some organizers. We all liked him and were prepared to assist in this ploy. When it came round to the knee reflex test, he would cross his left leg over his artificial one. The doctor would tap it, and find it satisfactory.

At this point one of us — usually Innes Ireland — would ask some pointless question to distract the doctor's attention. Alan would then perform a clever little shuffle which still left his good leg uppermost. This was always good for a chuckle among us as we filed out of the examination room.

Yes, it was a terrible race

From *Jim Clark at the Wheel* by Jim Clark (Arthur Barker, 1964)

Oh Deer Me

Nigel Roebuck

Shortly before the end of the Friday morning session, [Stefan] Johansson crested the blind brow before the Rindtkurve to find a large deer running left-to-right across the road. He swerved to avoid the unfortunate animal, but could not. The impact shattered the McLaren's nearside front suspension and the car then hit the left-hand guardrail, still travelling at close to 150 m.p.h.

Johansson, shaken and sickened, climbed from the wreckage more or less uninjured although he was later taken to hospital for X-rays and all weekend his neck was stiff, shoulders and ribs bruised and sore. All weekend, too, men with shotguns probed the foliage and forest around. Long-rumoured plans to ditch the Austrian Grand Prix from the Formula One schedule will indubitably have the support of local wildlife.

Unless there can be guarantees that such an incident will never recur, Johansson, too, would probably go along with that. 'I got a massive fright,' he said, 'and I was so lucky it hit the suspension. If it had been head-on – just a few centimetres to the right – I reckon that would have been it for me . . .'

From *Autosport* 1987

Haring off at Monza, 1969

Jackie Stewart

Shortly after I overtook Jochen [Rindt] I caught sight of a tiny movement well down the straight, a long way ahead. It was a hare. The cars approached at something like 190 m.p.h. into the curve when it suddenly darted out. First it made towards the pack of cars bearing down on it. Then it sprinted right into my path. My right front tyre hit it; there was no question of me deviating even a fraction to avoid it. I would have had an accident and taken half the starters in the Italian Grand Prix off the road with me.

My feelings were not entirely humanitarian towards the unfortunate animal, but they *were* humanitarian towards me. I went through agonies for the next few laps thinking a bone had lodged in the tyre, or its teeth were being beaten through the tread with every revolution. My acuteness of every movement of the car was sharpened and I could hardly take my eyes off the front tyre, or the rear which I watched through the mirror. The shape of the tyre is often the first warning you get of a puncture.

From *Jackie Stewart: World Champion* by Jackie Stewart and Eric Dymock
(Pelham Books, 1970)

Hogging the Limelight in Canada

Joe Saward

Things were looking up at Benetton with a good performance from a V-8-powered B190. Sandro [Nannini] worked at finding a balance on Friday morning, a process interrupted by an electrical fault. Set the fourth fastest time in the afternoon. Found a good wet set-up on Saturday morning, running with full tanks and sixth in the afternoon. Made a good start to run third behind the McLarens. Briefly led during the pit stop sequence. Pitted and rejoined only to hit a groundhog which damaged the front wing and caused a puncture.

From *Autosport* 1990

Snowmen

Paul Evans

Despite this being his first Monte Carlo Rally, Colin McRae had entered [the] Burzet [stage] in second position. However, although [François] Delecour was running just two minutes ahead of him when he arrived at the same corner that had claimed [Armin] Schwartz, McRae also saw no tyre tracks through the fresh snow which was callously positioned on the apex. Likewise, although the Scot had the corner cautioned in his notes, he wasn't expecting the sudden loss of grip and he had little chance of keeping his Subaru Impreza 555 on the road. It cleared the ditch Schwartz was still trying to get out of, and he lost over forty minutes trying to get back on the road, eventually completing the stage in 164th position.

'There were about fifteen spectators standing there with shovels, it was obvious they'd just shovelled snow on the road,' said an understandably angry McRae. 'I bet it was the same bastards that came to dig me out because they all had shovels as well.'

From Motoring News 1994

A Lot of Bull

Jim Clark is surrounded by photographers and receives his trophy from a local beauty queen, but Denny Hulme wanders off along the back of the pits and seems totally unconcerned about the World Championship he has just won. The crowd begins to drift away, and the drivers pile into their borrowed Renaults and head for the prize-giving, somewhat daunted by the fact that it is being held in a bull ring and they have been told they will have to 'fight' for their prizes.

Autocar 1967 after the Mexican Grand Prix

They were very small bulls. Calves, really.
Denny Hulme

CHAPTER TEN

JUST ME?

All But My Life

Ken Purdy

I don't know what makes me go on. People often ask me, do you think of giving up racing when someone's killed, a close friend perhaps? Yes, surely. You must think, there but for the grace of God . . . but you hope of course that you have a little more experience or a little more ability or a little more luck or a little more something, and so it's not going to happen to you. If I were killed racing I wouldn't want any driver to give up racing or even pull out of the race it happened in . . . it's not going to do me any good. [Talking to Walter Cronkite of the Columbia Broadcasting System in the United States, Moss said: 'I never say to anybody: "See you next week." If they say it, I say: "Well, I hope so."']
I understand racing, I know it may happen, and if I knew any way to lessen the chance I would do it – as I think I do now. I race as safely as I know how – with the possible exception that I drive cars that are more likely to fail than others, they are less robust, and in that I'm foolish, and I know it. But other factors enter there – my wish to drive British non-factory cars, and so on. . . .

But there's no point in looking into the past. I won't do it. I will not allow myself to live in the past, not the slightest bit. The only way I know what I did yesterday is to look it up in my diary. I keep a full diary, and I do it every night no matter what. If I'm conscious, I make an entry in my diary. If someone's in bed with me, I just say:

I've already discussed Ken but I'd like to explain the significance of our book *All But My Life* from which this extract comes. The book is beautifully written and easy to read. I hate reading galley proofs, although I must confess I find it easier reading about myself than other people! Ken was the first writer who took the subject of a racing driver away from concentrating entirely on the sport. *All But My Life* isn't about motor racing – it's about a person's life, and that person happens to be in racing. The book was the first that I know of which didn't concentrate on a blow-by-blow account of races and in that sense was ahead of its time.

S.M.

'Excuse me, sweetie, while I write a couple of things in m'book.' And do you know, sometimes I find it difficult to remember, at night, what I've done that day, never mind yesterday? I upset my friends. I said to David Haynes: 'You must see this terrific film,' and he said: 'Look, we saw it together last Thursday.' I said to him: 'My God, next year you must come with me to South Africa' and he said: 'You know, I was the one with you in Africa' . . . he understands, it's just that there's so much going on today and tomorrow and next week, and I *must* think that way, because there are so many heartbreaks for me in racing that if I worried about yesterday . . . as it is now, I can lose a race, I can lose the world championship on Sunday and I can be out enjoying myself on Monday, and I *mean* enjoying myself. Nothing is sillier than this notion that drivers have a death-wish. Most of them enjoy life infinitely more than the average man, and it's nothing to do with eat, drink and be merry for tomorrow we die, either. [Oddly, the Marquis de Portago said the same thing to me, in almost precisely the same words.] I've been accused of living a twenty-nine hour day and I plead guilty, with pleasure. I live for the day.

You could say it's an odd life, Ken, and I'd agree, but it's like a story I remember your telling me in a letter a long time ago, about the man who was told the roulette game was crooked, and he said: 'Yes, I know – but it's the only game in town.'

In the end, one has one's work – the only game in town. I wouldn't want any other work. Obviously the major satisfaction in my life is racing, and I enjoy it even when I'm frustrated, sometimes I think maybe *most* when I'm frustrated; I think, I can't damned well win, I've lost five laps in the pit, it's impossible to win now, mathematically impossible, but then I begin to think, well, my God, even if I can't win I'm going to damned well go, and then I can enjoy really fast motoring, for the exhilaration of it and because I'm trying to prove something to myself; they may have five laps on me, but I'm going to take one back, and the lap record is always there to be broken. . . . [Here Stirling is, eerily, describing precisely the situation he was to be in four days later at Goodwood.]

Another thing, you know, you say to yourself, let's really get going, let's try to drive the perfect lap, all the way around and not one mistake, not one mile an hour slow or ten revs down, and this to me is an interesting thing. Often I turn to myself and say, well, let's try to turn one perfect lap. Invariably something somewhere isn't just quite right, and you say, well, that's finished, now let's try another, try again. I've never made a perfect lap, although people have said I have.

'You go through a corner absolutely flat out, right on the ragged edge, but absolutely in control, on your own line to an inch, the car just hanging there, the tyres as good as geared to the road, locked to it, and yet you know that if you ask one more mile an hour of the car, if you put another five pounds of side-thrust on it, you'll lose the whole flaming vehicle as surely as if someone had smeared the road with six inches of grease; so you stay just this side of that fraction of extra speed, that fraction of extra weight that could ruin everything, and perhaps kill you to boot, you're on top of it all, and the exhilaration, the thrill is tremendous, you say to yourself, all right, you bastards, top that one, match it, even, and you feel like a painter who has just put the last brush-stroke on a canvas, after years of trying to catch a certain expression – it's rewarding. And you must grant that it's not monotonous. No art can be monotonous, and I believe that driving, as practised by some very few people in the world, is an art-form, and is related to ballet. I believe that when someone like Alfred Neubauer uses the term 'artist' in relation to a driver, he knows what he's talking about. Driving is certainly like ballet in that it is all discipline, rhythm, movement. I've had people tell me it's a mad thing to say that driving can be an art. After all, we can all of us drive, can't we? Of course, and we can all sing, and write, and most of us can dance, and draw some kind of picture, but some do it a little better than others, that's all.

I don't say that driving is an art-form *wholly* comparable with ballet. Certainly it's not creative in the sense that choreography is creative or that the composition of music for ballet is creative, but I think that in *execution* it is comparable. Ballet is movement, isn't it, rhythmic and disciplined movement, gracefully performed . . . the man doesn't do it, the driver, he makes the car do it . . . of course, to see it you must be at the right corner at the right moment. The straights don't count, the straights are just there to join the corners. But in the corners there is something to see, sometimes.

'The straight is the place to listen,' I said to Stirling. 'A few weeks ago I was listening to a race in France on the radio, and cars were going past the microphone, and I said to somebody who was with me: "That Ferrari is in F-sharp" – and of course I was told it was an absurd idea, I was out of my mind. And a couple of weeks later Anthony Hopkins, the composer, you know who he is, was on BBC, and he was talking about the musical sound cars make passing a given point. They're all quite different. Of course they have to be wound right out, the faster the engine's turning, the better; and there's that up and down as they come and go past a point, you know, the Doppler Effect. Of course you hear none of it, driving.'

'No . . . but I've sat out a few races, don't forget!'

'I have an idea for a ballet, the central theme, a thesis: "I don't know where I'm going, but I will be there ahead of you."'

Stirling said: 'At first, that sounds funny, but there's nothing funny about it, nothing at all.'

'No, there isn't.'

'In any case,' Stirling said, 'driving is a dance, in a way. And it's like skiing, too, very much like skiing . . . the same, but never the same, never monotonous . . . monotony in life would drive me mad. I can't bear inactivity; I get disheartened sometimes when I stop moving. If you turned to me right now and said: "We've finished, you're to go home and sit down and think for a while", I wouldn't dream of doing it. I would find that very bad. I fill every moment. When you leave me here Ken Gregory and some people are coming for a meeting. After that I'm going out to dinner. Then I'm going dancing. [Moss has been known to dance from early evening until dawn, almost without stopping.] I don't know how long I'll stay out, but one thing I'm sure of, when I go to bed tonight I hope to be very tired, because I don't want to think, I don't *like* thinking, unless it's about a specific solvable problem. As far as life is concerned, and what life is going to offer me, I find it terribly depressing. When I look at the future I find it terribly depressing!'

He spoke so vehemently, and it was so unlike anything I had heard him say before, that I was surprised. 'Do you really, Stirling?' I said.

'Yes, terribly, because I can't see, in the ultimate, what there can be of happiness. I know that to some people achievement in business, in work, is happiness. To me it's not, it's a fulfilment, but not happiness, or not necessarily happiness. It's a pleasure, but pleasure isn't happiness. My idea of happiness seems Utopian to me and it may seem absurd to you, so absurd I'm surprised I can bring myself to tell you, but it is to be married, and have two or three children, and a house in the country, if you like, and to go away for two weeks on holiday – and most of all, most importantly, to be able to *accept* that life as happiness. Do you understand? To be able to *accept* it, that's the whole heart of the matter. I'm trying to describe an attitude, I think, more than a way of life. A matter of *balance*. I know what it is, but I can't accept it, not at the moment. I'm hoping that with maturity I will be able to, or that at least some form of compromise with it will be possible. I'm not unhappy. I've had some tremendously good times. But right now I'm in a state of suspended animation, in a transition period which is tolerable, and which keeps me from being depressed. . . . I dance, I run about, I do a bit of designing and this and that, it's activity, I keep my finger in the dike, it's not going to patch the bloody thing but at least it's stopping the water pouring in. I'm waiting for maturity to come to me, and I'm doing what I can to bring it. I don't know if one ever feels happiness, or if contentment is the maximum we can hope for. As I said, I'm not unhappy. If I were to be killed tomorrow I wouldn't feel that thirty-two of my thirty-two years had been unhappy. . . .'

We talked, and the thin brown tape, shuffling through the recorder-heads, silently took it down. Dusk sifted out of a wet London sky. We had given ourselves three hours, and at five minutes short of seven the tape ran out. He made me a drink. He couldn't find a bottle-opener for the orange squash he wanted and I fiddled the top off with my knife. We talked about some other people for a few minutes. He telephoned for a taxi. I told the driver to go to Charing Cross. As I opened the cab door I looked back. Moss was standing in the middle of the little room, looking through the window. I waved to him. He waved, and moved away across the room. He looked grim and, somehow, weirdly, sheathed all in grey, or white. I was suddenly and inexplicably immersed in a crushing sadness and in pity for him. The cab moved away. I felt frightened, and very nearly ill. I remembered the only time such a thing had happened to me before, ten years ago, on a hot July day in Connecticut, again for no reason – except that at that moment, 1500 miles away, as I was to know later, a doctor was saying of my son: 'He may live forty-eight hours, but I doubt it.'

By next morning I had put all that out of my mind. I was in Belgium on Easter Monday and I didn't see Stirling Moss again until early June, when I went to the Atkinson Morley Hospital. I stayed a couple of hours. Judy Carne did a scalding imitation of her Hollywood manicurist phoning a boy-friend. I told the old story about Beatrice Lillie, Lady Peel, and the butcher's wife. The tape-recorder man came, tacking shyly into the room against a gale of laughter. I left.

'Come back soon,' Stirling said. 'I'm not going to hang about here for ever.'

From All But My Life Stirling Moss Face to Face with Ken Purdy
(William Kimber, 1963)

Hawthorn and Moss

John Blunsden

I have always been aware that while journalists are entitled to voice opinions they should never indulge in personal bias. However, I recall that back in the Fifties it was extremely difficult to be both a 'Stirling Moss' and a 'Mike Hawthorn' fan. Though united by their exceptional talent and in their burning ambition to knock 'all those bloody foreigners' off the motor-racing perch, they went about their business in such sharply contrasting styles that it was easy to identify with one or other of them, but very difficult to do so with both.

I've known John for years and years and he's one of the stalwarts of motor racing who sees things clearly and in their true context. He was always a good, solid writer who made sure he crossed his t's and dotted his i's, whether reporting for *The Times* or in his books. He respects the subject, and that alone demonstrates his love for it.
S.M.

The fact that I found myself more comfortable in the Moss camp probably dates back to one evening in 1951 – long before I was earning a living by putting words on paper, and at a time when I knew little of Mike Hawthorn other than that he had been driving a pair of prewar Riley sportscars very quickly indeed – when I first spoke to Stirling on the telephone (a mutual friend had given me his number). The details of the conversation, which must have gone on for more than an hour, are irrelevant, although they revolved around the possible purchase of a 500cc Formula Three car. What matters, and what impressed me so much at the time, was that a very busy and already highly successful racing driver was freely prepared to give so much of his time to a complete stranger, painstakingly and patiently offering the benefit of his knowledge and experience. His enthusiasm for the sport came pouring down the telephone, but equally impressive was the care with which he explained in great detail the various pitfalls and how to avoid them.

Through that rewarding and wide-ranging conversation, I was immediately convinced that Stirling's spectacular success so early in his career had been achieved not just through his exceptional virtuosity as a racing driver, but also because of his attention to all the extraneous factors which can impinge on the level of a driver's success in motor racing, things which so often were either unidenti-fied or ignored by other drivers.

He had set out as a teenager determined to prove to his parents that it was possible to make the grade as a professional driver at a time when racing was still essentially an amateur activity, and in pursuing this it became clear to me that he was applying a level of professionalism which extended far beyond its purely monetary con-notation.

At that time, remember, Britain was woefully short of competi-tive racing cars at the upper level, so it was essential that the perform-ance disadvantage of 'racing British' should be reduced by whatever legal means were available. Stirling voiced the opinion that a racing driver owed it to himself – and to the people he worked with and the public – to maximize the potential which his driving ability offered him, and this meant achieving the ultimate standards of personal as well as technical preparedness.

Whatever he was driving, he would seek to be that much better prepared than anyone else when he lined up on the starting grid. It was a level of dedication which caused a certain amount of amuse-ment in those days – motor racing still had much of the 'Tally-ho' atmosphere left over from the fighter pilots of the Second World War – and what has long since become standard practice in profes-sional motor racing was even regarded in some quarters as being slightly unsporting. Yet when the prospects of success at the highest level seemed so remote, Stirling's self-imposed standards of pre-race preparedness seemed to me to make a great deal of sense, and they tended to become the yardstick by which I began to judge the performance of others, including, in due course, Mike Hawthorn.

Like many people, I first heard of Hawthorn when I read of his exploits at the wheel of the two Riley sportscars, and then, of course, he hit the headlines early in 1952 with his first drives at Goodwood in Bob Chase's Formula Two Cooper-Bristol. He had already been christened 'The Farnham Flyer' by the media by the time I first came into contact with him at Silverstone a few weeks later, and I remem-ber clearly the minutes prior to his heat in the *Daily Express* Inter-national Trophy race. Inevitably, he and his car had become a centre of interest in the paddock, but I sensed he was finding it a distraction and couldn't wait to drive away from the crowd on to the track, where he could concentrate on the task ahead.

I watched his race from the inside of Woodcote Corner, and within two or three laps it was clear what all the fuss had been about. It was not just that Hawthorn was quick, very quick, it was that he looked even quicker. With the skinny tyres of the day, a long, fast, right-hander like Woodcote called for a lot of work on the steering wheel if you were really trying, and Hawthorn was certainly trying. His tall frame seemed to overflow out of the low-sided cockpit of the Cooper and his arms were pumping like an express train each time he swept through the corner, holding his car on the limit of adhesion. It was wonderful stuff to watch. I recall that he won that heat, but then had some sort of trouble in the final, a long pit-stop putting him out of the running, but though he went home empty-handed, no one had matched him for entertainment value that day.

While Moss's determination to 'drive British' whatever the odds was putting a brake on his own career, Hawthorn's leapt ahead when he responded to Enzo Ferrari's offer for the 1953 season, recognizing that it was the best possible passport to success in Formula One, as he was to prove in the French Grand Prix at Reims in that nail-biting photo-finish victory over Juan-Manuel Fangio's Maserati.

Over the next year or two, Moss had to work harder than Hawthorn for his success, not because of any deficiency of driving skill – on the contrary – but because of some of his decisions off the track, which all too often left him to fight his battles in inferior machinery. Then the tables were turned when Moss was invited to join Fangio in the Mercedes-Benz team, and Hawthorn began to struggle with the early Vanwall.

It was at this point that I thought Hawthorn's inconsistency compared with Moss began to become more noticeable. On occasions his driving would have a magical quality, but then would come a lack-lustre performance which the more cynical would put down to a manifestation of his pre-race partying and nocturnal activities. However, it has to be said that this was not always a fair accusation because what was not widely known at the time was that Hawthorn – who had been condemned by some sections of the media for avoiding his National Service – was not even eligible to serve because he was medically unfit, a fact which he chose not to reveal.

Nevertheless, I long felt that Mike, in enjoying life in the broadest sense, did his racing career no favours, and I think it was not entirely down to the cars they were driving that from 1956 to 1958, the year when Hawthorn narrowly beat Moss to the World Championship, he was able to score just one Grand Prix victory to Moss's nine, four of which came in Hawthorn's Championship season.

From the start, Hawthorn had been a fun-loving extrovert, but not everyone responded to his sometimes outrageous pranks; not that this seemed to worry him because I never thought he was overendowed with diplomacy. Also, towards the end of his all-too-short career I felt that even the humour and the pranks were sometimes a little contrived, that deep down he was not enjoying life quite as much as first impressions might have suggested.

It is widely known that he was emotionally crushed by the 1955 Le Mans accident and by the inevitable probing afterwards into the whys and wherefores of motor racing's biggest ever tragedy, in which he had been one of the drivers closest to the centre of the catastrophe. Thankfully, I was not there, but it has always struck me as cruelly ironic that the disaster should have occurred at the end of one of the finest demonstrations of sportscar racing between two artists at the wheel – Hawthorn in his Jaguar and Fangio in his Mercedes – ever seen at the circuit.

I believe that even after he had come to accept, as so many had insisted, that he should not shoulder the blame for what had been a classic motor-racing accident, he turned ever more closely to those who were part of his 'set' and raised the barriers that little bit higher to those who were not. His great pal Peter Collins ('Mon Ami Mate') was, I found, much more approachable, and though no wallflower himself was, I think, a little exasperated at times by Mike's more extreme behaviour.

Certainly, Collins' death at the Nürburgring in 1958 upset Hawthorn greatly, and it removed much of the enjoyment which his forthcoming World Championship might otherwise have yielded him. Given all the circumstances, it was not, perhaps, so surprising that he should decide to retire from racing rather than go on to defend his title in 1959. All the pleasure had gone out of it.

A few weeks later I was in Monaco covering the Monte Carlo Rally for *Motoring News* when the news filtered through that Mike had died in a road accident near Guildford. I can remember it as if it were yesterday. The first reaction was disbelief, then something bordering on annoyance that he would do something so foolhardy; without even knowing the facts, there was already the potentially dangerous assumption that he had done something wrong because it seemed to fit the image. (Years later – by a coincidence this was also in Monte Carlo – I related this feeling to Jean Howarth, Mike's fiancée and now Mrs Innes Ireland, and she rebuked me, saying that in all the time she had known him Mike had never scared her on the road. She was so convincing that I had to believe her.)

That day in 1959 I was thankful I was not working for a daily newspaper. Less fortunate was my future business partner Alan Brinton, who at that time was motoring correspondent of the *News Chronicle*. He knew the paper would have been trying to contact him so we rushed back to his hotel hoping to pool our combined memory bank (covering a rally, neither of us had any racing reference material with us). Sure enough, the paper had been on, and I think we had about twenty minutes for Alan to compile some material and phone it across.

Working for a weekly, of course, I had more time, and in any case the editorial team back in London would tackle the main story while I concentrated on the rally. But afterwards, I tapped out a piece for our 'Culpeper' column, which I repeat here because I think it accurately portrays what Mike meant to so many of us at the time of his death:

> For those of us who were in Monte Carlo last week, the first thing we heard was the question, passed by word of mouth, 'Have you heard about Mike?' The horrible news that followed shocked us, at first into disbelief. It just couldn't be true. It must be some garbled rumour – perhaps he has had a bit of a prang and is injured.
>
> All too soon we were to know that it was no rumour – that Mike was dead. Even then it took a long time before the full impact of the tragedy went home. Never again to see and enjoy the Hawthorn bonhomie around the circuits and in the club rooms was something not easy to grasp. For although he had vacated the cockpit, he was to remain a familiar figure wherever there was the sport of driving or talking about motor cars.
>
> In a way, we were proud when we saw the headlines in the eagerly awaited British papers the following morning. No event, even the end of the war, had carried such heavy print, and invariably he was identified not as 'Hawthorn' or 'World Champion', but simply as 'Mike'. To the whole country, it was like losing one of the family, and the papers paid the appropriate tribute.

Without doubt, Hawthorn was *the* personality of the race tracks, and his *joie de vivre* had a magnetic quality that instinctively drew people to him. He was the sort of character on which people tried – but never really succeeded – to model themselves. For Mike was always the individualist – he conformed to no set pattern, indeed he disliked convention for its own sake, just as he abhored fakes in any guise.

He was the chap who loved to 'have a real bash', even when the odds were stacked heavily against him, and some of his best drives during the past eight years are not even featured in the record books. He invariably gave of his best when fighting at close quarters, for 'pressing on' was the natural way for him to go motor racing.

Both on and off the track, he had to endure great tragedy during his all-too-short career, and many people did not realize that his overflowing sense of fun hid a far from happy young man, whose emotions had been severely strained.

Those of us who knew a little (few knew all) of the 'story behind the story' learnt to forgive his occasional outbursts of abuse, bad temper and non-co-operation. For even then, his steadfast insistence on doing and saying what he liked, regardless of the consequences, was most refreshing. Whatever Mike said, you knew he meant it, unless, of course, you were the victim of his tremendous wit and sense of fun.

As a driver, he was already lost to us, and who knows, time may prove that in that respect he was just about replaceable. But as a man, as a character, as a tremendous personality, there could never be another Mike Hawthorn. Long shall we mourn and remember you, 'Mon Ami Mate!'

Yes, he was quite a character, was Britain's first World Champion.

From *Champions!* by John Blunsden and Christopher Hilton (MRP, 1993)

Poet and Peasant

Godfrey Smith

I first began to regret the idea somewhere near Haslemere. It was a pleasant sunny afternoon and I was bowling along between stately Surrey oaks in my Morris Minor at a steady forty miles an hour. The notion that I should shortly be travelling nearly a hundred miles an hour faster seemed incredible, and not a little dismaying.

While what follows is self-explanatory, I'd like to point out that Godfrey, a noted contributor to the *Sunday Times*, wrote on many subjects, which gave him perspective for what I did to him.
S.M.

I had never travelled very fast in a car before. I had once driven a Renault flat out on the road to Le Mans, but even that amounted to only a wretched eighty-four miles an hour. Despite a mild interest in motor sport acquired through family enthusiasms, I was and am a very average driver – in the colourful parlance of the racing fraternity I am a *peasant*.

Nevertheless, I was excited by the possibilities for a writer in the limit of any human experience. And one day over a lunch a few months ago Stirling Moss offered to take me out with him. It was spring and the idea seemed, at that distance, highly agreeable.

He commands an annual income a prime minster would be glad to own. His name is a household word. 'Who do you think you are – Stirling Moss?' is part of the ordinary driver's vocabulary of abuse. He is a schoolboy's hero, one of the dream parts played by the Walter Mitty in every man. He is also a master craftsman, still striving for that last tantalizing degree of skill which will bring him as near perfection as man will ever get.

He was to drive me as fast as he liked in an open DB3'S' works car. It had been built only this year, and had raced four times. Driven by Moss and [Peter] Collins, it had come second at Le Mans, and had won the three-litre category. Moss had driven it to victory at Oulton Park only a few weeks before.

It would do about 135 m.p.h. down the Lavant straight at Goodwood. If you felt inclined to buy one, it would cost you £3,901.

Lloyds had sportingly bet me 2,000 to 1 that I would neither kill myself nor meet with a number of other unpleasant eventualities.

The first thing Moss asked after he had shaken hands was: 'Did you bring a helmet? No. We'll find you one. The visor will help your eyes, and is any case it's sensible.'

He decided to take the DB3'S' for a few trial laps. He leaped in, pressed the starter and roared off round Madgwick Corner.

Goodwood deserted is a very different place from Goodwood *en fête*. The stands seemed empty and forlorn and there was no one as far as the eye could see. No one, that is, but the three men Aston Martins had sent with the car. Two were mechanics, and the third was Roy Parnell, the racing superintendent and nephew of the famous driver. I strolled over to them.

Parnell is a quiet pipe-smoking Midlander. 'Have you ever been fast before?' he enquired. I confessed that I had not. 'Ah, well,' he said philosophically. 'I expect you'll get a bit of a shaking.'

We heard Moss busily negotiating Lavant Corner on the other side of the track, his gear changes like some angry hornet in flight. He came thundering down the Lavant straight and into Woodcote Corner. Coming out he grazed the earth at the side of the track, and a puff of dust rose into the air. The mechanics laughed appreciatively. 'He's really trying today.' They looked me over in a slightly cynical way. 'Don't you wish you hadn't come?' one asked sympathetically.

Moss came in after three laps. He was wearing blue overalls and a pair of mocassins. In ordinary clothes he always seems uneasy. Now he looked in his element. The mechanics told me to tuck the ends of my trousers into my socks as if I was going cycling. I noticed with a pang of embarrassment that my socks were now revealed up to the world as a violent buttercup yellow.

I was wearing a pair of suede boots, a grey lounge suit, and on to this already incongruous ensemble I lowered the helmet they had found for me. Because of the size of my head, I could fasten the strap only in the last hole. I looked like an adipose [fat!] Martian. Moss looked me up and down and grinned broadly. 'You brave devil,' he said ironically. 'If you want to say anything,' he said, 'do this.' He waved his hand palm downwards. 'I'll try to hear.' He started the engine and we were away.

To be frank, my first conscious thought was that Moss had gone berserk. He hurried the car into Madgwick Corner at such speeds that I was sure we would turn over. There was an appalling shriek from the tyres and the first black acrid stench of the rubber assailed me.

On that first lap I saw almost nothing. I did not exactly close my eyes, but I will admit to squinting. I was dimly aware that Moss was using his arms in a kind of legerdemain. Even in that first corner, I had been appalled to see him suddenly steer the wrong way, that is left into a right-handed corner. It was done so quickly that I might almost have imagined it. Later he told me that he probably used as much left lock as right to get round a corner at that speed.

When you are driving normally, the road unfolds before you in a pleasing continuous flow. Trees, posts and pillars mark your orderly progression.

But now I was presented only with disrupted snatches of experience. It was as if, instead of seeing a film unwind, I was watching an expert shuffler zip through a pack of cards. The road seemed to leap at me on one side, then the other, in random pieces of brute sensation. The line that marked the edge wriggled by us like some frantic white serpent.

It was during the first lap that we left the road altogether and ploughed through the grass. My weight had led Moss into a very slight and very rare miscalculation. He knew a long time before most people that he had made a mistake and, as he afterwards explained, he decided to cut his losses. Instead of fighting the car round the bend, as the ordinary motorist would do, he turned the other way and elected to go up on the grass.

The odd thing was that this did not frighten me in any special way. I was already in the grip of a vast and complex reaction.

It was compounded of strangeness, awe, exhilaration and panic. At first, my brain was only telegraphing urgent animal messages from my outraged body. It was rather like that moment when the dentist's drill hits the nerve. The body simply cannot believe the affront, and rebels, seizing the mind captive and clamouring for relief.

The moment soon passed. Round Lavant, which is nearly a hairpin, I lost all sense of space and direction. The world seemed to spin round us as if we were the centre of a pre-Copernican system geared up a million times too fast. And then we were into the Lavant straight.

Moss threw the car down the track with what seemed to me maniacal recklessness. The wind had almost blown my coat off. It had risen up under my armpits and the sleeves were up to my elbows. I was hanging on, not as if my life depended on it, but because I had convinced myself that it literally did depend on it. We seemed to be hammering a wall of solid air.

Just before the pits there is a chicane – a wall built out halfway across the track to form a man-made obstacle. Moss hurled the car round in what seemed to me roughly the right direction and then, to my horror, when the bricks and mortar were just about to go by on the left, he seemed to steer suddenly straight into them.

I hastily snatched my left hand off the cowling for fear of breaking my knuckles. There were certainly only inches to spare. Moss grinned. It was only when he did exactly the same thing in each successive lap that I began to appreciate the precision of his driving.

By about the third lap I had relaxed slightly from the condition of apparent rigor mortis into which I had frozen. Moss lifted a thumb as if to ask if I was all right, and I halfheartedly lifted a thumb in reply. I tried desperately to analyse my emotions, to collect the material for that piece of writing I had spoken of so airily.

Racing drivers are often criticized for being inarticulate. 'It's just a drive' is all they will say after a hair-raising race. In fact, the experience is eventually indescribable. It is in a different bracket of experience – a separate octave of sensation. You can know it or not know it. The words to describe it fail you.

We came into the pits after five laps. I asked Moss a number of questions and he answered them at length. To illustrate what he had done, he took me round the course in his Standard Ten and went through the whole thing again in slow motion.

We cruised along at forty miles an hour. It was delicious; like breaking into a guilty walk after running for ten miles in a cross-country race.

Parnell had written down our lap time. We had gone round the second lap in one minute thirty-eight and six-tenths seconds. Moss would have expected to do two seconds less without the encumbrance of my weight. The lap record for our sort of car stands in the name of Mike Hawthorn. He went four seconds quicker, but that was during a race and in a Ferrari.

As we cruised past Woodcote Moss pointed to the verge where

he had thrown up the dust going round by himself. 'There ought to be a wall there,' he said, 'but as there isn't we go over a little. It's poetic licence.'

Poetic licence! – it seemed an odd phrase to me. And yet, I reflected in the harmony and grace of what they do there is something not far removed from poetry.

Moss waved goodbye and drove off to Chichester. I dawdled towards home. Near Guildford there was a sudden roar, and the Aston Martin went by, driven by one of the mechanics.

I watched its red lights winking into the distance. It seemed immeasurably remote from the modest progress of my Morris Minor. Yet I felt a tenuous sympathy for those vanishing lights. A poet and a peasant may have little in common, but if their lives have overlapped by only a few minutes, it is enough.

From *Aston Martin: The Story of a Sports Car* compiled by Dudley Coram
(MRP, 1957)

Pockets in the Pockets

Innes Ireland

This great Scotsman died in 1993. No anthology of motor sport could be complete without a glimpse of his view of life, his devil-may-care approach which seems — and is — from another era altogether. We were doing some car testing of Porsches at their track at Stuttgart and Innes wrote a piece about it for the American magazine *Road and Track*. He couldn't get over my travel bag.

S.M.

Ireland drove in fifty Grands Prix from 1959 to 1966, and gave Lotus their first win, at Watkins Glen, USA, in 1961. It's fascinating to compare his reactions to being a passenger in a hot car with those of Godfrey Smith.

C.H.

I have never been at my best in testing of this nature, nor even in official practice for a race. From the Porsche figures it looks as if I learn circuits and cars more slowly than Stirling. We discussed gears and exiting revs, and I found Stirling was taking 5th on the straight in the non-turbo whereas I was holding 4th and just hitting the rev limiter at my braking point. I tried 5th a couple of times but was slower on both occasions. When I queried the use of 5th, Stirl said, 'Well, it saves a bit of petrol!'

I had to laugh. 'But Stirling, you're not having to pay for the bloody petrol!' Of course, what he meant was this would be his tactic in a long-distance race.

He drove me around the circuit in the Turbo to illustrate his lines, braking points and so on, and I must say sitting beside him at racing speeds is a lot less nerve-racking than sitting beside him in city traffic! He is incredibly smooth and still able to keep up a running commentary on what he's doing. He was always a master at late braking, and rolling off speed even well into the corner, and I think this is where I was losing on his. In one corner where I eased on the brakes Stirling just lifted the throttle momentarily without touching the brakes!

The proof of our differing sensitivity and approach became clear on the return journey. [At the airport] Stirl dived into that amazing bag of his and with paper all over the place, calculator in hand, he produced a set of figures. In the non-turbo my average times were 1.35 sec down on him. I was much closer in the Turbo, my average time just 0.40 secs down.

It was a very revealing day where my only consolation was that whereas Stirling did his best times early in each session, mine were coming down progressively until I came in. But then Stirling was always a hard man to catch!

We were just finishing a cup of coffee when our flight was called. Leaping to his feet, gathering up all his bits and pieces. Stirling suddenly exclaimed, 'Hey, Innes, have you seen my glasses?'

'No,' I replied, 'when did you last have them?'

He was already digging into the innards of that amazing bag – again – papers and all manner of things littering the table. 'They're not here,' he said, patting down all his pockets.

'Aren't they in that dinky little handbag of yours?' I asked, already sensing the beginnings of panic.

'No, I never put them in there.' By now the search was becoming frantic. I even started feeling through my pockets, hoping against hope that I hadn't picked them up by mistake. Stirling's amazing bag was really getting a hammering now! Still no sign of the glasses, the departure area now devoid of our fellow travellers.

'Are you sure they're not in that handbag, Stirl? They've got to be somewhere.'

'No. I never put them in that bag,' he repeated, a tone of desperation creeping into his voice.

'Well, they don't seem to be any place else, Stirl. It's worth a quick look,' I pleaded.

Unzipping the little bag, the first thing he came across were his specs! With a muttered 'I don't know how they got in there' he stuffed everything back into the amazing pockets of the amazing bag and we ran like jackrabbits for the plane.

From *Road and Track*, July 1985

Innes now hatched a plot to have some fun with *Road and Track*. He suggested that I wrote a letter to the editor about his article – with the understanding that he would help me with the letter so that I could use his writing talents. I agreed.
S.M.

Dear Sir,

I can't deny there was some confusion over the whereabouts of my spectacles. I was also impressed that Innes was accurate in pointing out that in both the turbo and non-turbo Porsche 944s we tested I was quicker than he was! In an effort to improve my packing and reduce confusion at critical moments I would like to inform you that I have purchased a new bag.

Like most bags it has a central compartment but it is the pockets that make it interesting. On both sides there are two pockets, an outside one and an inside one. The outside one has a pocket on the inside and another one on the outside, and the inside pocket has a pocket on the outside and another on the inside. The same thing is repeated on the other side of the bag, all with zip fasteners, but the outside pocket on this side, as well as having a pocket on the inside as well as the outside, has another pocket on the outside of the outside pocket which doesn't have a zip and is for newspapers or a magazine and suchlike.

That in itself is a lot of pockets, but if you're still with me, there are other pockets, one at each end of the bag. These are fairly straightforward pockets, useful for holding other small bags such as the one I never put my spectacles in, but they do have small pockets on their insides although none on their outsides . . .

(signed) Stirling Moss

Road and Track used the letter! S.M.

Mille Miglia 1955

Denis Jenkinson

On 1 May motor-racing history was made, for Stirling Moss won the 1,000-mile Mille Miglia, the first time in twenty-two years that this has been achieved by a British driver, and I had the very great privilege of sitting beside him throughout this epic drive.

But let us go back to the beginning, for this win was not a fluke on the spur of the moment; it was the result of weeks, even months, of preparation and planning. My enthusiasm for the Mille Miglia race goes back many years, among the reasons being the fact that it is permissible to carry a passenger, for this event is for all types of road-going cars, from family saloons to Grand Prix-type racing/sports cars, and when I had my first taste of the lure of the Mille Miglia as a competitor last year, with Abecassis in the HWM, I soon set about making plans for the 1955 event.

Regular *Motor Sport* readers will remember that last year I enthused over a little private dice that Moss gave me in a Maserati, and at the time I mentioned to him my desire to run in the Mille Miglia again. Then in September, while in discussion with the American driver John Fitch, we came to the decision that the only way a non-Italian could win the Mille Miglia was by applying science. At the time he was hoping to be in the official Mercedes-Benz team for the event, and we had long talks about ways in which the driver could use a passenger as a mechanical brain, to remove the responsibility of learning the circuit. When it is realized that the race is over a thousand miles of ordinary, unprepared Italian road, the only concession to racing being that all traffic is removed from the roads for the duration of the race, and the way through towns is lined with straw bales, it will be appreciated

Jenks is a genuine eccentric and a highly intelligent man. I asked him to come on the Mille Miglia with me because it was easy to find people who were prepared to be driven fast but difficult to get somebody who could keep their head at speeds of 170, 180 m.p.h. and give me instructions — acting as a sort of guide dog with the pace notes, was terribly important. Although he was a well-known reporter for *Motor Sport* I also knew he'd been World Champion three times in side-cars. To do that you've obviously got to be reasonably clear-thinking under pressure. A few years after the Mille Miglia I said to Jenks, 'Will you come with me for a try-out in an MG?' and he said, 'No, no.' I wondered why. He said he'd be scared stiff — his philosophy was that if it was a car he could drive, he could drive it as well as you. If, however, you went up a stratum to the Mercedes-Benz 300SLR he was quite content to be a passenger. That sort of thinking makes him unique.

S.M.

that the task of one man learning every corner, every swerve, gradient, hummock, brow and level-crossing is nigh impossible. Even the top Italian drivers, such as Taruffi, Maglioli, Castellotti and so on, only know sections of the route perfectly, and all the time they must concentrate on remembering what lies round the next corner, or over the next brow.

During the last winter, as is well known, Moss joined the Mercedes-Benz team and the firm decided that it would not be possible for Fitch to drive for them in the Mille Miglia, though he would be in the team for Le Mans, so all our plans looked like being of no avail. Then, just before Christmas, a telephone call from Moss invited me to be his passenger in the Mille Miglia in a Mercedes-Benz 300SLR, an invitation which I promptly accepted, John Fitch having sportingly agreed that it would be a good thing for me to try out our plans for beating the Italians with Moss as driver.

When I met Moss early in the new year to discuss the event I already had some definite plan of action. Over lunch it transpired that he had very similar plans, of using the passenger as a second brain to look after navigation, and when we pooled our accumulated knowledge and ideas a great deal of groundwork was covered quickly. From four previous Mille Miglia races with Jaguars Moss had gathered together a good quantity of notes, about bumpy level-crossings, blind hill-brows, dangerous corners and so on, and as I knew certain sections of the course intimately, all this knowledge put down on paper amounted to about 25 per cent of the circuit.

Early in February Mercedes-Benz were ready to start practising, the first outing being in the nature of a test for the prototype 300SLR, and a description of the two laps we completed, including having an accident in which the car was smashed, appeared in the March *Motor Sport*. While doing this testing I made copious notes, some of them rather like Chinese due to trying to write at 150 m.p.h., but when we stopped for lunch, or for the night, we spent the whole time discussing the roads we had covered and transcribing my notes. The things we concentrated on were places where we might break the car, such as very bumpy railway-crossings, sudden dips in the road, bad surfaces, tramlines and so on. Then we logged all the difficult corners, grading them as 'saucy ones', 'dodgy ones' and 'very dangerous ones', having a hand sign to indicate each type. Then we logged slippery surfaces, using another hand sign, and as we went along Moss indicated his interpretation of the conditions, while I pinpointed the place by a kilometre stone, plus or minus. Our task was eased greatly by the fact that there is a stone at every kilometre on Italian roads, and they are numbered in huge black figures, facing oncoming traffic.

In addition to all the points round the course where a mistake might mean an accident, and there are hundreds of them, we also logged all the long straights and everywhere that we could travel at maximum speed even though visibility was restricted, and again there were dozens of such points. Throughout all this preliminary work Moss impressed upon me at every possible moment the importance of not making any mistakes such as indicating a brow to be flat-out when in reality it was followed by a tight left-hand bend. I told him he need not worry, as any accident he might have was going to involve me as well, as I was going to be by his side until the race was finished. After our first practice session we sorted out all our notes and had them typed out into some semblance of order, and before leaving England again I spent hours with a friend, checking and cross-checking, going over the whole list many times, finally being 100 per cent certain that there were no mistakes.

On our second visit to Italy for more laps of the circuit, we got down to fine details, grading some corners as less severe and others as much more so, especially as now we knew the way on paper it meant that we arrived at many points much faster than previously when reconnoitring the route. On another lap I went the whole way picking out really detailed landmarks that I would be able to see no matter what the conditions, whether we had the sun in our eyes or it was pouring with rain, and for this work we found Moss's Mercedes-Benz 220A saloon most useful as it would cruise at an easy 85 m.p.h. and at the same time we could discuss any details.

Our whole plan was now nearing completion, we had seventeen pages of notes, and Moss had sufficient confidence in me to take blind brows at 90–100 m.p.h., believing me when I said the road went straight on; though he freely admitted that he was not sure whether he would do the same thing at 170 m.p.h. in the race, no matter how confident I was. He said he'd probably ease it back to 160 m.p.h. for, though that 10 m.p.h. would make no difference to the resulting crash if I had made a mistake, it comforted him psychologically! Throughout all this training we carefully kept a log of our running time and average speeds, and some of them were positively indecent, and certainly not for publication, but the object was to find out which parts of the thousand miles dropped the overall average and where we could make up time, and our various averages in the 220A, the 300SL and the 300SLR gave us an extremely interesting working knowledge of how the Mille Miglia might be won or lost.

Our second practice period ended in another accident and this time a smashed 300SL coupé, for Italian army lorries turn across your bows without warning just as English ones do. Rather crestfallen, we anticipated the rage of team-chief Neubauer when we reported this second crash, but his only worry was that we were not personally damaged; the crashed car was of no importance; these things happened to everyone and anyway their only interest was to win the Mille Miglia, regardless of cost.

Leaving Italy for another brief respite, we both worried out every detail we could think about, from every aspect, the car, the route, our hand signals – for we could not converse in the 300SLR – any emergencies that might arise, anywhere we could save seconds, details of our own personal comfort which would avoid fatigue, and so on. We lived and breathed Mille Miglia day in and day out, leaving no idea untried. The joy of all this was that Daimler-Benz were doing exactly the same things on the mechanical side, supervised by engineers Uhlenhaut, Kosteletzky and Werner, while the racing department were working unceasingly and Neubauer was worrying out every detail of the race organization in Italy. We were putting all our efforts into this race, knowing that they were negligible in comparison with those of the factory.

After Easter we went out to Brescia for our third and final practising session, the technical department, with Kling and Herrmann, having already made an extra one. During their practice period they had thrashed the prototype car up and down the section from Rome to Florence, for this part of the route was the hardest. There are few straights, but all the time the car is averaging nearly 100 m.p.h., the chassis being subjected to strains from every possible angle, and as the 58-gallon petrol tank would be full when leaving Rome, this part of the route would be the most likely on which a breakdown would occur.

By now our details of the route were perfected and I now wrote them all down on a special sheet of paper eighteen feet in length.

Moss had had an alloy case made, on the map-roller system, and for our final practice I employed this machine, winding the paper from the lower roller to the upper one, the notes being read through a Perspex window, sealed with Sellotape in the event of the race being run in rain. A complete lap in a 300SL was done as a sort of dress rehearsal, this car being ideal as it had a maximum of nearly 140 m.p.h., good acceleration, and was a very good approach to racing conditions, while at the same time we could speak to each other if the need arose, though normally all our conversation was done by hand signals, there being about fifteen altogether, to cover every aspect of conversation. During this dress rehearsal we employed an amusing technique in the more deserted parts of the route, especially in the mountains, where I kept an eye on the approaching road out of the side windows, and even out of the rear one on mountain hairpins and, by continually shouting 'Yes' while the road was clear, Moss could have a real go at 'nine-tenths' on the section of road just in front of him, certain in the knowledge that no traffic was approaching, for it must be remembered that all our practice was being done on normal Italian roads, open to the public. This technique, while being amusing to us, was also useful to Moss as it meant he could get the feel of the road surface conditions at racing speeds. By now the Mille Miglia date was approaching and all round the thousand miles we saw more and more signs of growing enthusiasm, occasionally seeing other competitors practising parts of the route, while the police were beginning to leap off the pavement, stop the traffic and wave us on over crossroads with excited cries of 'Mille Miglia – via' and, of course, the Italian populace were leaping straight up into the air with joy as Moss fought the sliding SL through many of the corners. It was interesting that the average English enthusiast would turn his head and look if he saw a 300SL being really motored, whereas the Italians, from errand boys to bank managers, will spontaneously leave the ground and spin completely round, with excited waves, at the same sight, and then rush to another point in the hope of getting a further glimpse of the speeding car. We completed our third practice period without any crashes, though the 'hack' SLR decided to give up the ghost while we were having a final run in it, but we were entirely blameless; old age creeps up on the best vehicles, and this one had done the equivalent of at least six Mille Miglias in the hands of Moss, Fangio, Kling and Herrmann, the four drivers for the race.

A week before the event we went to Stuttgart to try out the actual car we were using in the race, and several laps of the fast Hockenheim circuit convinced us that we had a truly magnificent 3-litre sports car under us, the eight-cylinder fuel-injection engine giving well over 290 b.h.p. on normal pump petrol, and the car geared to give a maximum of 170 m.p.h. at the peak revolutions of 7,500 r.p.m., though we were given no ultimate limit, should the car wind itself over this downhill. On this SLR the seats were made to measure for us, being cut and shut just like a tailor would make a suit, while every detail in the cockpit received our personal attention, and anything was altered to our desire without question. When we finally left the racing department at 5 p.m. on Tuesday 26 April, we had the pleasant feeling that we had just left an organization that knew no limit to the trouble they would go to in order that we might start the Mille Miglia with everything on our side.

Next day we flew to Brescia and when we went round to the garage in the evening the cars were already there, having been driven down in the fast racing lorries overnight. We were now satisfied with almost everything we could think about; we had practised wheel-changing over and over again, in case we had tyre trouble, and I would add that we impressed the Mercedes-Benz mechanics by changing a rear wheel in 1 min 25 sec from stopping the car to starting off again, including getting the tools and spare wheel out of the boot and putting everything back again. We had practised fitting the temporary aluminium aero-screens that went in front of the Perspex screen should it be broken by a stone – Mercedes-Benz engineers remembering how Herrmann Lang was nearly suffocated at 170 m.p.h. at Donington Park in 1938 when his windscreen was broken. We had tried changing plugs; we had studied the details of the pipes of the fuel-injection, the petrol pumps, various important parts of the wiring system, how the bonnet catches functioned; we were given spare ignition keys, shown where numerous small spares were stowed should we stop by the roadside with minor trouble; and by the end of the week we felt extremely confident that we could give of our best in this toughest of motor races, lasting for more than ten hours over every known road condition, over mountains and through cities, for a thousand miles.

On the Friday before the race we did a final test on the nearby Autostrada, to try out some windscreen modifications to improve the air flow along the cockpit sides. Moss also tried out a new mechanism fitted to the gear-change that would prevent him from changing from second gear to fifth gear. The gear-gate is exposed, with first left-forward, second centre-rear, third centre-forward, four right-rear, and fifth right-forward. Being used to four-speed boxes Moss was occasionally going across the gate from second to fifth, and when he told the engineers about this the racing department set to and designed, drew and made an entirely foolproof link-mechanism that fitted on the top of the gate that would prevent this. He mentioned this on Tuesday afternoon and on Friday morning the new parts arrived in Brescia and he was trying the mechanism out before lunch – at such speed does a true racing department work.

For the week before the race I had been going to bed extremely early and getting up extremely early, a complete reversal of my normal life, for to get up suddenly at 6 a.m. gives me a feeling of desolation until well past mid-morning. Moss had been employing similar tactics, so that when we went down to the start at 6.30 a.m. on the morning of 1 May we were both feeling ready for anything.

All the previous week a truly Italian sun had blazed out of the sky every day and reports assured us that race-day would be perfectly dry and hot, so we anticipated race speeds being very high. I had a list of the numbers of all our more serious rivals, as well as many of our friends in slower cars, and also the existing record times to every control point round the course, so that we would have an idea of how we were doing. We had privately calculated on an average of 90 m.p.h. – 2 m.p.h. over the record of Marzotto, providing the car went well and the roads were dry. Mercedes-Benz gave us no orders, leaving the running of the race entirely to each driver, but insisting that the car was brought back to Brescia if humanly possibly. Moss and I had made a pact that we would keep the car going as long as was practicable having decided in practice at which point we could have the engine blow-up and still coast in to the finish, and how many kilometres we were prepared to push it to the finish, or to a control. At Ravenna, Pescara, Rome, Florence and Bologna there were Mercedes-Benz pits, complete with all spares, changes of tyres should it start to rain, food, drink and assistance of every sort for in this race there are no complicated rules about work done on the car or outside assistance; it is a free-for-all event.

The enormous entry had started to leave Brescia the previous evening at 9 p.m., while we were sleeping peacefully, the cars leaving at one minute intervals, and it was not until 6.55 a.m. on Sunday morning that the first of the over-2,000 cc sports cars left. It was this group that held the greatest interest, for among the thirty-four entries lay the outright winner of this race, though many of the 2-litre Maseratis and smaller Oscas and Porsches could not be over-looked. Starting positions were arranged by ballot beforehand and the more important to us were: Fangio 658, Kling 701, Collins (Aston Martin) 702, Herrmann 704, Maglioli (Ferrari) 705; then there went off a group of slower cars and Carini (Ferrari) 714, Scotti (Ferrari) 718, Pinzero (Ferrari) 720, and then us at 7.22 a.m. There was no hope of seeing our team-mates, for they left too long before us, as did Maglioli, but we were hoping to catch Carini before the end. Our big worry was not so much those in front, but those behind, for there followed Castellotti (Ferrari 4.4-litre) 723, Sig-hinolfi (Ferrari 3.7-litre) 724, Paulo Marzotto (Ferrari 3.7-litre) 725, Bordoni (Gordini 3-litre) 726, Perdisa (Maserati 3-litre) 727 and, finally, the most dangerous rival of them all, that master tactician, Taruffi (Ferrari 3.7-litre) 728. With all these works Ferraris behind us we could not hang about in the opening stages, for Castellotti was liable to catch us, and Sighinolfi would probably scrabble past us using the grass banks, he being that sort of driver, and Marzotto would stop at nothing to beat the German cars, so if we didn't press on straight away there was a good chance of the dice becoming a little exciting, not to say dangerous, in the opening 200 miles.

Neubauer was ever present at the start, warning Moss to give the car plenty of throttle as he left the starting ramp, for Hermann had nearly fluffed his take-off; he also assured us that we could take the dip at the bottom of the ramp without worrying about grounding. The mechanics had warmed the engine and they pushed it up on to the starting platform to avoid unnecessary strain on the single-plate clutch, one of the weak points of the 300SLR. The route-card which we had to get stamped at the various controls round the course was securely attached to a board and already fitted in its special holder, the board being attached by a cord to one of my grab rails, to avoid losing it in the excitement of any emergency. We both settled down in our seats, Moss put his goggles on, I showed him a note at the top of my roller device, warning him not to apply the brakes fiercely on the first corner, for the bi-metal drums needed a gentle application to warm them after standing for two days.

Thirty seconds before 7.22 a.m. he started the engine, the side exhaust pipes blowing a cloud of smoke over the starter and Sig. Castegnato and Count Maggi, the two men behind this great event, and then as the flag fell we were off with a surge of acceleration and up to peak revs. in first, second and third gears, weaving our way through the vast crowds lining the sides of the road. Had we not been along this same road three times already in an SLR amid the hurly-burly of morning traffic, I should have been thoroughly frightened, but now, with the roads clear ahead of us, I thought Moss could really get down to some uninterrupted motoring. We had the sun shining full in our eyes, which made navigating difficult, but I had written the notes over and over again, and gone over the route in my imagination so many times that I almost knew it by heart, and one of the first signals was to take a gentle S-bend through a village on full throttle in fourth gear, and as Moss did this, being quite unable to see the road for more than a hundred yards ahead, I settled down to the job, confident that our scientific method of equalling the Italians' ability at open-road racing was going to work. At no time before the race did we ever contemplate getting into the lead, for we fully expected Fangio to set the pace, with Kling determined to win at all costs, so we were out for a third place, and to beat all the Ferraris. Barely ten miles after the start we saw a red speck in front of us and had soon nipped by on a left-hand curve. It was 720, Pinzero, number 721 being a non-starter. By my right hand was a small grab rail and a horn button; the steering was on the left of the cockpit, by the way, and this button not only blew the horn, but also flashed the lights, so that while I played a fanfare on this Moss placed the car for overtaking other competitors. My direction indications I was giving with my left hand, so what with turning the map roller and feeding Moss with sucking sweets there was never a dull moment. The car was really going well now, and on the straights to Verona we were getting 7,500 in top gear, a speed of 274 k.p.h., or as close to 170 m.p.h. as one could wish to travel. On some of these long straights our navigation system was paying handsomely, for we could keep at 170 m.p.h. over blind brows, even when overtaking slower cars, Moss sure in the knowledge that all he had to do was to concentrate on keeping the car on the road and travelling as fast as possible. This in itself was more than enough, but he was sitting back in his usual relaxed position, making no apparent effort, until some corners were reached when the speed at which he controlled slides, winding the wheel from right to left and back again, showed that his superb reflexes and judgement were on top of their form.

Cruising at maximum speed, we seemed to spend most of the time between Verona and Vicenza passing Austin-Healeys that could not have been doing much more than 115 m.p.h., and, with flashing lights, horn blowing and a wave of the hand, we went by as though they were touring. Approaching Padova Moss pointed behind and I looked round to see a Ferrari gaining on us rapidly, and with a grimace of disgust at one another we realized it was Castellotti. The Mercedes-Benz was giving all it had, and Moss was driving hard but taking no risks, letting the car slide just so far on the corners and no more. Entering the main street of Padova at 150 m.p.h. we braked for the right-angle bend at the end, and suddenly I realized that Moss was beginning to work furiously on the steering wheel, for we were arriving at the corner much too fast and it seemed doubtful whether we could stop in time. I sat fascinated, watching Moss working away to keep control, and I was so intrigued to follow his every action and live every inch of the way with him that I completely forgot to be scared. With the wheels almost on locking-point he kept the car straight to the last possible fraction of a second making no attempt to get round the corner, for that would have meant a complete spin and then anything could happen. Just when it seemed we must go head-on into the straw bales Moss got the speed low enough to risk letting go the brakes and try taking the corner, and as the front of the car slid over the dry road we went *bump*! into the bales with our left-hand front corner, bounced off into the middle of the road and, as the car was then pointing in the right direction, Moss selected bottom gear and opened out again.

All this time Castellotti was right behind us, and as we bounced off the bales he nipped by us, grinning over his shoulder. As we set off after him, I gave Moss a little handclap of appreciation for showing me just how a really great driver acts in a difficult situation.

Through Padova we followed the 4.4-litre Ferrari and on acceleration we could not hold it but the Italian was driving like a maniac, sliding all the corners, using the pavements and the loose edges of the road. Round a particularly dodgy left-hand bend on the outskirts of the town I warned Moss and then watched Castellotti sorting out his Ferrari, the front wheels on full understeer, with the inside one off the ground, and rubber pouring off the rear tyres, leaving great wide marks on the road. This was indeed motor-racing from the best possible position, and beside me was a quiet, calm young man who was following the Ferrari at a discreet distance, ready for any emergency. Out of the town we joined an incredibly fast stretch of road, straight for many miles, and we started alongside the Ferrari in bottom gear, but try as the Mercedes-Benz did the red car just drew away from us, and once more Moss and I exchanged very puzzled looks. By the time we had reached our maximum speed the Ferrari was over two hundred yards ahead, but then it remained there, the gap being unaltered along the whole length of the straight. At the cut-off point at the end we gained considerably, both from the fact that we knew exactly when the following left-hand corner was approaching and also from slightly superior brakes. More full-throttle running saw us keeping the Ferrari in sight, and then as we approached a small town we saw Castellotti nip past another Ferrari, which we realized we were going to have to follow through the streets until there was room to pass. It was number 714, Carini, so soon, and this encouraged Moss to run right round the outside of the Ferrari, on a right-hand curve, confident from my signals that the road would not suddenly turn left. This very brief delay had let Castellotti get away from us but he was not completely out of sight, and after waving to Peter Collins, who had broken down by the roadside before Rovigo, we went into that town at terrific speed. Straight across the square we went, where in practice we had had to go round the island; broadside we left the last right turn of the town, with the front wheels on full opposite lock and the throttle pedal hard down. Castellotti was in sight once more but out on the open roads he was driving so near the limit that on every corner he was using the gravel and rough stuff on the edges of the road. This sent up a huge cloud of dust, and we could never be sure whether or not we were going to enter it to find the Ferrari sideways across the road, or bouncing off the banks and trees, for this sort of hazard a scientific route-navigating method could not cope with. Wisely, Moss eased back a little and the Ferrari got ahead of us sufficiently to let the dust clouds settle.

Along the new road by the side of the River Po we overtook

Lance Macklin in his Austin-Healey, and he gave us a cheery wave, and then we went through Ferrara, under the railway bridge, over the traffic lights and down the main streets and out onto the road to Ravenna. All the way along there were signs of people having the most almighty incidents, black marks from locked wheels making the weirdest patterns on the road, and many times on corners we had signalled as dangerous or dodgy we came across cars in the touring categories lying battered and bent by the roadside, sure indication that our grading of the corner was not far wrong. To Ravenna the road winds a great deal and now I could admire the Moss artistry as he put in some very steady 'nine-tenths' motoring, especially on open bends round which he could see and on those that he knew, and the way he would control the car with throttle and steering wheel long after all four tyres had reached the breakaway point was a sheer joy, and most difficult to do justice to with a mere pen and paper. Approaching the Ravenna control I took the route-card board from its holder, held it up for Moss to see, to indicate that we had to stop here to receive the official stamp, and then as we braked towards the CONTROLLO banner across the road, and the black and white chequered line on the road itself, amid waving flags and numerous officials, I held my right arm well out of the car to indicate to them which side we wanted the official with the rubber stamp to be. Holding the board on the side of the cockpit we crossed the control line, bang went the rubber stamp, and we were off without actually coming to rest. Just beyond the control was a row of pits and there was 723, Castellotti's Ferrari, having some tyre changes, which was not surprising in view of the way he had been driving.

With a scream of 'Castellotti!' Moss accelerated hard round the next corner and we twisted our way through the streets of Ravenna, nearly collecting an archway in the process, and then out on the fast winding road to Forli. Our time to Ravenna had been well above the old record but Castellotti had got there before us and we had no idea how Taruffi and the others behind us were doing. Now Moss continued the pace with renewed vigour and we went through Forli, waving to the garage that salvaged the SL we crashed in practice, down the fast winding road to Rimini, with another wave to the Alfa-Romeo service station that looked after the SLR that broke its engine. I couldn't help thinking that we had certainly left our mark round the course during practice. Ever since leaving the start we had

had the rising sun shining in our eyes and, now, with the continual effects of sideways 'G' on my body, my poor stomach was beginning to suffer and, together with the heat from the gearbox by my left buttock, the engine fumes and the nauseating brake-lining smells from the inboard-mounted brakes, it cried 'enough' and what little breakfast I had eaten went overboard, together with my spectacles, for I made the fatal mistake of turning my head sideways at 150 m.p.h. with my goggles lowered. Fortunately, I had a spare pair, and there was no time to worry about a protesting stomach for we were approaching Pesaro, where there was a sharp right corner.

Now the calm, blue Adriatic sea appeared on our left and we were on the long coastal straights, taking blind brows and equally blind bridges at our full 170 m.p.h., and I chuckled to myself as I realized that Moss was not lifting his foot as he had threatened. We were beginning to pass earlier numbers very frequently now, among them some 2-litre Maseratis being driven terribly slowly, a couple of TR2 Triumphs running in convoy, and various saloons, with still numerous signs of the telling pace, a wrecked Giulietta on the right, a 1,100 cc Fiat on the left, a Ferrari coupé almost battered beyond recognition and a Renault that had been rolled up into a ball. Through Ancona the crowds were beautifully controlled, barriers keeping them back on the pavements and we were able to use the full width of the road everywhere, and up the steep hill leaving the town we stormed past more touring-car competitors who had left in the small hours of the morning while we were still asleep. All this time there had been no signs of any of our close rivals. We had passed the last of the Austin-Healeys, driven by Abecassis, a long way back, and no Ferrari had appeared in our rear-view mirror.

It was a long way down to the next control point, at Pescara, and we settled down to cruising at our maximum speed, the car giving no impression at all of how fast it was travelling, until we overtook another competitor, who I knew must be doing 110 m.p.h., or when I looked sideways at the trees and hedges flashing past. It was now mid-morning and the sun was well above us but still shining down on to our faces and making the cockpit exceedingly hot, in spite of having all the air vents fully open. Through the dusty, dirty Adriatic villages we went and all the time I gave Moss the invaluable hand signals that were taking from him the mental strain of trying to remember the route, though he still will not admit to how much mental strain he suffered convincing himself that I was not making any mistakes in my 170 m.p.h. navigation. On one straight, lined with trees, we had marked down a hump in the road as being 'flat-out' only if the road was dry. It was, so I gave the appropriate signal and with 7,500 r.p.m. in fifth gear on the tachometer we took off, for we had made an error in our estimation of the severity of the hump. For a measurable amount of time the vibro-massage that you get sitting in a 300 SLR at that speed suddenly ceased, and there was time for us to look at each other with raised eyebrows before we landed again. Even had we been in the air for only one second we should have travelled some two hundred feet through the air, and I estimated the 'duration of flight' at something more than one second. The road was dead straight and the Mercedes-Benz made a perfect four-point landing and I thankfully praised the driver that he didn't move the steering wheel a fraction of an inch, for that would have been our end. With the heat of the sun and the long straights we had been getting into a complacent stupor, but this little 'moment' brought us back to reality and we were fully on the job when we approached Pescara. Over the level crossing we went, far faster than we had ever done in practice, and the car skated right across the road, with all four wheels sliding, and I was sure we were going to write-off some petrol pumps by the roadside, but somehow 'the boy' got control again and we merely brushed some straw bales and then braked heavily to a stop for the second control stamp. Approaching this point I not only held the route-card for the driver to see, but also pointed to the fuel filler, for here we were due to make our first refuelling. However, I was too late, Moss was already pointing backwards to the tank himself to tell me the same thing. Just beyond the control line we saw engineer Werner holding a blue flag bearing the Mercedes-Benz star and as we stopped everything happened at once. Some eighteen gallons of fuel went in from a gravity tank, just sufficient to get us to our main stop at Rome; the windscreen was cleaned, for it was thick with dead flies; a hand gave me a slice of orange and a peeled banana, while another was holding a small sheet of paper; someone else was looking at the tyres and Moss still had the engine running. On the paper was written 'Taruffi, Moss 15 seconds, Herrmann, Kling, Fangio', and their times; I had just yelled 'second, fifteen seconds behind Taruffi' when I saw a uniformed arm trying to switch off the ignition. I recognized an interfering police arm and gave it a thrump, and as I did so, Moss crunched in bottom gear and we accelerated away as hard as we could go. What had seemed like an age was actually only twenty-eight seconds!

Over the bridge we went, sharp right and then up one of the side turnings of Pescara towards the station, where we were to turn right again. There was a blue Gordini just going round the corner and then I saw that we were overshooting and with locked wheels we slid straight on, *bang* into the straw bales. I just had time to hope there was nothing solid behind the wall of bales when the air was full of flying straw and we were on the pavement. Moss quickly selected bottom gear and without stopping he drove along the pavement, behind the bales, until he could bounce down off the kerb and continue on his way, passing the Gordini in the process. As we went up through the gears on the long straight out of Pescara, I kept an eye on the water temperature gauge, for that clonk certainly creased the front of the car, and may have damaged the radiator, or filled the intake with straw, but all seemed well, the temperature was still remaining constant. There followed three completely blind brows in quick succession and we took these at full speed, the effect being rather like a switchback at a fair, and then we wound and twisted our way along the barren valley between the rocky mountain sides to Popoli, where a Bailey Bridge still serves to cross a river. Along this valley I saw the strange sight of about fifty robed monks, with shining bald pates, standing on a high mound and waving to us as we went by with a noise sufficient to wake the devil himself. Up into the mountains we climbed, sliding round the hairpins with that beautiful Moss technique I described two months ago in *Motor Sport*, and then along the peculiar deserted plateau high up in the mountains we held our maximum speed for many kilometres to be followed by a winding twisting road into Aquila, where up the main street the control was dealt with while still on the move. We certainly were not wasting any seconds anywhere and Moss was driving absolutely magnificently, right on the limit of adhesion all the time, and more often than not over the limit, driving in that awe-inspiring narrow margin that you enter just before you have a crash if you have not the Moss skill, or those few yards of momentary terror you have on ice just before you go in the ditch. This masterly handling was no fluke, he was doing it deliberately, his extra special senses and reflexes allowing him to go that much closer to the absolute limit than the average racing driver and way beyond the possibilities of normal mortals like you or me.

On the way to Rome we hit a level crossing that had been just 'bumpy' in the SL and smooth in the 220A; the resultant thud threw us high out of our seats into the airstream, and with a crash we landed back again, nearly breaking our spines but the Mercedes-Benz suspension absorbed it all without protest and there was no feeling that anything had 'bottomed' unduly severely. This sort of thing had happened three or four times already, for our route-noting was not infallible, and it seemed unbelievable that nothing broke on the car each time. Although we occasionally saw a train steaming along in the distance we never came across any closed level crossing, though if we had we had a remedy. In practice we had tried lifting the barrier, Italian gates being two long poles that lower across the road, and found that the slack on the operating cables was just sufficient to allow the car to be driven under the pole, much to the annoyance of the crossing-keeper. However, this did not arise and down into the Rome control we had a pretty clear run, being highly delighted to overtake Maglioli soon after Rieti, he suffering from an arm injury received in practice and a car that was not going well. With a grin at each other we realized that one of our unseen rivals was now disposed of, but we still had Taruffi behind us on the road, and no doubt well ahead of us on time, for all this ground was local colour to him. Coming down off the mountains we had overtaken Musso driving a 2-litre Maserati and as we had calculated that we were unlikely ever to catch him, if we averaged 90 m.p.h. for the whole race, we realized we must be setting a fantastic record speed, but as Taruffi had been leading at Pescara, his average must be even higher.

The last six miles into the Rome control were an absolute nightmare; there were no corners that needed signals, and we would normally have done 150–160 m.p.h., but the crowds of spectators were so thick that we just could not see the road. The surface was bumpy and Moss dared not drive much over 130 m.p.h. for there was barely room for two cars abreast. It seemed that the whole of Rome was out to watch the race, all oblivious of the danger of a high-speed racing car. While I blew the horn and flashed the lights Moss swerved the car from side to side and this had the effect of making those on the very edge leap hastily backwards, thus giving us a little more room. The last mile into the control was better organized and I was able to show Moss the control card, point backwards at the fuel tank and also at the fibre disc wired to the steering column which had to be punched at this control. 'Bang' went the stamp and we then drew into the Mercedes-Benz pit and switched off the engine; this was our first real stop since leaving Brescia nearly 3½ hours ago, and our average speed to this point was 107 m.p.h., the average to Pescara having been 118 m.p.h., the mountain section causing it to drop from there to Rome.

As we stopped Moss leapt out to relieve himself, I felt the car rise up on the jacks and heard the rear hub nuts being beaten off, the windscreen was cleaned and a welcome shower of water sprinkled over me, for I was very hot, very tired, very dirty, oily and sweaty and must have looked a horrible sight to spectators. The fuel tank was being filled, someone handed me a drink of mineral water and an orange, and offered a tray of sandwiches and cakes, but I felt incapable of eating anything firmer than a slice of orange. A hand appeared in front of me holding a sheet of paper and I snatched it and read 'Moss, Taruffi, Herrmann, Kling, Fangio' and the times showed we had a lead of nearly two minutes. Bump went the car as it was dropped down off the jacks, and with a lithe bound Moss was into the driving seat again and as we took the hairpin after the control I managed to yell in his ear, 'First by more than one minute from Taruffi,' and then the noise of the exhaust and wind prevented any further words. On the next bend we saw a silver Mercedes-Benz, number 701, well off the road among the trees and badly wrecked. We knew it was Kling and exchanged long faces with each other, wondering how badly hurt he was, but this had no effect on Moss and he now began to put everything he knew into his driving, on this most difficult section, while I had to concentrate hard in order to give him warnings and signals of the approaching road conditions, for this was indeed a difficult section for both of us. Past Monterosi we waved to the 'Agip' service station, where we had a sheep-killing incident in practice, and then we sped on our way through Viterbo, sliding this way and that, leaving the ground on more occasions than I can remember, yet all the while feeling completely at ease, for such is the confidence that Moss gave me, and round the corners I never ceased to marvel at the superb judgement with which he weighed up the maximum possible speed at which he could go, and just how far he could let the car slide without going into the ditch or hitting a wall or rock face. Now there was the continual hazard of passing slower cars, though it must be recorded that most of them gave way splendidly, keeping one eye on the mirror. Just after Acquapendente I made my first and only mistake in navigating – that it was not serious is why you are reading these words now; having just given warning of a very dodgy right-hand bend I received a shower of petrol down my neck and looking round to see what had happened we arrived at another similar corner, and I missed the signal. Fortunately Moss had recognized the corner, for he knew many parts of the course extremely well, and after seeing that the petrol was coming from the filler due to surge, I looked back to see an irate Moss face saying very rude things at me and shaking his fist, all the while cornering at a fantastic speed. How serious the fuel surge was I did not know, and as the exhaust pipes were on the side of the car I decided it would be all right and said nothing to Moss, as he appeared not to have received any of the spray. For the next ten or fifteen miles I received this gentle spray of cold fuel, cooling in the enormous heat of the cockpit, but a little worrying in case it got worse. Up the Radicofani Pass we stormed and the way the car leapt and slithered about would have really frightened me had I not already had a lot of experience of its capabilities and of the skill of Stirling Moss; as it was I sat there and revelled in the glorious feeling of really fast motoring. Over the top of the pass we swept past a saloon car competitor, into a downhill right-hand bend followed by a sharp left-hander. Now, previous to this Moss had been pointing to the front of the car and indicating that a brake was begining to grab on occasions, and this was one of them. Without any warning the car spun and there was just time to think what a desolated part of Italy in which to crash, when I realized that we had almost stopped in our own length and were sliding gently into the ditch to land with a crunch that dented the tail. 'This is all right,' I thought, 'we can probably push it out of this one,' and I was about to start getting out when Moss selected bottom gear and we drove out – lucky indeed! Before we could point the car in the right direction we had to make two reverses and as we accelerated away down the mountainside I fiddled about putting the safety catch back on the reverse position of the gear-gate, while we poked our tongues out at each other in mutual derision.

At the Siena control we had no idea of whether we were still leading or not, but Moss was quite certain that Taruffi would have had to have worked extremely hard to catch him, for he had put all he knew into that last part of the course, he told me afterwards. Never relaxing for an instant he continued to drive the most superb race of his career, twirling the steering wheel this way and that, controlling slides with a delicateness of throttle that was fairy-like, or alternatively provoking slides with the full power of the engine, in order to make the car change direction bodily, the now dirty, oily and battered collection of machinery that had left Brescia gleaming like new still answering superbly to his every demand, the engine always being taken to 7,500 r.p.m. in the gears, and on one occasion to 8,200 r.p.m., the excitement at that particular instant not allowing time for a gear change or an easing of the throttle, for the way Moss steered the car round the sharp corners with the back wheels was sheer joy to experience.

On the winding road from Siena to Florence physical strain began to tell on me, for with no steering wheel to give me a feel of what the car was going to do, my body was being continually subjected to terrific centrifugal forces as the car changed direction. The heat, fumes and noise were becoming almost unbearable, but I gave myself renewed energy by looking at Stirling Moss who was sitting beside me, completely relaxed, working away at the steering as if we had only just left Brescia, instead of having been driving for nearly seven hundred miles under a blazing sun. Had I not known the route I would have happily got out there and then, having enjoyed every mile, but ahead lay some interesting roads over which we had practised hard, and the anticipation of watching Moss really try over these stretches, with the roads closed to other traffic, made me forget all about the physical discomforts. I was reminded a little of the conditions when we approached one corner and some women got up and fled with looks of terror on their faces, for the battered Mercedes-Benz, dirty and oil-stained and making as much noise as a Grand Prix car, with two sweaty, dirty, oil-stained figures behind the windscreen, must have looked terrifying to peaceful peasants, as it entered the corner in a full four-wheel slide. The approaches of Florence were almost back-breaking as we bounced and leapt over the badly maintained roads, and across the tramlines, and my heart went out to the driver of an orange Porsche who was hugging the crown of the steeply cambered road. He must have been shaken as we shot past with the left-hand wheels right down in the gutter. Down a steep hill in second gear we went, into third at peak revs, and I thought, 'It's a brave man who can unleash nearly 300 b.h.p. down a hill this steep and then change into a higher gear.' At speeds up to 120–130 m.p.h. we went through the streets of Florence, over the great river bridge, broadside across a square, across more tramlines and into the control point. Now Moss had really got the bit between his teeth, nothing was going to stop him winning this race, I felt; he had a rather special look of concentration on his face and I knew that one of his greatest ambitions was to do the section Florence–Bologna in under one hour. This road crosses the heart of the Apennines, by way of the Futa Pass and the Raticosa Pass, and though only just over sixty miles in length it is like a Prescott Hill-Climb all the way. As we got the route-card stamped, again without coming to rest, I grabbed the sheet of paper from the Mercedes-Benz man at the control, but before I could read more than that we were still leading, it was torn from my grasp as we accelerated away among the officials. I indicated that we were still leading the race, and by the way Moss left Florence, as though at the start of a Grand Prix, I knew he was out to crack one hour to Bologna, especially as he also looked at his wrist-watch as we left the control. 'This is going to be fantastic,' I thought, as we screamed up the hills out of Florence, 'he is really going to do some nine-tenths-plus motoring', and I took a firm grip of the 'struggling bar' between giving him direction signals, keeping the left side of my body as far out of Moss's way as possible, for he was going to need all the room possible for his whirling arms and for stirring the gear-lever about. Up into the mountains we screamed, occasionally passing other cars, such as 1900 Alfa-Romeos, 1100 Fiats and some small sports cars. Little did we know that we had the race in our pocket, for Taruffi had retired by this time with a broken oil pump and Fangio was stopped in Florence repairing an injection pipe, but though we had overtaken him on the road, we had not seen him, as the car had been hidden by mechanics and officials. All the time I had found it very difficult to take my eyes off the road. I could have easily looked around me, for there was time, but somehow the whole while that Moss was really dicing I felt a hypnotic sensation forcing me to live every inch of the way with him. It was probably this factor that prevented me ever being frightened, for nothing arrived unexpectedly. I was keeping up with him mentally all the way, which I had to do if I wasn't to miss any of our route marking, though physically I had fallen way behind him and I marvelled that anyone could drive so furiously for such a long time, for it was now well into the Sunday afternoon. At the top of the Futa Pass there were enormous crowds all waving excitedly and on numerous occasions Moss nearly lost the car completely as we hit patches of melted tar, coated with oil and rubber from all the other competitors in front of us, and for nearly a mile he had to ease off and drive at a bare eight-tenths, the road was so tricky. Just over the top of the Futa we saw a Mercedes-Benz by the roadside amid a crowd of people, it was 704, young Hans Herrmann, and though we could not see him, we waved. The car looked undamaged so we assumed he was all right.

Now we simply had to get to Brescia first, I thought, we mustn't let Taruffi beat us, still having no idea that he had retired. On we went, up and over the Raticosa Pass, plunging down the other side, in one long series of slides that to me felt completely uncontrolled but to Moss were obviously intentional. However, there was one particular one which was not intentional and by sheer good fortune the stone parapet on the outside of the corner stepped back just in time, and caused us to make rude faces at each other. On a wall someone had painted 'Viva Perdisa, viva Maserati' and as we went past in a long controlled slide, we spontaneously both gave it the victory sign, and had a quiet chuckle between ourselves, in the cramped and confined space of our travelling hothouse and bath of filth and perspiration. On another part of the Raticosa amid great crowds of people we saw an enormous fat man in the road, leaping up and down with delight; it was the happy body-builder of the Maserati racing department, a good friend of Stirling's, and we waved back to him.

Down off the mountains we raced, into the broiling heat of the afternoon, into Bologna, along the dusty tramlined road, with hordes of spectators on both sides, but here beautifully controlled, so that we went into Bologna at close on 150 m.p.h. and down to the control point, Moss doing a superb bit of braking judgement even at this late stage in the race, and in spite of brakes that were beginning to show signs of the terrific thrashing they had been receiving. Here we had the steering column disc punched again and the card stamped, and with another Grand Prix start we were away through the streets of Bologna so quickly that I didn't get the vital news sheet from our depot. Now we had no idea of where we lay in the race, or what had happened to our rivals, but we knew we had crossed the mountains in 1 hr 1 min, and were so far ahead of Marzotto's record that it seemed impossible. The hard part was now over, but Moss did not relax, for it had now occurred to him that it was possible to get back to Brescia in the round ten hours, which would make the race average 100 m.p.h. Up the long fast straights through Modena, Reggio Emilia and Parma we went, not wasting a second anywhere, cruising at a continuous 170 m.p.h. and cutting off only where I indicated corners, or bumpy hill-brows. Looking up I suddenly realized that we were overtaking an aeroplane, and then I knew I was living in the realms of fantasy, and when we caught and passed a second one my brain began to boggle at the sustained speed. They were flying at about three hundred feet, filming our progress, and it must have looked most impressive, especially as we dropped back by going round the Fidenza bypass, only to catch up again on the main road. This really was pure speed, the car was going perfectly and reaching 7,600 r.p.m. in fifth gear in places, which was as honest a 170 m.p.h. plus as I'd care to argue about. Going into Piacenza where the road doubles back towards Mantova we passed a 2CV Citroën bowling along merrily, having left Brescia the night before, and then we saw a 2-litre Maserati ahead which shook us perceptibly, for we thought we had passed them all long ago. It was number 621, Francesco Giardini, and appreciating just how fast he must have driven to reach this point before us, we gave him a salutary wave as we roared past, leaving Piacenza behind us. More important was the fact that we were leaving the sun behind us, for nice though it was to have dry roads to race on, the blazing sun had made visibility for both of us very tiring. Through Cremona we went without relaxing and now we were on the last leg of the course, there being a special prize and the Nuvolari Cup for the fastest speed from Cremona to Brescia. Although the road lay straight for most of the way, there were more than six villages to traverse, as well as the final route card stamp to get in the town of Mantova. In one village, less than fifty miles from the finish, we had an enormous slide on some melted tar and for a moment I thought we would hit a concrete wall, but with that absurdly calm manner of his, Moss tweaked the wheel this way and that, and caught the car just in time, and with his foot hard down we went on our way as if nothing had happened. The final miles into Brescia were sheer joy, the engine was singing round on full power, and after we had passed our final direction indication I put my roller-map away and thought, 'If it blows to pieces now, we can carry it the rest of the way.' The last corner into the finishing area was taken in a long slide with the power and noise full on and we crossed the finishing line at well over 100 m.p.h., still not knowing that we had made motor-racing history, but happy and contented at having completed the whole race and done our best.

From the finishing line we drove round to the official garage, where the car had to be parked and Stirling asked, 'Do you think we've won?' to which I replied, 'We must wait for Taruffi to arrive, and we don't know when Fangio got in.' At the garage it was finally impressed upon us that Taruffi was out, Fangio was behind us and we had won. Yes, won the Mille Miglia, achieved the impossible, broken all the records, ruined all the Mille Miglia legends, made history. We clasped each other in delirious joy, and would have wept, but we were too overcome and still finding it hard to believe that we had won. Then we were swept away amid a horde of police and officials, and the ensuing crush amid the wildly enthusiastic crowds was harder to bear than the whole of the thousand mile grind we had just completed.

Our total time for the course was 10 hr 07 min 48 sec, an average of more than 157 k.p.h. (nearly 98 m.p.h.) and our average for the eighty-five miles from Cremona to Brescia had been 123 m.p.h. As we were driven back to our hotel, tired, filthy, oily and covered in dust and dirt, we grinned happily at each other's black face and Stirling said, 'I'm so happy that we've proved that a Britisher can win the Mille Miglia, and that the legend "he who leads at Rome never leads at Brescia" is untrue – also, I feel we have made up for the two cars we wrote off in practice.' Then he gave a chuckle and said, 'We've rather made a mess of the record, haven't we – sort of spoilt it for anyone else, for there probably won't be another completely dry Mille Miglia for twenty years.'

It was with a justified feeling of elation that I lay in a hot bath, for I had had the unique experience of being with Stirling Moss throughout his epic drive, sitting beside him while he worked as I have never seen anyone work before in my life, and harder and longer than I ever thought it possible for a human being to do. It was indeed a unique experience, the greatest experience in the whole of the twenty-two years during which I have been interested in motor-racing, an experience that was beyond my wildest imagination, with a result that even now I find it extremely hard to believe.

After previous Mille Miglias I have said, 'He who wins the Mille Miglia is some driver, and the car he uses is some sports car.' I now say it again with the certain knowledge that *I know* what I'm talking and writing about this time.

From *Motor Sport*, June 1955

INDEX

Daimler, Gottlieb, 1–4
Darniche, Bernard, 225
Davenport, John, 218–23
Davis, Cliff, 180
Daytona Beach, Florida, 205–11
de Cadenet, Alain, 46
de Graffenreid, E., 58
Dean, James, 221
Delage, Louis, 10
Delecour, François, 235
Dennis, Ron, 160
Depailler, Patrick, 88, 113, 168, 171
Dijon circuit, 161
Divo, Albert, 11–15
Donaldson, Gerald, 122–6, 198–203
Donington circuit, 146
Donnelly, Martin, 162
double-declutching, 136
Driven to Win (Mansell), 7, 172
driving techniques, 92–7, 135–8
Dubonnet, André, 11
Dumfries, Johnny, 125
Durand, Georges, 40, 42

Ebblewhite, A. V., 10–11
Ecurie Ecosse, 71, 177
Elford, Vic, 100
England, Lofty, 48, 50
Etancelin, P., 17–25, 58
Evans, Paul, 235–6
Eyston, George, 10–15

Fagioli, Luigi, 17–25, 150
Fangio, Juan-Manuel,
    Alfa-Romeo driver, 150–51
    German Grand Prix 1957, 30–39
    Le Mans crash 1955, 43–6
    Mille Miglia (1955), 264, 270, 273,
        276, 279
    on Nürburgring, 26
    pre-race calmness, 100
    World Championships, xv, xvii, 33
Farina, Giuseppe, 58, 144–53
Faroux, Charles, 41
Fenn, Alan, 15
Ferrari, Enzo, 82–5, 115, 146, 197,
    202–3, 245
Ferrari cars, 35–7, 82–5, 146–7, 224,
    266–7
financial rewards of racing, 158
Fittipaldi, Emerson, 90, 114
Flockhart, Ron, 49
Forghieri, Mauro, 82, 194, 200
Foster, Trevor, 161
Foyt, A. J., 61
Fraichard, Georges, 40–42

French Grand Prix,
    1934, 16–25

Gallop, Clive, 10
Garnier, Peter, 56–60
Garrett, Richard, 98–107
Gauld, Graham, 64
Gavin, Bill, 229–30
Geistdorfer, Christian, 222
Gendebien, Olivier, 49, 51, 53
German Grand Prix,
    1967, 77–81
    1976, 169–70
    see also Nürburgring
Giardini, Francesco, 278
Gibson, John Eason, 149
Giraud-Cabantous, Y., 58
González, Froilán, 31–4, 144, 150
Goodwood circuit, xiii, 139, 244–5,
    249–53
Granatelli, Andy, 65–6
Grand Prix Drivers' Association, 56, 199
Gregory, Ken, 129
Grimsley, R. H., 216
Gross, Paul, 42

Hailwood, Mike, 46, 127–34
Halford, Major Frank, 10–15
Hamilton, Maurice, 5–9, 163, 212–17
Hansgen, Walt, 65
Harper, Bob, 160
Harryman, Terry, 220
Hartmann, Laszlo, 147
Hawthorn, Mike,
    death, 246–8
    German Grand Prix 1957, 30–39
    Le Mans crash 1955, 43–6
    Moroccan Grand Prix 1975, 48–55
    Moss, rivalry with, 245–6
    on Nürburgring, 27
    sports-car racing, 243–5
    World Championship, xvii, 55, 248
Hayes, Walter, 154–8
Haynes, David, 237–8
Healey, Donald, 216
Hémery, Victor, 41
Henry, Alan, 162, 176–81
Herbert, Johnny, 174
Herrmann, Hans, 264, 270, 277
Hertz, Arne, 221
Hesketh, Alexander Fermor-Hesketh,
    Baron, 165–6
Hewetson, Henry, 3–4
Hill, Bette, 68, 187–92
Hill, Graham,
    Belgian Grand Prix 1966, 74